SIR CHARLES WOGAN

Jacobite, Soldier, Royal Agent & Man of Letters

For my grandparents, Kevin and Angela Brazil

SIR CHARLES WOGAN

Jacobite, Soldier, Royal Agent & Man of Letters

Richard K. Maher

PEN & SWORD HISTORY
AN IMPRINT OF PEN & SWORD BOOKS LTD.
YORKSHIRE – PHILADELPHIA

First published in Great Britain in 2025 by
PEN AND SWORD HISTORY
An imprint of
Pen & Sword Books Ltd
Yorkshire – Philadelphia

ISBN 978 1 03613 409 9

A CIP catalogue record for this book is available from the British Library.

Typeset in Times New Roman 11.5/15 by
SJmagic DESIGN SERVICES, India.
Printed and bound in the UK by CPI Group (UK) Ltd.

The Publisher's authorised representative in the EU for product safety is Authorised Rep Compliance Ltd., Ground Floor, 71 Lower Baggot Street, Dublin D02 P593, Ireland.
www.arccompliance.com

For a complete list of Pen & Sword titles please contact
PEN & SWORD BOOKS LIMITED
George House, Units 12 & 13, Beevor Street, Off Pontefract Road,
Barnsley, South Yorkshire, S71 1HN, England
E-mail: enquiries@pen-and-sword.co.uk
Website: www.pen-and-sword.co.uk

or

PEN AND SWORD BOOKS
1950 Lawrence Rd, Havertown, PA 19083, USA
E-mail: uspen-and-sword@casematepublishers.com
Website: www.penandswordbooks.com

MIX
Paper | Supporting responsible forestry
FSC® C013604

Contents

Acknowledgements

I wish to extend my sincere gratitude to Dr Declan Downey, whose encouragement and generous support helped me find my feet in my research and writing. To Dr Éamonn Ó Ciardha and Dr Harman Murtagh, I would like to give my thanks for taking time out of their busy schedules to read my draft chapters and help sharpen the work. I am grateful to my hawk-eye mother, Ms Patricia Maher, for doing the final proof-read to catch the remaining elusive errors. I would like to thank my colleagues Mr Liam Moloney and Mr James Grannell for their encouragement and practical support while I completed this project. I extend my thanks to Mr Mario Luis López Durán who shared files relating to Wogan that he found during his own research. I thank the man who started the whole thing, An tUasal Pól MacGrennachain, who handed me a copy of Wogan's *Female Fortiude* in 2014. I am very grateful to Mr Rafael Torres of Madrid, who allowed me to stay at his apartment for free while I consulted the archives there. I wish to thank Ms Lisset Jara who found Wogan's final resting place at Barcelona Cathedral. To all my dear family, friends and colleagues who have given me endless encouragement to finish this project, I would be lost without you all.

I would like to thank the wonderful staff of the following institutions who assisted me and, in some cases, put up with my dreadful Spanish and French while I was working at their archives: the National Library of Ireland, National Archives of Ireland, Galway Kilmacduagh and Kilfenora Diocesan Archive, Registry of Deeds Archive Services. In the UK, the National Archives at Kew and the British Library, the Bodleian

Library at Oxford University, and Cambridge University Library. In Spain, Archivo General de Simancas, El Archivo General de Palacio, Archivo Histórico Nacional, Collegi Notarial de Catalunya, and Arxiu de la Catedral de Barcelona. In France, Bibliothèque Nationale de France and Service Historique de la Défense at Vincennes. In Italy, Archivio Apostolico Vaticano.

Introduction

I first read about Sir Charles Wogan while completing my master's degree at University College Dublin. By happenstance, my housemate, Paul, handed me a facsimile reprint of the account of the rescue of Princess Maria Clementina Sobieska in 1719 titled *Female Fortitude*, attributed to Wogan. Of all the interesting topics covered during the MA, this was immediately different. There was something about the style of writing, the subject matter and the context that made the individuals and places described seem almost tangible and it drew me in. After taking a trip to the Galway, Kilmacduagh and Kilfenora Diocesan Archive located at Galway Cathedral and successfully finding very useful material there, my thesis supervisor, Dr Declan Downey, observed with a wry smile that I had been bitten by the research bug. Now, more than ten years later, I have collected documents from archives in Rome, Madrid, Barcelona, Paris, London, and Dublin and Galway in Ireland, towards completing this critical biography of Sir Charles Wogan.

Sir Charles can be described as one of the *Wild Geese*, a term used to describe migrants of various professions from Ireland to continental Europe after the Treaty of Limerick of 1691, signed between the armies of King William III (Williamites) and that of James Stuart II (Jacobites), which brought an end to the War of the Two Kings (1689–1691). According to Irish tradition, Patrick Sarsfield, the hero of the defeated army of King James II, is said to have seen flocks of migrating geese from the deck of the transport ship that was taking him and his troops to France and vowed that like them, they would soon return to retake Ireland.[1] The war in Ireland caused a new wave of migration which continued for decades to come. The new migrants would benefit from institutions in their new host countries such as Irish colleges and Irish army regiments already in existence from previous waves of migration from Ireland. The various needs of the Irish community in Europe were serviced by their compatriots, whether legal, educational, spiritual, logistical, or financial. The largest professional group among the migrants were soldiers, which were welcomed into armies across Europe. The Irish regiments in the service of the Kingdoms of France and Spain would become known as the Irish Brigade and presented a dangerous standing threat to the British government for half a century. The Irish regiments typically wore the red coats of the Stuarts and fought under banners showing the Irish harp. Cognisant of reduced conditions of their compatriots and co-religionists at home, the Irish Jacobite migrants drank to the health of the Stuart monarch upon recruitment, vowed to restore them to their ancestral thrones, to return to liberate Ireland from the oppressive regime there, and reestablish Roman Catholicism at the expense of Protestantism. The latter point, an aim incomprehensible to English and Scottish Jacobites, indicates a distinct Irish Jacobite identity, rooted in Roman Catholicism, determined to recover lost lands and rights in Ireland, and the acknowledgment of the legitimacy by birthright and lineage of the Stuarts as the rightful rulers of Ireland. Recruitment to the Irish regiments abroad provided the main link between those at home and those in Europe. It was a capital offence to recruit or to sign up to serve the Pretender, as James III's Whig opponents dubbed him, and those caught in the act in Ireland could be hanged. Despite repeated government proclamations against the practice, thousands would successfully leave over the following years.

The Catholic clergy formed another important link. The Stuart monarchs retained the right granted by the papacy to nominate bishops to vacant sees in Ireland. The movement of clergy to and from Ireland occurred in tandem with successful smuggling by Irish mercantile families based in all the major ports from the Ostend to Cadiz. The focal point of the exiled Irish Jacobite community was the Stuart court in exile based at Saint-Germain-en-Laye outside Paris, where Sir Charles's wife, Anne O'Driscoll, was born and raised like many others. The Stuart monarchs provided patronage, financial support and letters of recommendation for their subjects as they attempted to make their fortunes in their new supporting societies. James III, obliged in 1716 to remove his court from Saint-Germain to the Palazzo del Re in Rome, was very obliging in this regard to Sir Charles who would have frequent need of his assistance.

It is into this context that Sir Charles can be situated. An avowed and dedicated Jacobite, surviving letters and official documents give us keen insight into the ebb and flow of life for a military migrant during the eighteenth century. His family tradition and the experience of his immediate relatives in both the Wars of the Three Kingdoms (1639–1653) and the War of the Two Kings (1689–1691) clearly made its mark on him. Identifying his specific outlook and sense of identity requires a nuanced approach. The Wogans were an Anglo-Norman settler family with roots in Pembrokeshire in Wales. In the thirteenth century they settled on lands around their main familial estate at Rathcoffey in County Kildare where they remained until the nineteenth century. Sir Charles was an Old English Palesman (landowners of an area around Dublin under the control of the English Government known as the Pale), traditionally loyal to the English Crown and steadfast in his Roman Catholicism). He identified as an Irishman, but was also Anglo-centric, having spent time in England during his youth among his relatives. This distinguished him from those of Old Irish (Gaelic) stock. His letters give voice to the persecution mentality common among the Irish Jacobite community, which itself drew on the grievances of the Irish Catholic community from the seventeenth century. Sir Charles gave expression to the military threat to the British and Irish authorities mentioned above. He helped to organise the 1715 insurrection against George I in Britain and fought at the Battle of Preston; he secured the prestigious Stuart-Sobieski royal match in 1719 for his royal master, James III, to the chagrin of his rival; he was involved in the Atterbury Plot to restore James III to power; he advocated for a military expedition to Ireland as part of a plan to affect a restoration; he acted as the official Stuart representative to the royal court in Madrid during the 1745 insurrection, successfully soliciting aid; and eventually led a body of Irish officers to attempt to join Prince Charles Edward in Scotland.

The full review of his letters provides a window into the life of a migrant and its attendant difficulties in eighteenth-century Spain. Although Spain in the early eighteenth century was still a considerable military power, its military might had been eclipsed by the French, and the British were asserting themselves successfully. Irishmen such as Toby Bourke, Sir Patrick Lawless, and Count Daniel O'Mahony had risen to considerable positions of influence in the court of Philip V during the War of the Spanish Succession (1701–1714). Wogan arrived in 1719 during a lull between two periods of significant Irish influence there: firstly the War of Succession, secondly the development of the Irish party around Richard Wall, Spanish prime minister (1754–1763). As such, the timing of his arrival and its coincidence with relative peace during his military career in Spain meant that there were fewer opportunities for promotion available. The Kingdom of Spain suffered fiscal problems which Wogan would experience directly through arrears in his pay. Throughout this frustrating period, his membership of the exiled Jacobite community and his correspondence with the Stuart court in exile in Rome sustained and supported him. After providing such high-profile service to the Stuarts, it is likely that his fortunes were impacted by successful lobbying by British representatives in the Kingdom of Spain against his promotion there. His dual loyalty to James III and Philip V of Spain may also have offered a barrier to his advancement, which was very slow and frustrating for him. His proximity to the Stuart court between 1715 and 1719 and the successful services he provided there leads one to question why a place was not made for him there. He would continue to the very end in his support for the Stuarts, eventually succeeding in gaining positions of authority in his latter years in Barcelona.

This work is based on extant documents housed in archives and libraries in Ireland, Britain, France, Spain and Italy. Undoubtedly, the main stumbling block facing scholars of the Wild Geese is the fact that the source material can be scattered over a wide area. Furthermore, the difficulty presented by processing documents written in multiple European languages offers a significant but not insurmountable barrier. In any case, the most useful collection has been the Stuart and Cumberland Papers which are scanned and available to access free of charge at The National Archives at Kew in London. Wogan's letters to the Stuart court are numerous and verbose and, most importantly, legible and mostly written in English. They have enabled a detailed view of the vicissitudes of his fortunes, his family life, and how he came to grips with his life in exile. His correspondence with Jonathan Swift, Dean of Saint Patrick's Cathedral in Dublin, has already been published in full and provides a fascinating historiographical reaction by a member of the Irish exile community to the Irish experience during the seventeenth century. The unpublished 'Wogan Manuscript' housed at the Galway, Kilmacduagh and Kilfenora Diocesan Archive offers further enthralling glimpses of contemporary Spain and on aspects of his life. His military service record is available to view at the Archivo General de Simancas in Spain as well as other related documents and letters that have been useful. Combined, the sources used here have allowed the telling of his story largely in his own words which is appropriate and agreeable for a man who expressed that wish.

Chapter One outlines his family background, early life, education and the question of his position as an officer in an Irish regiment in France. The second chapter deals with his involvement in the 1715 insurrection against the unpopular George I, while Chapter Three tells of his escape from Newgate and his role at the Stuart court in exile. Chapter Four describes the part he played alongside James Butler, second Duke of Ormond, on a diplomatic mission to Russia and Sweden and his identification of Princess Maria Clementina Sobieska as a potential marriage match for James III. After the princess's arrest in Innsbruck at the insistence of the British government, Chapter Five shows how Wogan masterminded and affected her rescue and escape into Italy, where she was married to James III. The solemnisation of the royal marriage, Wogan's elevation by James III to a knight-baronet and his being awarded with Roman senatorial honours by Pope Clement XI is the subject of Chapter Six. Chapters Seven and Eight detail the early years of his career in Spain and his marriage to Anne O'Driscoll, a *camarista* (maid) of Queen Elizabeth Farnese of Spain. The eddying rumours of international intrigue, European power-politics, a potential invasion plan for Ireland, and his impression of Spain provide the basis for Chapter Nine. Chapter Ten delves into the detail surrounding Spain's reconquest of Oran in the Maghreb and the vital part played by Wogan in relieving the beleaguered hilltop fortress of Santa Cruz outside the city. His correspondence with Swift, his relationship with Philp Wharton, first Duke of Wharton, and Wogan's possible membership of the shadowy quasi-masonic Order of Toboso are discussed in Chapter Eleven. Chapter Twelve tells of his return to Spain after his tour of duty at Oran and his unsuccessful attempts to gain promotion at the royal court in Madrid which resulted in his subsequent depression and withdrawal. The end of the chapter tells of his long-awaited promotion to a civil position in 1744. Chapter Thirteen describes his agonising attempts to hurry the Spanish government to commit soldiers, materiel and money to assist Prince Charles Edward in his insurrection in Scotland in 1745. The final chapter covers the twilight years of the old Jacobite in Barcelona where he held the acting governorship of the city while it lay vacant. His death in July 1754, the identification of his final resting place, and his son's adoption of knight-baronetcy are also discussed. The short epilogue is written to provide a signpost to any future scholar interested in Wogan and where they might be likely to find further letters and documents.

Chapter 1

Charles's Early Life and a Brief History of the Wogan Family

The main branch of the Wogan family held lands around the original medieval castle in Rathcoffey, County Kildare, the ruined gatehouse of which is all that remains today. Sir Charles was a member of a junior branch of the family as the first-born son of Patrick Wogan of Richardstown and Maria (née Dempsey).[2] Only rubble remains of Richardstown Castle today but its location was found marked on maps produced during the Ordnance Survey of Ireland of 1829–1842.[3]

A description underneath its location on the map described it as a ruin, but an entry in the OSI letters describes it as 'a square building about 60 feet in height'.[4]

The most extensive study undertaken on the Wogan family was conducted by Le Comte Alphonse Charles Albert O'Kelly de Galway and its title is *Mémoire historique et génealogique sur la famille de Wogan avec une relation inédite de l'evasion de la princesse Marie-Clémentine Sobieska, femme de Jacques III, roi de la Grande-Bretagne et d'Irlande, 1719*. While it has been criticised for inaccuracies by historians of Wogan such as Hugh Law and Frank D'Arcy, like many other studies of its day it still remains a very useful repository of the memory of what was once a major family of the Pale in Ireland.

The Wogans established themselves as members of a new ruling class in Ireland during the fourteenth century in County Kildare after the Anglo-Norman invasion of Ireland. O'Kelly traced their origins to a patrician family from ancient Rome by the name *Ughi*, providing an agreeable link to classical antiquity.[5] Later, according to O'Kelly, they would have links with nobility and royalty in Angevin Normandy and in medieval England. Before coming to Ireland, the Wogans occupied land in Pembrokeshire in Wales[6] after the Norman conquest of England. Through Justiciar of Ireland, John Wogan (d. 1321), the family became established in County Kildare in Ireland.[7] Even taken with the proverbial pinch of salt, O'Kelly provides an illustrious background for a family obsessed with lineage and adds a flourish to the more recent and tangible sources which could be drawn upon for his study. The immediate subject of this book, Sir Charles Wogan, knight-baronet of Ireland, brigadier (graduato) of the Spanish army, special operative of King James III of Britain and Ireland, Senator of Rome, and acting Governor of Barcelona, had a deep sense of pride in the origins of his family and in the performance of some of his relatives in the more recent unsettled times in early modern Ireland.[8]

Before the Protestant Reformation in the sixteenth century, two groups lived in and contested the patchwork of lordships and large estates which then existed in Ireland, namely the Gaelic Irish and the Anglo-Normans.[9] Until the Reformation, Gaelic and Anglo-Norman families vied with each other to expand their territories and influence in Ireland. As England emerged as a Protestant nation, Ireland stubbornly refused to convert to the new religion despite the wishes and actions of the Tudor monarchs in London. Their efforts included translating the Holy Bible into Irish and instructing English Protestant ministers to conduct their ministries through the medium of Irish; but where the carrot failed, the English monarchs took up the stick and fought brutal wars to bring Ireland completely under English rule. A solution to Ireland's resistance to Protestantism had been trialled which saw the first attempts to plant Protestant English and Scottish settlers in Ireland as a means of providing long-term stability for English rule in Ireland. The new settlers were given lands in Ireland at the expense of those already living there and they were referred to in Ireland as the 'New English'; and so, we return to the original point. The Gaelic Irish (Uí Bhriain [O'Briens], Uí Néill [O'Neills], Uí Dhomhnaill [O'Donnells]), the Old English (Wogans, Warrens, Fitzgeralds, Dillons, Nugents), and the New English (Hunts, Fletchers, Beales) now vied for control of Ireland. The Gaelic Irish and the Old English largely remained Catholics, and the New English followed the new religion.

Thus, the Wogans and other Old English families began to find it difficult to maintain their position of status and their loyalty to the English Crown since the New English in Ireland, and the English government, distrusted their adherence to the Catholic religion. As shall be demonstrated in Wogan's own writings, the Old English identified strongly both with Ireland and with their English and French heritage and attempted to straddle both worlds and maintain their loyalty to the Crown. This position became all the more difficult during the Wars of the Three Kingdoms and Interregnum (1638–1660) when the Old English had to choose between remaining loyal to their monarch or siding with the English parliament.[10] In the end, most of the Old English supported Charles I.

Edward Wogan, a relative of Sir Charles, fought creatively and won a reputation for himself as a brave, resourceful and loyal soldier of the king. The young Charles doubtlessly was influenced by stories of his gallant relative and his sacrifice for the Royalist cause.[11] As a young boy, Charles lived through the War of the Two Kings of 1690–1692 in which his father, Patrick Wogan of Richardstown, was listed as a lieutenant in Lieutenant-Colonel John Wogan's company in Sir Maurice Eustace's regiment of foot of the Irish Jacobite army.[12] The Wogans were fortunate to retain their family holdings at Rathcoffey following severe land confiscations during and after Cromwell's rule. A schedule of deeds contained in the collection titled 'Deeds and papers of the Wogan family of Rathcoffey, 1648–1802', contained in the 'Archive of the Talbot family, Barons Talbot de Malahide' (housed at the Bodleian Library), shows that Willam Wogan received the deed of Rathcoffey from James Butler, Duke of Ormond, dated 2 February 1666.[13] Ormond was serving as Lord Lieutenant of Ireland[14] at the time. John Wogan succeeded William to Rathcoffey, receiving a letter of patent from King Charles II dated 27 November 1683.[15] After the Wars of the Three Kingdoms, the Old English had earned a permanent distrust of the New English, who increasingly became the only reliable vehicle in the English government's eyes for Ireland's peaceful governance in England's interest. Wogan would later correspond with Swift stating that the king gave lands of those who fought for him to those who fought against him.[16]

When the Catholic Duke of York as James II succeeded his brother Charles II as king in 1685, the English found it difficult to stomach; but when his wife Mary's pregnancy and delivery of a healthy male heir secured the Catholic succession, James's daughter, Mary, and her husband, Dutch stadholder Prince William of Orange, were encouraged to invade England which precipitated the so-called glorious revolution. James II would ultimately be deposed and William and Mary received the crown in his stead. The episode was triumphantly referred to by subsequent English historians as the 'Glorious Revolution' but characterised by a historian with a different view as an adventure of backstairs intrigue and foreign invasion![17] The Wogans had to choose again, but similarly to most of the Old English and Gaelic Irish, they viewed James II and his male heirs as the only legitimate kings of England, Scotland and Ireland.

Charles referred to Richard Talbot, Duke of Tyrconnell (James II's last confidant), as his uncle, but the veteran duke would have been quite a distant relative of his. Nevertheless, these two venerable Old English families of the Pale had formed tight connections over the centuries.[18] During the Jacobite-Williamite war (also known as the War of the Two Kings), the lines became more clearly drawn in Ireland than ever before. For the most part, the Gaelic Irish and the Old English sided strongly with James II and the New English sided with William III. James II's Jacobites fought William III's Williamites in a series of battles including at the Boyne (1690), Aughrim (1691) and Limerick (1690–1691), the consequences of which were largely disastrous for the Irish Catholics, both Gaelic and Old English, as the New English would soon repudiate the letter or at least the spirit of the Articles of Limerick in which William had largely set lenient terms for the defeated. A new Protestant ascendancy of Ireland enacted Penal Laws, making life very challenging for Irish Catholics living in Ireland. Many chose to follow James II into exile,[19] taking honourable employment in the military service of major European powers and awaiting the opportunity to restore James II and his family to the thrones of the three kingdoms. This provided the context for the young Charles Wogan, then being raised in close proximity to the long-occupied Wogan lands around Rathcoffey, County Kildare.

Traditional familial loyalty to the Stuart dynasty found new expression through Charles and his brother, Nicholas. The date of Charles's birth has been the source of some confusion. His Spanish military service record and his own correspondence indicate the year 1685.[20] Although, in one of his later letters in the year 1746 he referred to his upcoming 63rd birthday as being in mid-September, which would give us the year 1683 as his year of birth.[21] Even though little is known of his early years, it has been suggested that Charles was sent to England for his education at some point in the late seventeenth or early eighteenth century. Irish Catholics had been prohibited by law from receiving a formal education by an act of the Irish parliament passed in September 1695.[22] Prior to this, it had often been the case for Catholics of gentle birth to be sent to the Continent to be educated at the Irish, English and Scots colleges already established there. Glickman writes that even foreign education had been proscribed officially and that Catholic children had to be sent abroad under aliases. Foreign schooling would become a natural extension of family life that resulted in building a more resilient character with which to endure hard times. Thus, this practice affected Jacobite ideology, preserving 'the transmission of a certain habit of mind ... the intransigent vocab of English Catholicism. "The noble power of suffering bravely", as Pope put it, would be rekindled generation-by-generation'.[23] Wogan would have great need of this personal quality but as regards the transmission of a particular mindset it appears that his son certainly inherited his father's zeal for the cause.

Winch asserts that Wogan resided in Binfield, Berkshire in 1705 and there made friends with Alexander Pope. The only source for this is from Wogan's later correspondence with Jonathan Swift of his relationship with Pope, that he lived 'in perfect union and familiarity, for two or three summers' and that Wogan 'had the honour to bring [him] up to London, from our retreat in the forest of Windsor, to dress *à la mode*, and introduce at Will's coffeehouse', however, he does not mention a specific year.[24] If 1705 and preceding years is accurate for Wogan's 'two or three' summers, that would mean that he would have been roughly between the ages of 17 and 20, and Pope between the ages of 13 and 17. The fact that he mentions the area as a 'retreat' and not a more permanent residence is significant, lending itself to the notion that perhaps he resided there during breaks in the latter stages of his continental education. His name appears in the continental regimental lists immediately after the period in question here – and the Wogan family had branches in Norfolk and Pembrokeshire. They owned a substantial 424-hectare estate in Norfolk,[25] inherited through marriage in the mid-seventeenth century, so it is possible that a British relative supported and housed the young Charles. His education must have been broad enough for him to acquire Latin and to communicate effectively in both English and French, as evidenced by the large body of his letters and poetry.[26] He also seems to have had an in-depth knowledge of classical literature and history. Similarly, the legal impediments to education for Catholics did not prevent Pope from acquiring an outstanding education at home in England. Two early biographers of his give glimpses of the nature of educational opportunities then available. Dilworth states that his father and an aunt taught him to read and write from an early age. At 8 he learned basic Latin and Greek from a priest named Taverner. Two years later he attended a school at Hyde Park Corner before transferring to a 'popish seminary at Twinford near Winchester'. In the early eighteenth century, Pope and his father moved to Binfield near Windsor Forest where a local gentleman named Sir William Trumbull, a fellow of All Souls College at Oxford, became an important patron for the aspiring poet.[27] Ayre's biography, which appeared one year after Pope's death in 1745, asserts that Pope received a private education by a Mr Deane who introduced him to English and Latin poets. By 15 (*c.*1703), Pope 'had a very good acquaintance among people of fashion, who […] had great judgement of men and manners'.[28] Charles Wogan could conceivably have been one of those people of fashion. Wogan's own letters to Swift may not have been known to Ayre when he was writing his biography, so his own reference to having dressed Pope 'à la mode' supports Wogan's inclusion among those anonymous people of fashion. The image of a young and flamboyant Charles Wogan dressing Alexander Pope is quite comical, especially given Pope's prickly reputation.

In the interim between his summers in England (and possibly Ireland) there is a strong possibility that Charles obtained a military post as an officer in an Irish regiment in the French army. The surname 'Woghan' appears in the regimental list, *Contrôle des officiers 1706–1710*, as a lieutenant in the second battalion of the Duke of Berwick's Regiment.[29] The surname is crossed out at the bottom of the section, Captain Dauchimoury's company, and moved up to replace that of an officer by the name of Hide whose name had been crossed out. While there is a chance that this could be another Wogan, since the French military archive contains the records of a few of them, the Wogan name, or any variation of it, does not appear anywhere else in any contemporary regimental lists. His brother Nicholas would probably have been too young at that stage to hold a military post, so Charles may have been serving long enough in that regiment to be promoted to first lieutenant in that company and it presents a credible timeline for his reference to his time with Pope and his joining Berwick's Regiment.[30] No reference appears in Wogan's Spanish military service record to his participation in Berwick's Spanish campaign during the War of the Spanish Succession, an intriguing omission during a particularly active time for the French military. By comparison, his compatriot, John Misset, who accompanied him to Spain after their successful rescue of Princess Clementina Sobieska in 1719, appears regularly during the same period as an officer in Dillon's Regiment. Furthermore, at no stage in his later writings did Wogan mention his involvement in military action during these early years. His appearance on the French army list but lack of military experience or action could suggest that he had already made connections at the Stuart court in exile in Saint-Germain-en-Laye outside Paris.

The court at Saint-Germain was the heart of the Jacobite community of Irish, English, Scots and Welsh exiles and all plans to bring about a restoration emanated from it. It functioned like any royal court with the exception of its prime goal: affecting a restoration. From there, Jacobite ambassadors and agents were sent to the courts of European powers in the constant campaign to garner support for a restoration. The queen dowager, Mary of Modena, consort of the deceased James II, still resided there and provided crucial support to the needy subjects who had followed her and her late husband into exile. Artists and musicians visited, resided and composed new works of art there. High-ranking members of the exiled aristocracy of England, Scotland and Ireland held full-time positions at the court.[31] In addition, Cardinal Filippo Antonio Gualtiero, the Roman Catholic cardinal protector of the three kingdoms resided there. The papacy, in its refusal to recognise British monarchs in the aftermath of the deposition of James II, granted the right to confirm appointments to vacant Catholic sees and positions in Britain and Ireland exclusively to the Stuart kings in exile. With the cooperation of Cardinal Gualtiero, James III fulfilled it, providing him with a direct means of influencing the internal affairs of the three kingdoms.[32] The familiar tone of one of the surviving letters written by Wogan to Gualtiero in March 1716 suggests that he already knew the cardinal.[33] The young Irishman's selection by James III to undertake the risky job of infiltrating England in the late summer of 1715 also suggests that he had made himself known to his superiors and to his liege at Saint-Germain. That his name appears in the French military service records suggests that he drew pay from Berwick's Regiment; the lack of evidence of active duty indicates that he may have been selected to play a more creative a part in the restoration of the Stuarts.

Chapter 2

The Fifteen

It is a testament to the prestige of Charles and Nicholas Wogan among the Jacobite high command that both performed at the highest level of the Jacobite army with important duties in Northumbria at the beginning of the 1715 rebellion. The Wogans formed part of a small group of military officers who travelled north from London disguised as tourists to inform James III's supporters to be ready to rise up against 'German' George, the Hanoverian successor to Queen Anne. O'Callaghan claims that up to nine-tenths of the population of Britain and Ireland opposed the Hanoverian Succession.[34] It is notable that the Irish remained totally quiet during this rebellion; reasons suggested for this inactivity include the draining of men of fighting age from Ireland into the continental services and a lack of planning and weaponry (owning arms and horses was prohibited for Catholics under the Penal Legislation). Despite this, four of the twelve men instructed to prepare the rebellion in northern England were Irish: Colonel Henry Oxburgh, Captain James Talbot, and both Charles and Nicholas Wogan, and all have come in for some criticism. Szechi notes that 'when the Northern English rebellion broke out in October observers were moved to comment on how ill-prepared most of the participants were, despite the fact that Jacobite agents – who included a number of Irish officers formerly in French Service – had been sent out by the conspirators in London since at least August'.[35] Any explanation as to what the expectations were from a dozen officers sent forth with no weapons or money to a place the size of Switzerland is not forthcoming or immediately apparent. In any case, the Jacobite officers secured enough support in northern England to begin marching south. Thomas Forster was nominated for command of the English Jacobite forces. He had no military experience and it has been suggested that his selection stemmed from a need to gain the support of English Protestants.[36] This tendency to make political selections for key roles instead of appointing those most competent to achieve results would continue to haunt and hamper the Jacobite cause. It would appear in hindsight that Colonel Henry Oxburgh, a veteran of the Irish Jacobite army and of Louis XIV's wars in Europe, would have been the better choice as a military leader; however, as an Irish Catholic from County Offaly, his command of the English Jacobite army would have been unpalatable to potential English leaders and recruits. On this occasion, Forster's selection for this command did not go well for the Jacobites.

Charles Wogan served as *aide-de-camp*[37] to Forster. His brother Nicholas, 'a gentleman of a most generous mind and a great deal of bravery', took command of the fifth troop of English Jacobites suggesting that he led a detachment of cavalry.[38] The force traversed northern England during September 1715, gathering supporters, arms and provisions on their march. They were joined by Brigadier William Macintosh and William Gordon, sixth Viscount Kenmuir, from the main Jacobite army under John Erskine, Earl of Mar, in Scotland. The joint forces pressed south from Kelso towards Manchester numbering about 4000 men with plans to seize the city and capture Warrington Bridge to secure Liverpool. The cavalry vanguard of the Jacobite army entered Preston on 9 November to be followed the next day by the main force.[39] However, the Jacobite leaders failed to observe the movements of King George's army and by 12 November they faced six regiments under the command of General Charles Wills at Preston.[40] A hastily assembled Jacobite army, without adequate weapons, lacking serious training, experience or pay, faced fully-trained and equipped professional soldiers.[41] General Wills moved his men towards Preston from the south and found that the Jacobites had left the narrow bridge over the River Ribble totally undefended. This would be decisive, since this single crossing over the river less than a kilometre from the town would have provided an ideal place for an advanced defensive position and any attempt to take the bridge could have been made very costly indeed for the Hanoverian forces. A rare contemporary account[42] asserts that a Captain Wogan commanded an advance party which defended the approach to the town from the bridge and that his defensive position centred upon a barricade erected across the road. The position was also defended by some buildings at the edge of the town.[43] Wills ordered the attack and the Jacobites repulsed the first attempt with heavy losses for the government forces. His men had better luck on the second attempt and managed to occupy some buildings after which fires were lit and the chaos of street-fighting characterised the day's combat. After another day of indecisive action, Wills's reinforcements from Newcastle under General Carpenter moved into position north of Preston on 13 November, effectively surrounding the Jacobite forces. Many of these subsequently slipped away that night in the darkness, obviously mindful of their untenable position. Nicholas Wogan distinguished himself through chivalrous action in the heat of the battle. He saved a Hanoverian officer, Captain Preston, who had been wounded, from being summarily killed by Jacobite soldiers. This would later save Nicholas from execution. Fighting continued throughout the weekend, until government reinforcements arrived from the north and surrounded the Jacobite army on 13 November.

Forster sent Colonel Oxburgh to conduct negotiations for surrender to General Wills, without the knowledge of the Jacobite junior officers or the rank and file.[44] It is telling of the general hostile[45] sentiment in the town towards capitulation that Forster did not appear publicly during this time. Indeed, the news so incensed James Murray that he drew a pistol on Forster only to have his aim skewed by the intervention of Robert Patten, Forster's chaplain and later author of *The History of The Rebellion in the Year 1715*.[46] Murray had arrived in Scotland from the exiled Stuart court in France by way of England on 2 October, apparently referring to himself as James III's secretary of state.[47]

Despite their misgivings, the Jacobite force obtained a cease fire on 13 November and laid down arms the following day.[48] Wills divided and confined them in the subsequent days. 1301 Scottish Highland clansmen were transported to North American plantations to serve as indentured labourers for a limited term.[49] About a fortnight later, Wills removed the Wogan brothers and 174 other officers to London.[50] At Highgate Hill, he divided the prisoners between the Marshalsea, the Tower, the Fleet, and Newgate where he confined the Wogans.[51] This was only an early phase of the 'Fifteen', which ran into 1716 but, after the Preston debacle was confined to Scotland. The rebellion got substantial support from Phillipe d'Anjou de Bourbon, victor of the War of the Spanish Succession, now Philip V of Spain. Documents in the *Archivo Historico Nacional* in Madrid shed light on the substantial financial support that was sent by the Spanish state to assist James III in this latest attempt at his restoration.[52] The French proved less forthcoming, as they had just entered a period of entente with the government of George I and they seemed reluctant to jeopardise it. At the same time, they played a balancing act, pledging money and some supplies. Crucially though, they refused to send any Irishmen serving in the ranks of the French military to assist the rebellion because this clearly would have breached the new understanding with Britain.[53] On the other hand, in the unlikely event of the rebellion achieving its goal, they needed to appear to have assisted this happy result, thereby setting themselves up for a positive relationship with the new government in Britain. Without serious military assistance from France or Spain, however, the rebellion was doomed. Furthermore, George I's government had taken very effective action in the summer of 1715 to neutralise the potential leadership of the rebellion in the West Country and in traditional Royalist/Jacobite strongholds such as Oxford. They took effective action to control the situation and they could rely on Dutch military assistance which would be deployed to good effect. Their pre-emptive action is significant because it points to their excellent intelligence and information network. This became one of the most effective weapons that the Hanoverian regime would develop and use to devastating effect against the Jacobites throughout this period. James III arrived in Scotland on 22 December 1715, but without trained soldiers, supplies or money, he returned to France on 5 February 1716. The rebellion petered out and the consequences for its leadership, including Charles Wogan, would be very serious indeed.

Chapter 3

From Newgate to the Palazzo Ducale

According to Daniel Defoe's *The History of the Pressyard* (London, 1717), 174 Jacobite prisoners 'were marched from the Hill of Highgate through the streets of London to their respective places of durance amid jeers and hoots encouraged by their captors'.[54] Approximately seventy prisoners were received by the officers of Newgate, had their names called out, but then had their bindings removed and were treated to refreshments of French wine.[55] This contrasts sharply with their earlier treatment of being paraded as criminals. The prisoners could thank Mr Pitts, governor of Newgate, for this hospitality which suggests that they had entered into friendlier custody. It may also point to some sympathy with their cause, or at least a muted expression of dissatisfaction with the Whig establishment and 'German George'. This source also provides insights into the relatively relaxed conditions of the prison, which were quite surprising particularly for those who had taken up arms against state authorities. The Jacobite prisoners received regular visits from supporters and family members who provided them with material and financial help. They also received aid from foreign benefactors. Their financial wherewithal meant that they could pay turnkeys to have their shackles removed, enjoy a wide variety of food and wine, and in General Forster's case, to be housed and fed in the governor's residence itself.[56] In Wogan's case, he was able to acquire all he needed to write and post letters and even compose poetry.

Until recently, scholarship concerning Charles Wogan seems to have been unaware that he had engaged in a poetic correspondence with William Tunstall, another Jacobite taken at Preston but imprisoned in the Marshalsea. Tunstall, a pro-Stuart propagandist and pamphleteer, had joined the Jacobite cause in northern England and became paymaster general of the Jacobite army.[57] Robert Patten's *The History of Rebellion in the Year 1715* described Tunstall as 'a Yorkshire man, second son to a gentleman of that county, of a plentiful estate'.[58] He is therein described as a somewhat older, well-educated, Catholic gentleman with a cheerful nature. From his cell in Marshalsea, Tunstall initiated a poetic correspondence with Wogan.[59] Their verse later appeared under the title *Poems of Love and Gallantry*,[60] set to the old English tune *To all ye ladies now at land*, a ballad which laments sailors' departure from shore leaving their sweethearts behind them. Tunstall is doubtless jesting at their being deprived of female company. The title also alludes to the strong possibility that they would most certainly face a life in exile after sentencing. Despite the gravity of their circumstances, the content struck a light-hearted tone. The first piece begins thus:

> From me, dear Charles, inspired with ale
> To thee this letter comes
> To try if scribbling can prevail
> To moderate our dooms
> Tho' pent in cage the blackbird swings
> Yet still he hops, and struts, and sings!

Tunstall's introductory piece is ten stanzas in length and it abounds with classical references and light-hearted appraisals of his incarceration, including a comparison to the confines of marriage. To the same tune, Wogan wrote a reply dedicated 'to the ladies about court and town from the Preston prisoners'. The tone remained light-hearted, though the latter's lines do not exhibit the same flourish as the former's, whose benefit of years shone through. Tunstall humorously replied to Wogan not to doubly shackle himself, at once being imprisoned in Newgate and again for the sake of the affections of the fairer sex. Under the burden of the charges against them, one imagines that such cheerful rhymes brought a welcome comfort.[61]

The executions of James Radclyffe, third Earl of Derwentwater, and William Gordon, sixth Viscount Kenmuir, for their leadership roles in the 'Fifteen' dashed whatever sense of comfort the prisoners might have felt. In a classic example of Whiggish quippery, the anonymous author of *The Secret History of the Rebels in Newgate* wrote:

> After the execution of the two lords, they [the prisoners] received orders to prepare for their trial, then their *Jacobite courage* did quickly appear in its proper colours: they knew that in such circumstances, one pair of heels was worth two pairs of hands: so that having as little stomach to die for the cause as they had to fight for it, they began seriously to contrive an escape.[62]

In March an escape attempt by breaking through the Press Yard wall failed, at which our Whig author remarks, 'this prevented their dearly beloved practice of running away'.[63] On 7 April 1716, the authorities brought bills of high treason against Forster, Oxburgh, the two Wogans and several other Jacobite leaders.[64]

This expedited the escape attempts and on 10 April, Forster slipped his loose confinement. Governor Pitt, now suspected of Jacobite sympathy, was arrested and charged with treason but he was later acquitted.[65] Security at Newgate was increased. On 26 April Charles, Nicholas and a number of others appeared at the bar and pleaded not guilty.[66] Quite literally at the eleventh hour, on the night before Wogan's trial, Brigadier Macintosh, Charles, and a number of other prisoners surprised a turnkey and forced their way out of the gaol.[67] Ever fond of a dramatic story, Wogan later recalled the event:

> tho' laden with irons, I forced with the help of a few unarmed companions, all the doors and bolts of a prison, manned with treble guards already aware of the attempt; and wrenched muskets and bayonettes out of the hands of those that never knew, until then, what it was to lay down or give up their arms.[68]

The contemporary Whig commentator seems to have fallen silent on this matter, and one wonders how he might have riposted to Wogan's parry. In his later correspondence with Jonathan Swift, Dean of St Patrick's Cathedral, Dublin, Wogan refrains from the use of the word 'flight' in favour of 'honourable retreat' when describing this event.[69] James Talbot, one of the Irish instigators of the rebellion, was retaken shortly afterwards with some others, but Wogan and Macintosh made good their escape.[70] Colonel Henry Oxburgh had no such luck. He was sentenced to death on 10 May, and executed four days later; his head ended up on a spike on Temple Bar, London, as a grisly reminder to Jacobite sympathisers of the consequences of their political allegiance. This backfired on the Whig government, as it provoked widespread sympathy among the public for the Newgate prisoners and would prove fortunate for the Jacobites.[71] Nicholas, who had remained at Newgate, was tried on 18 May and received a death sentence. However, his earlier chivalry at Preston provided a form of life insurance. Captain Preston, whose life he had saved, testified in his favour and he secured a reprieve on 22 May 1716.[72]

Charles's correspondence of 1732 with Swift provides the details of his escape from Newgate and flight to France. Wogan's own copy of his epistolary exchanges with the anti-Whig, politically suspect Swift in *The Wogan Manuscript* provides insights into many of the finer details, though embellished with a literary flourish.[73] Nevertheless, Wogan's first package to Swift in 1732 gave a brief description of his time as a fugitive. Shortly after his escape, the British authorities offered a bounty of £500 for his recapture. He evaded his pursuers, almost being discovered in a building in which he had taken refuge, narrowly avoiding detection by hiding on a rooftop[74] 'while the whole neighbourhood stood gazing out of the garrett-windows adjacent; and the houses, as well as the streets about me; were crowded with a posse and its ever-attending mob'.[75] News of the escape of such a large number of high-profile prisoners from Newgate would indeed have travelled fast and, as has been noted, public sentiments had been warmed in favour of the Jacobites in the wake of the executions at Tyburn. Wogan fled the city and sought refuge 'in the thick forest of the city of London'.[76] He wrote to Swift that he had settled for a night beneath the walls of Arundel Castle, the seat of Thomas Howard, eighth Duke of Norfolk, whose brother, Edward, had participated in the ill-fated rebellion the previous year.[77] As has been noted, the Wogan family had properties in Norfolk. It is unclear whether Wogan had been actively assisted by Norfolk or by members of his household to escape to the coast when his pursuers made such 'noise and bustle in all corners of the castle' trying to find him.[78] Eventually, Wogan obtained transport from a sympathiser from Chichester to Courcelles-sur-Seine, within easy reach of Paris where he arrived 'towards the end of June in 1716'.[79]

As stated above, it has been claimed that Wogan had served in Arthur Dillon's Irish regiment, part of the Irish Brigade in the French army, for a period after his flight to France. An examination of French military records and his correspondence indicates otherwise. Letters in the *Calendar of Stuart Papers* collate Wogan's own approximated time of arrival in France with a missive between William Gordon and John Patterson, two Parisian Jacobites, dated 8 July 1716:

> …give my son the enclosed bill of 128 livres on Mr. Wogan. If he don't [*sic*] pay it, cause him to speak to General Forster, who ordered me to advance Wogan what he wanted for his journey, and I thought I might repay this gentleman who had so seasonably assisted him.[80]

When testifying to Wogan's prowess at Preston, Robert Patten echoed the admirable terms used to describe Wogan's service to Forster as his *aide-de-camp* during the 'Fifteen'. The journey that Gordon referred to in the above-cited letter could refer to Wogan's travel expenses from his crossing the channel or, perhaps, a new venture, as shall be seen. By this date it is most likely that he was in Paris. His relative, Major Richard Gaydon of Dillon's Regiment, frequented the city as evidenced in subsequent letters in the *Stuart Papers*.[81] In November 1716, correspondence between Father Thomas Innes, prefect of studies at The Scots College in Paris, and John Erskine, Earl of Mar, James III's secretary of state, mentions Wogan as part of their correspondence network. It is evident that Wogan swiftly returned to James's service in a similar capacity to that which he held before the 'Fifteen'. On 16 November 1716, the

Earl of Mar sent instructions to Wogan, then based in Lyons, to act as a conduit through which Jacobite correspondence could flow with the decreased possibility of being detected by the ever-watchful agents of John Dalrymple, Lord Stair, George I's ambassador to France, and his allies in the French establishment. As has been noted, the British intelligence system became more effective and sophisticated during that era. The Mar-Wogan correspondence refers to the Jacobite court in exile's need to use complex ciphers to protect sensitive information in their letters. Once established in Lyons under a false name and with various secure delivery addresses, Wogan would provide a secondary route for correspondence between the papal enclave of Avignon, James III's contemporary residence, and Paris.[82]

It is clear that from November 1716 until February 1717, Wogan was posted at Lyons, and a letter from Mar states that James III required him to follow the king to his new residence in Bologna.[83] Wogan's letters from Lyons require extensive examination; suffice to say that his correspondence brims with intrigue and intelligence from a multitude of sources on a wide range of issues, all of which are linked to the ultimate goal of a Jacobite restoration.

Wogan's trail may be picked up again in correspondence between John Patterson and the Earl of Mar, dated 5 June 1717, in which he is mentioned as having set out in the company of Lieutenant-General Arthur Dillon from Paris to Rome.[84] This letter may well explain the origin of the notion that Wogan had served in Dillon's Regiment and it is possible that he had served there at an earlier stage as an ensign or cadet before he attained his rank of lieutenant at Berwick's. Even though he accompanied Dillon to Paris in 1717, it is very unlikely that it was in a soldiering capacity. It is more likely that Wogan served as James's agent, and that he had been sent him to Paris in that capacity on special business. Thereafter it seems that Wogan resided at the Jacobite court in exile in Urbino until summoned to join James Butler, 2nd Duke of Ormond, on a diplomatic mission to make peace between Charles XII of Sweden and Czar Peter the Great of Russia and unite them against George I.[85] A secondary objective was to visit various courts to identify suitable princesses who might be considered as potential brides for James III in 1718.[86]

Chapter 4

Diplomacy and Strategy

The failure of the 'Fifteen' proved that without serious diplomatic, material and financial support from allies in Europe, future attempts would meet a similar end. After the rebellion, George I had put renewed pressure on the regency of Prince Philippe d'Orléans, nephew of Louis XIV, to have James III and his court in exile removed from French territory. This had been a condition of the peace of Utrecht (1713), which concluded the War of the Spanish Succession. The French government had initially done nothing but now George I forced its hand; so in the aftermath of the 'Fifteen' they complied with his wishes that James be removed first to the Duchy of Lorraine et Bar, then to Avignon, Pesaro, Urbino, and eventually to Rome. This British diplomatic success severely hampered James's ability to affect his restoration and to recruit members of the British and Irish nobility to staff his court in exile. From 1717–1719 the British, Dutch, French and Austrians formed the quadruple alliance to shore up peace and stability in Europe and to act as a counter-weight to Bourbon Franco-Spanish might.[87] While the British government settled into a new era of power-politics based on effective diplomacy, James retained many supporters and sympathisers in places of authority in all the major powers of Europe.

During the same period, the Stuart monarch deployed some of his most capable and prestigious supporters on diplomatic and strategic endeavours in Europe. He could already count on Cardinal Giulio Alberoni, secretary of state in Spain, to act in his interest at the court of King Philip V and Queen Elizabeth Farnese in Madrid. The papacy with all its contacts and influence scattered throughout Europe also proved supportive and reliable. James decided that for now his best chances lay in enticing the support of Sweden and Russia for his cause. Rebecca Wills details the diplomatic efforts of Jacobite agents and of members of the extensive Jacobite network in Europe to form new alliances and to disrupt George I's plans in Europe. One such effort in Summer 1717 included an attempt by James to broker a peace between King Charles XII of Sweden and Czar Peter the Great of Russia to put an end to the great northern war and form an anti-Hanover alliance in support of James III. James Butler, second Duke of Ormond, would be accompanied in his diplomatic endeavours by George Jerningham, Charles Wogan and Daniel O'Brien. They aimed to bring Sweden and Russia in concert with Spain, then isolate and weaken the quadruple alliance, and plan a military intervention to restore James III. The British government protested repeatedly at the Czar's willingness to meet with Jacobite representatives, while their intelligence intercepted letters which showed Peter's enthusiasm for the Pretender's cause. In the end, this diplomatic mission floundered due to the sudden death of Charles XII of Sweden and the loss of Robert Erskine, the main Jacobite connection in Russia and a personal friend of Czar Peter. The repeated protestations and diplomatic efforts on the part of the British government indicate the seriousness with which they treated the Jacobite threat.[88]

That Wogan played a key part in this affair shows James's growing confidence in him as a capable agent, moreover, this particular diplomatic effort provides an excellent example of the extensive Irish Jacobite network throughout all Europe. Ormond, Wogan and O'Brien formed the contingent from the Jacobite court in exile; Sir Patrick Lawless who was an influential Jacobite agent in Spain and was very close to King Philip V, joined in the efforts as the Spanish representative to Russia; as did Peter Lacy, one of the most influential military officers in Russia who was close to the czar himself and who consistently advocated in favour of James III's interests.[89] As for Wogan, he had been given a secondary objective to scout possible marriage matches for James III, whose unmarried status caused consternation among his supporters because of its implications for the continuation of the Stuart royal line. Furthermore, the use of marriage as a means of gaining important strategic relationships, increased prestige, and access to wealth became an important part of planning and strategy for all royal families and members of the aristocracy during this era. Regarding Wogan's selection for this mission, the Earl of Mar wrote to him on 25 November 1717:

> I had occasion to tell you before of the king's good opinion of you; I now have orders to write to you of an affair he is to employ you in, and I am persuaded he will have to be pleased at your discretion, secrecy, and good conduct, in going about it, with all the diligence and zeal it requires, and saving time in consequence.

In fact, the czar had offered his own daughter's hand in marriage to James but a defect in her lineage coupled with Charles XII's death and the changing diplomatic situation were all circumstances that may have stifled the match.[90] Wogan had orders to travel incognito through central Europe to find a suitable match for James. It is unclear whether he was still accompanied by Ormond but it is unlikely, as the latter would have been easily recognisable to Whig spies and informers.

Towards the end of his journey he stopped at Ohlau, the residence of Prince James Louis Sobieski (son of John Sobieski III, King of the Commonwealth of Poland and Lithuania and victor over the Turks at Vienna in 1683).[91] There, Wogan met with the 15-year-old Princess Maria Clementina Sobieska and wrote favourably to his master of this charming young princess with a wealthy, well-connected family. Her mother, Countess Palatine Hedwig Elisabeth of Neuberg, was aunt of the Holy Roman Emperor, Charles VI, sister of the Duchess of Parma, and of the queen-dowager of the late Charles II of Spain.[92] Wogan surmised that the cheerful Clementina would be the perfect match for James who suffered from bouts of depression. She would also be able to provide valuable connections and financial resources to the House of Stuart. James quickly agreed to the idea of this match and began making preparations for a formal proposal.

Soon after he returned to James's court at Urbino, an event characterised as 'a foolish thing' involving Wogan took place in July

1718.[93] After successfully gaining the consent of Princess Clementina and her father, Prince James Louis, Wogan retained his position at the Stuart court as part of the military detail providing security. The small court remained in transition while James III strategised on where best to set up his permanent residence. Housed at the magnificent Palazzo Ducale in Urbino, the professional military officers at the court included a number of prominent Catholic Irishmen: Major Donald MacMahon; Captain John O'Brien; Captain Charles Wogan; and another O'Brien, Captain Sir John O'Brien, later promoted to colonel by James III in October 1717. Wogan and McMahon shared an apartment at the Palazzo Ducale. The pair had enjoyed good companionship and had taken trips to the countryside together and seemed to the other members of the small court-in-exile to be on good terms. At the Palazzo Ducale, the boredom of exile gave ample time to ruminate on perceived slights, and at the exclusively male court, King James could not always maintain discipline.[94] Mar's letter outlined the circumstances in detail describing how Wogan and McMahon had hosted a party and had taken drink, but at the end of the party were left by one who attended 'hugging and dancing together'.[95] Despite this, Wogan challenged McMahon on a number of minor incidents about which he was unhappy; McMahon dismissed them, and in the end the two fought a duel on the streets during which both men were lightly wounded.[96] Duelling over insults to one's honour was a feature of life among gentry and aristocracy during the period. It had become enough of a social issue to be banned by temporal and spiritual authorities alike.[97] Some of the townsfolk had seen them and it became the subject of much gossip. James III reacted with fury to this lapse of discipline among his trusted courtiers. He had just been required to make a humiliating move from France, dealing a serious blow to his chances of a restoration; an embarrassing episode like this allowed his Whiggish detractors to heap more scorn on him and his cause. Mar remarked that it would 'take some time before they can pacify their master. In order for them to appear publicly in his presence they will first have a public and severe reprimand with a certification to all his people that if any such thing happens again, how severely he will use them'.[98] James duly reprimanded both men and confined them to their quarters.[99] He could ill-afford such bad publicity at a time when a serious change of a prestigious and advantageous royal match had presented itself. Regardless of this minor embarrassment, James soon have reason to call on Wogan.

Shortly after this, James III sent James Murray to negotiate the marriage contract with the Sobieskis at Ohlau. Aware that the majority of his would-be subjects in Britain were Protestants, he therefore decided that it would be prudent to send one of his Protestant officials to lead the embassy and make the marriage arrangements. The Earl of Mar suggested his protégé, Murray, who had been released in the post-1715 amnesty in Britain.[100] The suitability of Murray for this important task jars with contemporary accounts of his character and conduct by other high-profile Jacobites. Captain John Ogilvie alluded to Murray as 'that busy young gentleman' and characterised him as 'a young, vain, white-livered Jackanapes'.[101] A more serious complaint had been made against him by Robert Harley, Earl of Oxford, who had been first lord of the treasury under Queen Anne from 1711–1714. Harley complained that Murray had written him a letter in a very superior tone and that he had badly failed to observe appropriate protocol:

> ... I am afraid his vain conduct will create more mischief and do more harm to the king's service than all his family and he can ever be capable to retrieve.[102]

Mar, the unsuccessful leader of Jacobite forces in the 'Fifteen', and thereafter secretary of state in the exiled Stuart court, had brought Murray into the office as his assistant. That he benefitted from Mar's patronage can be discerned by his commission to present James III's formal proposal of marriage. However, he soon undermined his patron's position at the Jacobite court, which may explain Mar's growing disillusionment with the Stuart cause, which led him to gravitate towards a reconciliation with George I and accept a British pension in 1721.[103] Murray ultimately displaced Mar and he began to exert a lasting influence over James. Wogan expressed his deep unhappiness at not being able to conclude what he had prepared and balked at Murray's selection over him.[104] Years later, in his account of the rescue written in 1744, he laid the blame squarely on Mar:

> … the duke of Mar … made him [the king] understand (with more ruse than truth) the harm he could do himself among the English in general and the umbrage the English would inevitably take if the services of an Irish Catholic were used in such an important affair…This would have very unfortunate consequences for his majesty, were these consequences not prevented and rendered ineffective thanks to the intelligence and intrepidity of this same Irish Catholic.[105]

This comment provides us with a glimpse of an undercurrent of resentment in Wogan's writings which also surfaced in his correspondence with Swift in the 1730s. He himself identified the apparent issue of his nationality and his religion in the eyes of the English and Scottish Jacobites around James, as rendering him unworthy of certain responsibilities. The true extent of any damage that could be caused by Wogan's selection is unknowable, but James III wanted to be prudent and sensitive in his politics on such occasions. This remained a source of anger for Wogan, as will be discussed below.

Murray went to Ohlau and he concluded negotiations with Prince James Sobieski for the marriage in May 1718. However, according to a letter from James Hamilton to Mar, dated London, 24 October 1718, Murray had been overheard talking, despite the need for discretion, about the plans for Princess Clementina's marriage to James III.[106] Evidently, the news quickly spread. Murray returned to Rome with the good news but fell ill and could not return to Ohlau to escort Clementina and her retinue to Rome. John Hay, Murray's brother-in-law, deputised but whether by bad planning or plain incompetence, Hay and his companions would be openly mocked by British officials and agents when they arrived at Innsbruck to meet the princess and her mother, as the two women were en route to Rome. The secrecy of their mission had been compromised and their incognito became nothing more than a farce.[107]

In the aftermath of the War of the Spanish Succession, tensions between King Philip V of Spain and the Emperor Charles VI continued to simmer. Philip wished to assert himself as the new Spanish Bourbon monarch and to recover former Spanish territories in Italy. Charles VI had gained territory from the Treaty of Utrecht but he considered unacceptable the splitting apart of the 'Two Sicilies', (Naples and Sicily), and the awarding of part of Sicily to Victor Amadeus of Savoy.[108] Having negotiated a favourable peace for Britain and Hanover at Utrecht, George I and his ministers continued to play a delicate diplomatic game in Europe. George wished to maintain an image of himself as both a defender of British Protestants and the wider Protestant interests. George's envoy in Vienna at the time, the Swiss Seigneur Francois Louis de Pesmes de Saint-Saphorin, aggressively supported the Hanoverians both to retain the three kingdoms and to promote the Protestant interest in Europe.[109] He had an accomplished military career in both the Dutch and Austrian services before entering the diplomatic service of Britain and Hanover. Similar to James Stanhope, first Earl Stanhope, George I's chief minister and principal foreign secretary, commenced machinations to prevent the proposed union between James III and the illustrious and extremely wealthy Sobieski family. At this time the British had become irritated with Charles VI for various reasons. Despite an article of the Treaty of Utrecht forbidding his setting up of an Ostend East India company, the Emperor had proceeded to do just that.[110] Despite this, George, as Elector of Hanover, had been very supportive of Charles, particularly during the War of the Spanish Succession. Therefore, the Emperor could not afford to ignore or refuse George's request that he do everything to obstruct the proposed Stuart-Sobieski marriage. Meanwhile, Stanhope dispatched a letter to Saint-Saphorin in Vienna strongly insisting the Imperial authorities immediately detain the Princess Clementina. En route to Italy, the princess was detained by General Hester at Innsbruck, on the orders of Charles VI, and placed under guard outside the old city walls in what is today the Palais Trapp, but was then known as the Greffensche Haus, 38 Marie-Theresien Strasse.[111] This incident seems to have caused alarm across Europe,[112] as the detention of a royal princess, a child of 16, and her mother at the behest of the British government was regarded as highly undignified and distasteful. The detention, though necessary for British support to safeguard his Italian territories against Spain, did not sit well with Charles as he had no wish to separate man and wife. One of Stanhope's letters warned the Emperor of the implications of failure regarding his obstruction of the match, stating that while 'conscience would have him avoid the greatest of two evils, so prudence should make him choose the least of two inconveniences'.[113] James III soon despaired, perceiving yet another manifestation of a curse upon the House of Stuart. He returned from Bologna to the Palazzo del Re in Rome where his safety was guaranteed.[114] A letter allegedly written by Clementina encouraging James to rescue her would circulate in his English kingdom among *Poems on Several Occasions* (1719):

> O Thee, my dear James, my lover and my friend, From Innsbruck's tow'rs these mournful lines I send, where I in a cloister, by unjust alarms, the German pow'rs with-hold me from thy arms. To thee, Britannia's native, exil'd king, I send in writing what I fain would bring, long health I send, and, void of winning art, the kindest wishes of a love-sick-heart.[115]

It is most probable that an English Jacobite enthusiast penned it as a piece of anti-Hanoverian propaganda. Its tone not only appeals to pro-Stuart romanticism, but may have been intended to strike a chord with current popular disdain for 'German George'. Furthermore, no original letter expressing such sentiments in Clementina's own handwriting exists. At this stage, she would not have been fluent in English. However, the idea of rescuing Clementina had not yet occurred to James, who soon left his papal refuge to join Cardinal Alberoni and Ormond in Madrid as they prepared another expedition to restore him to the thrones of the three kingdoms. Fate intervened once again against the hapless James as the Mediterranean winds prevented him from linking up with Ormond before their departure. The expedition failed as the fleet was dispersed by a storm before reaching British waters. While Clementina remained under house-arrest in Innsbruck, James III called on Wogan to affect her rescue and escape.

Chapter 5

The Rescue and Escape of Princess Maria Clementina Sobieska

Although the rescue has been the subject of many publications already, it is important for the purposes of this book to identify all of the various sources of information surrounding this event. In itself, the rescue and escape of Princess Clementina was to be the most impactful and memorable act of Wogan's service to the Jacobite cause, for along with success in achieving the goal, James III and his queen consort would produce two royal princes and continue the Stuart dynastic line. A synopsis of the delicate preparation and effective execution of the rescue is necessary here. On its own merits, it is one of the most remarkable acts of bravery, skill and daring in the annals of eighteenth-century Europe – the rescue of a royal princess from the custody of the Holy Roman Emperor and her escape with her Irish liberators over the Alps. Sir John Gilbert collated, edited and published the original accounts in 1894. He published five accounts of the rescue under the title *Narratives of the Detention, Liberation, and Marriage of Maria Clementina Stuart, styled Queen of Great Britain and Ireland, with contemporary letters and papers for the first time published*. Of the five accounts, there is one in English published in 1722 under the title *Female Fortitude* which is attributed to Wogan himself; a second version in French by Wogan written in 1744; another version in French by Major Richard Gaydon from 1719; one contemporary Italian version by an unknown author; and an account by Bonaventure Boylan, an Irish Franciscan at Louvain in Belgium.[116] Cathy Winch also reported that she was shown three accounts of the rescue written in German at the Innsbruck City Archive. Peggy Miller wrote in her introduction of *A Wife for the Pretender*[117] that copies of an account of the rescue and original letters between James III, Prince James Louis Sobieski, Princess Clementina and Pope Clement XI were made by a Polish noble named Prince Henri Lubomirski in 1845. The collection was housed in the National Library in Saint Petersburg but was later transferred to the Ossolinskich National Library in Wroclaw. There is a good chance that others exist in archives throughout central Europe, for the audacious event would have provided very entertaining reading for those fond of gazettes and other such publications.

Wogan received permission from King James to attempt a rescue of Clementina.[118] Prince James Louis Sobieski also gave him leave to carry it out.[119] He ordered Clementina and her mother to do as Wogan requested. In Wogan's version of the rescue, penned in 1744 which he dedicated to Queen Marie Leszczyńska of France, Clementina's cousin, he gives a very detailed account of how delicately he preserved his incognito in Ohlau while under the scrutiny of George I's spies and informers. Wogan places more emphasis on his own cunning and skill in the 1744 version than in the 1722 account, which served more to position James III as a prudent monarch and Clementina as the brave heroine, cheerfully overcoming all adversity and danger.[120] When he set out from Rome to attempt the rescue, only a small number of people knew of the plan, including James III, Pope Clement XI (Clementina's godfather), Cardinal Origo of Bologna, and Prince James Sobieski. Using his experience and his connections to safely send messages, letters travelled between Rome, Bologna, Vienna, Innsbruck, Ohlau and Strasbourg in the coordination of the daring rescue. He first travelled to Ohlau to secure Prince James's permission to attempt the rescue. Sobieski came under mounting pressure from Emperor Charles VI to call off the engagement. On New Year's Day 1719, Prince James originally declined Wogan's rescue plan but offered him a priceless gift to assuage his disappointment:

> A snuff box carved from turquoise, which King John, his father, had found in the tent of the Grand Vizier on the day of the famous battle of Vienna. It was unique of its kind, mounted in gold, and priceless, there being nothing like it in all Christendom, so much so that the jewellers of Augsburg, who know as much about their profession in Europe, declined to put a price on it.[121]

King John led 3000 Winged Hussars over a hill to the rear of the Ottoman camp which broke the exhausted Ottoman formations. He captured the personal tent of Grand Vizier Kara Mustafa Pasha with all his papers and possessions.[122] Wogan refused the gift stating that he could not return to Rome with such a gift without having secured the objective of his purpose there.[123] This display of steadfast loyalty won over the Sobieski patriarch, and he finally agreed to a rescue attempt. Along with the original 1744 version presented to Queen Marie Leszcyńska, Wogan included copies of the original written orders given to him by Prince James:

> … I give Monsieur de Wogan by the present note full powers to plan everything to carry out my daughter's escape: obliging me, furthermore, to lose my life rather than consent to Princess Clementina, my daughter, being the wife of any man, other than His Majesty King James III of England…[124]

Wogan then proceeded to Selestat, a garrison town near Strasbourg where Arthur Dillon's Irish Regiment were stationed. From its ranks, he recruited relatives of his to accompany him on the rescue attempt including Major Richard Gaydon, Captain John Misset, Lady Eleanor Misset, Captain Luke O'Toole and Lady Misset's servant, Jeanetton, who would take the princess's place at her lodging in Innsbruck. The party would be joined by Michel Vizzozi, a valet[125] sent by James III, and one Konski, a member of Prince James Louis's household.[126] Lady Misset agreed to play the important role of lady of honour to Princess

Clementina while on the road to Rome. In undertaking this task for his royal master, Wogan took a serious risk, given that he was a fugitive from the British authorities for the part he had played in the 1715 rebellion there. If captured, the British envoys in Vienna would have demanded that he be handed over. Likewise, the Irish officers of Dillon's Regiment ran the risk of the being denied re-entry to France, then at peace with Britain. Lieutenant-Colonel Lally had full knowledge of the rescue and allowed it, though his superior Lieutenant-General Arthur Dillon may also have been in James's confidence. In addition to these risks, they faced extreme weather, treacherous roads and precipitous cliffs. They shared these dangers, and as they set out from French territory, with the tacit blessing of the Governor of Strasbourg, Monsieur d'Angervilliers bid them 'Adieu, mes enfants, you are not crossing the Rhine for nothing, and you seem to be engaging in an attempt to make a hole in the moon. May God guide you, for I know you … will conquer or die'.[127]

The rescue party maintained contact with the princesses in Innsbruck through their servant, Monsieur de Chateaudoux, formerly a servant at the Stuart court in exile at Saint-Germain and well-disposed to the Jacobite cause. For this reason, she was told she was to trade places with a young countess who was, as the fib went, eloping with Captain O'Toole.[128] She had been promised both safety and a reward in gold for the part she would play; however, when it came time to prepare Jeanetton for the role, the plans almost completely collapsed. Jeanneton was quite tall, and she was proud of it, and, believing it gave her an unusual point of distinction, she always wore heels to accentuate this feature. When Wogan and the rescue party told her that she was going to have to wear flat shoes, since Clementina was much shorter, Jeanneton obstinately refused. She became so implacable for half an hour that the group were in despair. At great length, it was a tearful Lady Misset who finally succeeded in persuading the young woman to wear the shoes despite her misgivings.

Finally, Wogan and Jeanneton left the inn at 11:30 pm and they trudged through the atrocious weather and muddy streets. Jeanneton continued to curse the Ostrogoth shoes and the shabby English coat she had to wear, but they finally arrived at the house just after midnight.

The weather was so bad that the guards had left their posts and taken shelter in an inn across the street. They had assumed that no one would attempt to abduct a royal princess in such awful weather conditions. With this good fortune, Jeanneton was in the door and up the stairs without any trouble. She was met by Clementina's chamberlain, Monsieur de Chateaudoux (an experienced attendant of Saint-Germain-en-Laye) at the top, who escorted her into the princess's chambers. Clementina made her final preparations to leave and then bid her dear mother an agonised goodbye. She put on the heavy English coat and left a letter which gave the impression that her mother had nothing to do with the escape; but eventually Chateaudoux had to physically separate mother and daughter and help Clementina down the stairs. Wogan stood three doors down for an interminable half hour, until, after the clock had struck 1:00 am, Clementina emerged onto the street and they set off towards the Black Eagle. The sleet was beating down so furiously that at one point on their way they encountered a substantial channel of water running across their path. Being in a rush to get across, Wogan directed the princess to step on a stone and reach the other side, but when the princess stepped onto it, she sank into the muddy channel. This threw Wogan into much confusion as he helped the princess out of the water, but they pressed on. Her page, Konski, had caught up with them carrying a bundle of Clementina's effects, which he neglected to mention to Wogan had contained all of her priceless crown jewels. At about 1:30 am they arrived at the inn where the harrowed rescue party were waiting. Addressing them all, the princess said, 'Welcome to you my brave rescuers ... may the good God, who brought you to me, be our guide from now on'. While they prepared to leave, Konski, obviously terrified of the consequences he might face if he were seen there since he was staying behind in Innsbruck, simply flung the bundle behind the door in the room and quietly but speedily left without saying a word.

The party left the inn at about 2:00 am; Clementina, Lady Misset, Wogan and Gaydon in their carriage with Vezzosi on horseback in front of them and O'Toole behind. They were ten minutes out the road when Clementina asked about her jewels, but Wogan didn't know what she was talking about. All the horses were ordered to halt. The whole party had to wait another excruciating half hour while O'Toole galloped back to the inn. Finding the front door unlocked, he quietly let himself in, and as discreetly as possible searched in the dark until at last he found the bundle behind the door, and he rejoined the elated party where he had left them. They made slow progress on the steep road up Mount Brenner but reached the summit at dawn on 28 April, where Captain Misset was waiting for them.

While they changed horses for the next phase of the journey, Clementina fainted. Panic ensued until Lady Misset used a bottle of Eau de Carmes,[129] the smell of which revived the princess, who said, 'Ah my little woman, and you my poor marmosets, take courage; there is nothing to worry about'. She used pet names after this point – Wogan became 'Papa Warner', the original name he used while incognito when he first met her at her home in Ohlau. Lady Misset permanently became her 'little woman'. The harsh weather which battered them on the north side of Mount Brenner gave way to much gentler and milder conditions on its southern face. They only stopped to change horses and kept moving, entertaining the princess with stories. The princess acclimatised very well to the discomforts she faced in the small carriage. Wogan, wishing to remain alert, fought sleep as best he could using snuff and tobacco, but at one point he dosed off with something in his hands which promptly clattered Clementina on the head. Frozen in fear and mortified all he could manage was to murmur that '... it will never happen again', but Clementina made light of it.

Calamity seemed to hover around the rescue party as they sped towards the safety of the Italian States. One serious incident occurred as the carriage was travelling on the old and narrow Roman road through the mountains. The road was bordered by a wall on one side and a sheer precipice on the other, down to the River Adige. At one point on this dangerous road, the driver was speeding as instructed but took a dangerous risk by attempting to overtake a merchant wagon which hugged the wall. Those in the carriage only felt a jolt, nothing more; but then O'Toole rode up and furiously whipped at the driver, cursing him in a hushed voice. Wogan emerged and asked what the matter was but he knew O'Toole was not easily rattled, and seeing his distress, waited until later to shield the princess from seeing his demeanour. Apparently, the two outer wheels of the princess's carriage had gone off the road and dangled over the edge of the cliff. O'Toole, riding behind, thought for a horrifying second that the princess and his dear friends were about to tumble off the edge and plummet to their deaths, when the driver urged the horses back towards the middle of the road after he passed the wagon and the outer wheel of the princess's carriage hit an old tree trunk which knocked it back onto the empty road.

Wogan instructed Misset and O'Toole to remain at Wellishmile[130] in anticipation of the Emperor's first move to attempt to recapture Clementina. The Irishmen were instructed to intercept any courier passing through the town, as they would likely be carrying orders to the governors of Trento and Roveredo for the arrest of Clementina and her party. The Irish officers' orders were not to kill, but to delay by any other means. Meanwhile the others were making slow progress. The Princess of Baden and her son, the young prince, happened to be on the road just ahead of the rescue party – taking every fresh horse along the road ahead of them. There was a danger that the Badens would recognise Clementina if they encountered her on the road, since they had visited her at Innsbruck on their way to Loreto. They continued warily on their way.

In Wellishmile, Misset and O'Toole waited at the inn, masquerading as travelling merchants keen to attend a local fair, and as expected, towards 2:00 am that night, they spotted a courier arriving, his horse completely exhausted beneath him. O'Toole, who spoke German, cordially called out to him to come and sit with them and take a drink since he looked so tired and thirsty. The tired officer sat and complained about the lack of fresh horses and the bad road, while Misset *sneakily* spiked his wine with a powerful eau-de-vie made locally in Strasbourg, and poured the rest of it into a large water jug nearby. The officer drank down his wine, noting its peculiar strength. The Irishmen acknowledged this, saying that it was a local product, and cautioned him to water it down to mediate the strength, which he did liberally. As his wits became progressively annihilated, the disguised culprits made a show of their drinking prowess, and wanting to save face, of course, the courier had to at least attempt to keep up. Within the hour, the poor man was completely incoherent and soon very ill. The Irishmen quietly removed his orders from his satchel and destroyed them, all the while consoling their new friend and helping him up to bed, where he could do no harm at all.

Later that morning, on 29 April, the rescue party reached the town of Trento as the Badens were leaving, and, as before, there was not a single fresh horse to be found for the next stage of the journey. Princess Clementina was obliged by the circumstances to remain in her coach while the sun's heat increased throughout the morning, since many notables of Trento had visited her at Innsbruck. The local people were mystified by this strange situation, a carriage full of gentlefolk sitting inside, and they began to chance glances at who might be within. The group had to act quickly, so they came up with a plan to trick the governor, Prince de la Tour Taxis. Fortunately, the prince was indisposed due to an attack of gout, and Vezzosi was sent to his residence on behalf of the Count de Cernes and his family to ask for some horses to be released from fieldwork so that the count might catch the Badens. After an initial refusal, Vezzosi returned to say that the count was on his way to make a personal application to the prince. The prince was unwilling to embarrass the count by a further refusal, so he relented, and the party were moving again by 1:00 pm, with just two field horses swapped for the two most tired.

They pushed on to Roveredo where they made a simple meal of bread and tea to sustain Clementina who had felt faint again. There were no fresh horses there either, so they had to continue with the same tired horses towards Alla, the last town in the Emperor's territory, leaving Roveredo at about 3:30 pm. A detachment of mounted Imperial dragoons gave them a moment's fright, but they passed them at a gallop without paying the slightest heed. A few hours later they were almost halfway to Alla when the carriage struck a stone on the road followed by a loud crack and the carriage came to sudden halt. Wogan got out to check the carriage only to find that the axel shaft had broken in two! He had only descended when behind him there was a shrill cry. He looked back to see Clementina, who'd lost her footing descending from the carriage, knee deep in a stream rushing by the roadside. She was pulled out easily though, and Lady Misset helped her change. An attempt by Wogan and Vezzosi to replace the axel only brought them a little further along until it broke again at about 10:00 pm. The party were forced to continue in the darkness on foot with the horses until they reached Alla. As they entered the town it was clear to them that they had finally caught up with the Badens and the town was busy with activity. They found lodging away from the fuss where Clementina could refresh herself; meanwhile Wogan searched high and low around Alla for any type of carriage that would allow them to keep travelling. The only thing he could find was a shoddy two-seater vehicle which he himself labelled 'a most wretched conveyance'. Wogan wrote that 'it was in this ridiculous contraption and predicament, that the cousin of Emperor Charles VI, and of the Queen of Spain, and grand-daughter of King Jan Sobieski III, left Alla at 2am on 30 April'. It was ten miles from Alla to the Venetian town of Peri, and so the weary group set out slowly and quietly. Gaydon twisted his ankle on the road and advised Wogan to move on and that he would wait at the roadside for Vezzosi to arrive with the Berlin carriage fully repaired. Onward they went. The exhausted Wogan walked alongside the two ladies in their conveyance. They were watching for a part of the road where it was bordered on either side by thick walls, as it demarcated the territories of Trentino of the Holy Roman Empire, and that of Venice ... and after some hours walking they perceived with quiet joy what they were waiting for. Once the little chariot passed the walls, they knew they had entered friendly territory, and Clementina, Wogan and Lady Misset sang out a *Te Deum* in thanks for their safe conduct to Venetian territory.[131] On Sunday 30 April, the three companions arrived at Peri at about 8:00 am to the sound of ringing church bells. The small church in Peri was holding an early service in honour of the Princess of Baden, who they knew would be passing through the town on her way to Verona. Clementina had the chariot driven straight to the church where she attended the service, careful to remain veiled.

They took a small room in a local inn where they arranged for dinner to be served at 2:00 pm, and finally Clementina and Lady Misset were able to comfortably sleep while Wogan awaited the arrival of his friends. At 1:00 pm the rest of the rescue party rode in, carriage and all, safe and sound; and at 2:00 pm the whole party was reunited and sat down to dinner together. Wogan wrote that 'the sudden meeting of the whole company together after so many mishaps and adventures and in a safe country created in everyone a feeling of pure and perfect joy the likes of which is hardly ever found in life'. They arrived at Verona at dusk on 30 April, and all of them slept a full night soundly and peacefully for the first time in four days.

Next, they made for Bologna, avoiding the Imperial territory of Mantua, by taking the road through Pepoli and Caprara, until they crossed the Po at Stellata. They arrived in Bologna on 2 May and took lodgings at the Pilgrim Inn at 11:00 am. The inn was crammed full of boisterous English gentlemen who couldn't help themselves commenting on Clementina's loveliness, which to Wogan displayed a complete lack of manners and he commented sourly that 'the English feel that in Italy they can behave in whatever way they like'. This situation wouldn't do, so Wogan paid a visit to his friend Cardinal Origo. The Kildare man decided to play a trick on him, since the cardinal had doubted that he would succeed in his plans to rescue Clementina. He called on the papal legate with a solemn expression, upon seeing which Origo said, 'Monsieur Wogan, I have known you for long time as a very accomplished gentleman: I was expecting to find you as a man of your word'. To which Wogan replied, 'In what way have I failed your eminence?' The cardinal replied shortly, 'The Princess Sobieski!' Wogan allowed a slow smile to creep across his face, 'She is here, Monsignor: and I am a man of my word'. The cardinal leapt out of his chair and exclaimed the words 'Qui! Qui!' banging his hands off the walls as he did. He made such a racket that his attendants ran into the room white-faced thinking he was being attacked.

The cardinal agreed to obtain quieter lodgings for Clementina and her beloved marmosets, and he had a small house near the city walls prepared for her. It was thought best to keep her identity secret, in order to maximise the effect of her arrival in Rome on the envoys of George I and Charles VI. This need for secrecy unwittingly led to a bit of controversy for the honourable cardinal. He visited Clementina every evening between 9:00 and 11:00 pm and in order to keep the secret of her identity, he would ask his retinue to remain on the street while he continued the final 200 yards on foot and alone, with only a dark lantern to guide his way to the house. The Bolognese, being none the wiser, made the assumption that their beloved and pious cardinal had succumbed to the fruits of Eve, and that he was visiting a mistress near the walls of the town.

James Stuart had travelled to Spain to lead a military expedition to Britain aimed at his restoration to his ancestral thrones and for that reason he was not there to welcome Clementina in person at Bologna. He had left powers and instructions with his chief minister, James Murray, to carry out a marriage-by-proxy in the event that Clementina escaped captivity. On 9 May, Clementina was married by proxy to James Stuart III. His representative, James Murray, had arrived with his sister, Lady Marjorie, the day before with a much more suitable carriage with which to convey Clementina to Rome. They set out on 10 May, stopping along the way as they deemed appropriate or entertaining. As they approached the city on 15 May, they stopped near the Pontemolle on the Tiber where they remained until 4:00 pm, while Cardinals Aquaviva, Gualtiero and many other high notables of the Church came to pay their respects to Clementina. At 5:00 pm on 15 May 1719, Maria Clementina Sobieska Stuart crossed the bridge onto the avenue of the Porta del Popolo and into Rome as queen *de Jure* of Britain and Ireland. Wogan wrote that 'The entry to Rome was a veritable Triumph'. The avenue was lined on both sides by the fine carriages of the Roman nobility and her passage was greeted with the cheers and acclamations of all who witnessed. Clementina took lodgings and remained at the Ursuline Convent with her little woman, Lady Misset, until James Stuart returned to Italy.

Chapter 6

Of Knights and Roman Senators

Though Wogan had been warmly welcomed at Bologna and received a hero's welcome in Rome, he and his companions encountered a cool unease at the Jacobite court. The 1720 narrative of events by Lord Pitsligo illuminates the following months with great clarity. He was a senior Jacobite at the court at the time. From the moment Clementina arrived in Rome, despite a warm welcome from the Pope and his senior clerics, James Murray isolated her from the Jacobite court, only allowing her access to members of his own inner circle.[132] James III had named him acting-secretary of state while he travelled to Spain. The main members of Murray's inner circle included Colonel John Hay, his wife Marjorie Hay (Murray's sister), and initially Wogan and his companions. Despite Clementina's expressed desire to meet her subjects and the Jacobite court's wish to express their loyalty, Murray disallowed any introductions to be made.

After members of the Jacobite court expressed their dismay, Murray nominated Wogan to make formal introductions to the new queen.[133] However, this move caused a breach of protocol at the Jacobite court as introductions to a person of higher rank had to be carried out by a person of equal or higher rank. As Wogan had not yet even received a knighthood, this opened him up to criticism by members of the court. Lord Pitsligo noted that Wogan informed him the following day that he had been privately uneasy in making those introductions and suspected that Murray had 'made use of him as the cat's foot [*sic*]', with a view to diverting some of the ill-will in the Jacobite court onto Wogan.[134] Not long after this, Cardinal Aquaviva consulted Murray on the guest list while planning a dinner party, initially inviting twenty of the king's followers to attend. Murray replied that 'the four Irish gentlemen' (Wogan, Misset, O'Toole and Gaydon) would be fit and nobody else, resulting in only those of Clementina's rescue party being invited. This would have further opened Wogan and his companions up to the jealousies and contempt of the Jacobite court.[135] It seems that Murray, unable to reconcile the growing tide of anger and protestations against him at the Jacobite court, used any opportunity he could to direct the negative sentiments onto others.

Pope Clement XI conferred the rank of Senator of Rome upon Wogan and his companions in June 1719.[136] The extant original patent articulates their achievement in glowing and ornate language. This honour, normally reserved for kings, relatives of the Pope or the Roman nobility was bestowed by Monsignor Bianchini, papal penitentiary, and Count Ippolito Albani and Wogan later recollected the occasion to Swift:

> I have been led to the Capitol with the applause of thousands and received in the Roman Senate, at the immortal sound of the Litui and Tubae of the ancients. I have been dignified in all form, with an hereditary title, that once made the chief civil distinction of the Faby [Fabia] and the Scipios. Since the Saxon usurpation, no man of the birth of our islands has ever been invested with that honour… I am the first of my countrymen that has made a triumphal entry into Rome, the metropolis of the world, since the great Constantine.

The title allowed those who held it to be addressed as 'Your Excellency.'[137]

The following day, Bianchini sent a letter to James III outlining his plans to give further honours to Wogan and his companions. Plans were afoot to hold a special ceremony at the Basilica de Santa Maria

Maggiore where a *Te Deum* would be sung in honour of the Irish who brought Clementina to safety. The letter stated that:

> The four gentlemen who partook in the mission are to be honoured for their great success as the Chapter [of the Basilica] of Santa Maria Maggiore propose to celebrate a Te Deum to which Your Majesty and her Serene Highness [the king and Maria Clementina] are to be invited with Wogan and his officers in Dillon's regimental uniform, and Madame Misset.[138]

This splendid occasion bears further testimony to the sense of wonder and gratitude towards Wogan and his companions, felt at the highest levels in Rome.

During the turbulent first three weeks after Clementina's arrival in Rome, Wogan had managed to keep peace at court between Lady Mar and Murray.[139] By this time Murray had found himself in difficult circumstances at the Jacobite court, and later conveyed to James III his sense of gratitude to Wogan for his intervention in this matter, 'I must do Wogan the justice to let you know that he has behaved himself extremely well'.[140] While one would not doubt Murray's gratitude, his remark is mildly patronising. As mentioned above, Wogan had quarrelled with Lady Mar, laying blame on her that Murray had been sent to Ohlau to finalise the marriage arrangements in late 1718. Lord Pitsligo noted that upon meeting Wogan in Genoa, he had since apologised to Mar for his quarrel with his wife:

> Sir Charles Wogan told me at Genoa a great deal concerning his behaviour and that he himself had had a great quarrel with my Lady Mar who he supposed had been the cause of Mr. Murray's going to Innsbruck [*sic*. recte Ohlau] to manage some formalities about the articles of marriage, which he thought should belong to him as having done the difficult part before, but own'd he was mistaken as to my Lord Mar.[141]

King James, who had just seen the latest attempt at a restoration dashed, would have been in an ill humour to address the quarrels of the Jacobite court. Daniel Szechi has shown that the frustration and tedium of exile had led to much fractiousness, petty jealousies and quarrelling among the Jacobite exiles.[142] The king sent a letter to Wogan from Spain chastising the court for their undutiful behaviour towards Clementina in his absence. Clearly Murray had been misrepresenting the court to the king all along. It seems that Wogan, perhaps attempting to avert further discontent within the court, did not show the king's letter publicly while in Rome. It is likely that the king learned of Wogan's attempt at courtly prudence for he had a copy of the letter sent to Major Gaydon in Rome. Gaydon did not show the same discretion his companion had and shared the contents of the letter from the king, stating his anger at their perceived ill treatment of Clementina, creating even more tension there.[143]

After the king returned to papal territory in August 1719, arrangements were made for the solemnisation of his marriage to Clementina. James met his royal consort for the first time near Montefiascone, north of Rome, where the solemnisation of their marriage took place on 1 September, at which Wogan acted as a witness. King James knighted Wogan and granted him a baronetcy. The king also knighted Misset, O'Toole and Gaydon, and provided brevets of advancement to be used to obtain promotion in the military service of any of the Catholic powers of Europe. James recognised Lady Misset's important role and honoured her by granting a brevet of advancement for her father who was also an officer in Dillon's Regiment.

According to the patent which created Wogan a knight-baronet, he received this elevation from James on the same day as the marriage. His name is written on the certificate of marriage which is housed in Trinity College Dublin.[144] The Hays and Murray also attended the marriage, solemnised by the Bishop of Montefiascone. Carlo Maratti later painted the scene and Norbert Pottiers also struck a historic medal of the matrimonial scene.[145]

The king's decision 'to honour' Wogan for his gallant service is worth consideration here. Having been awarded the highest honour possible by Pope Clement XI, his receipt of a knight-baronetcy from

James III seemed a paltry reward for such extraordinary and strategic service. Nevertheless, the wording of the royal patent itself, bears ringing testimony to the king's gratitude:

> ... our trusty and well-beloved Charles Wogan Esq. has executed our commands in every respect to our entire satisfaction. He did contrive with so much prudence and execute with so much dexterity the means of her [Clementina's] escape that he conducted her safe [*sic*] into Italy through immeasurable difficulty and dangers to our inexpressible joy and to his own immortal honour.[146]

It must be noted that Wogan had declined James's offer of the rank of brigadier, as his comrades had only been offered the rank of colonel. Thus, he received a brevet of military advancement to the rank of colonel in a Catholic power of his choosing. In Wogan's view, his friends had shared an equal part of the danger and he thought it would be improper for him to receive a higher rank, though he would later come to regret this decision. Gaydon and O'Toole received the same rank that they had previously held in Dillon's Regiment in France, despite the brevets they received from James. The contrast between the Pope's honouring of Wogan and that of his king is difficult to explain. Wogan's refusal to join James in Spain after his rescue of Clementina may perhaps have irritated the king. Conversely, one might charitably conclude that James simply did not have the resources to award Wogan a position at court or a high ennoblement.

By late October 1719, Wogan's companions, Gaydon and O'Toole, had become irked with Murray for their own reasons.[147] One comical scene contained in the *Narrative of Lord Pitsligo*, printed in full in Henrietta Talyer's *The Jacobite Court in Rome 1719*, describes how the Irish around Clementina had entertained their new queen by doing impressions of Murray's carry-on at the court for her amusement:

> The particulars are too frivolous to insert. He [Wogan] said the queen was not only angry with Mr Murray but

> despised him and was content to see old Chateaudoux[148] and [John] Misset mime his grimaces. Hereupon Mr Misset fell to work before us and acted him to life. I protest I was sorry things were so low, the Queen might have had more proper diversions, but it is natural to a young body to like such comical representations. Among the rest of our familiarities Sir Charles showed me the account he had written in French of the Queen's escape from Innsbruck. Sir John Misset and he took ship for Spain and young Mr [Nicholas] Wogan and I went to Paris through Piedmont and Savoy.[149]

A letter between Mar and John Hay dated Paris, 19 April 1722 postulated the true reason behind the failure to find a place for Wogan at the Jacobite court:

> He [Wogan] at last compassed the affair [rescue] contrary to expectation, which naturally speaking gave him a very good title to the king's favour, as well as for his companions, and though the king did put a feather in his cap and got him provided for elsewhere, everybody who knew anything of his people knew that Murray was not well pleased.

The earl continued:

> But since Murray did go away, to his post, why was he let return without the king's being fully satisfied with him, seeing the part he would act when he did, was plain? And it was natural to believe that Clementina would have a favourable ear for Wogan and Lady Misset who had so eminently assisted her and brought her out of her difficulties, and the more because she thought (as I know she did) that they had been in a manner sacrificed upon her account to Murray and his sister's jealousy and resentment for her having looked favourably on them.[150]

The letter indicates clearly that Wogan, and later Lady Misset, were dismissed from the Jacobite court as a result of Murray's jealousy and his influence over the king. While James continued to support Murray for a time after Wogan's departure, eventually he would have to dismiss him in early 1721.[151] The conflict and ill-feeling which arose from Murray's actions since 1719 would resurface to plague King James's marriage a few years later, as will be discussed below.

Wogan and Misset proceeded to Spain to enter the Spanish military service, while O'Toole and Gaydon had been permitted to rejoin Dillon's Regiment in their previous positions.[152] This could be considered fortunate for them given the political position of the French government towards the Stuarts at the time. While with Pitsligo in Leghorn, Wogan surmised that given the king's strong position taken in defence of Murray, perhaps he did not want to replace members of his inner circle too frequently, thereby indicating instability in the court.[153] Pitsligo bade Wogan farewell at Genoa but shared the road to Paris with his brother, Nicholas. Meanwhile, Wogan and Misset were received warmly by King Philip V of Spain and made colonels of the Spanish army upon their first audience.

Chapter 7

Early Years in Spain, 1719–1722

James III had given Wogan instructions to continue to act as the eyes and ears of his monarch at the Spanish court and gain support for his interests where necessary, under the direction of the Duke of Ormond.[154] Having obtained brevets of advancement to the rank of colonel to be used there, on their arrival in late 1719 Wogan and Misset gained positions in the *Regimiento de Infantería de Limerick* under the command of James Fitzjames, Duke of Berwick y Liria, a natural son of King James II. However, it appears that although these brevets recognised their prior military experience and service, the two Irishmen held the actual rank (and pay) of captain in their new positions. A brevet is a military document that provides recognition that the officer who holds it is entitled to receive that rank but not necessarily the pay of that rank, and that they have only limited exercise of the rank. Essentially it is like a recommendation that the person who holds it could be trusted to perform well at that rank. As Wogan later remarked, he would rue the fact that he had turned down James III's original offer of a brigadier's brevet, because shortly after their arrival in Spain a new round of appointments to positions of military command overlooked the two Irishmen. His letter of 28 May 1720 is written in a despondent, resigned tone regarding the low pay of his position and his inability to live well in Madrid. He mentions having transferred what little money or property he had to his mother and to his sister-in-law 'in order to make what amends lay in my power to that unfortunate family'.[155] This could indicate a feeling of guilt – perhaps his relatives in Ireland were being made to suffer for their relationship to such a notorious Jacobite.

It seems that Wogan let his disappointment be known to his Spanish hosts and when news of this reached James, the king communicated his displeasure to Wogan. In a letter from Wogan to James III on 3 June 1720 it is clear that the king had written to him warning him to stop complaining, though the letter that James sent does not appear to have survived.[156] Clearly within the first six months he had irritated those in positions of power around him, referring to 'those expressions of ill-humour were only to paint the distress I was in by a painful and rebutting attendance on some Spanish ministers, by cross accidents that happened in the course of that ungrateful way of solicitation, and by the wants I was upon the point of being reduced to'.[157] Much can be gleaned from this passage regarding the situation in Spain and the *modus operandii* of the early Bourbon state. As shall be seen later, this was probably Wogan's first experience of having his pay delayed and also of the slow-moving nature of Spanish administration. James's reply of 21 July 1720 left no uncertainty of the meaning of his previous letter, stating that he was 'edified with your having taken in so right a manner my exhortation against the spleen, for I can assure you my last letter had no other meaning, and as such was but the part of a friend which I shall ever be to you'. The final qualifying remark seems to have been truly meant. The letter also mentions that should Spanish troops be sent to Italy, Ormond would solicit for Wogan and Misset to be among their number. The king ends with the warm regards of both he and the queen and assures both Wogan and Misset that 'we shall never forget the great merit both of you have with us'.[158]

Wogan had also asked for a congé, or official permission to depart from his post with the Limerick Regiment. Although the purpose of this request is not stated, it could have been that he and Misset would continue to receive pay but still be at liberty to rejoin the court in exile in Rome without having to burden James with their upkeep. In asking for this so soon after obtaining his commission in Spain however, he overlooked the consequential damage to his own prospects for advancement and promotion down the line by causing difficulty, not only with the Spanish ministers but also with the Duke of Berwick, his new commander, now prominent and influential at Philip V's court. Wogan looked on 'this misfortune [an angry spat with the Spanish ministers] as a friendly vicissitude from heaven to check my last year's vanity', possibly providing us with an important glimpse at another source of annoyance to his new hosts: his boastfulness and pride about Clementina's rescue.[159] While it is natural for him to celebrate the truly extraordinary feat, harping on it could have drawn the ire of his contemporaries. Indeed, one of his later letters states that Berwick had tired of Wogan's recounting of his story and that he had used his own influence to negatively mark him in the eyes of others in his milieu, including major players at the Spanish court.[160] Years later Wogan wrote of it thus, 'the duke of Liria found his account formerly in lessening that pretension here (to the colonelship of the Regiment of Limerick), and making it appear elsewhere as my perpetual echo, or the burden of my song, in which he did me a prodigious injustice. The duke found this injustice necessary in order to make room for another very crying one … in procuring the regiment called Limerick's, for a lieutenant-colonel to my manifest prejudice'.[161] Wogan and Misset subsequently transferred to the *Regimiento de Irlanda* in protest.[162] Downey observed of that regiment that:

> … their standards bore the heraldic escutcheon of the arms of Ireland: a gold harp upon a shield azure (blue) surmounted by a gold crown, superimposed on the top-left corner of the Burgundian Cross of Saint Andrew gules (red), on a field argent (white). Each regimental flag had its respective name embroidered in the lower section. The brigade was dedicated to the Irish national patron, Saint Patrick. They wore the traditional Jacobite red uniforms with blue Irish facings.[163]

Wogan's first experience of southern Spain gives a fascinating glimpse into life there in the early eighteenth century. Writing from Cartagena in

Murcia, he wrote that 'things as to complexions, customs and the way of living are so perfectly Moorish that if the court should order our whole regiment to remove into Africk [*sic*] we should scarce be sensible of having left Europe'.[164]

Meanwhile, in the Stuart court in Rome, the state of discontent between Clementina and James III's favourites had continued to deteriorate.[165] The dispute which would eventually lead to a breach between the royal couple began over the question of the new queen consort's household; chiefly the question of whether she could control her own household and make her own appointments to it. This would have been a reasonable expectation under normal circumstances at a royal court, but James presided over a financially-challenged court-in-exile. Between this consideration and the influence of his much-maligned favourites (John and Marjorie Hay, and James Murray), ultimately he decided that those responsibilities would be his. Arguably, the first flashpoint for this conflict occurred in the spring and summer of 1719 when Murray, acting as secretary of state in Rome in the king's absence, botched the management of the introductions to Clementina to the senior Jacobites at the court. In 1720, the conflict flared up again as Clementina's pregnancy progressed and the question arose of who would fill important positions for the new prince or princess. Lady Eleanor Misset had remained at the court as an attendant to Clementina since she had arrived there in May 1719. Lady Misset had been with child herself during Clementina's rescue and had in fact given birth to a baby girl on 10 September 1719, whom she named Maria Clementina. Later baptised in the Church of San Lorenzo in Luchina, on 11 February 1720, the king and queen stood as her godparents and were represented at the font by Lord and Lady Nithsdale.[166] Initially the king decided that Clementina would look after her new child alone with the assistance of Lady Misset.[167] Shortly after this, however, he sought an under-governess and had difficulty securing a person of sufficient rank for the important role, having refused Lady Nithsdale the position. Clementina despised Marjorie Hay, and senior Jacobites in France and in Britain openly criticised her and her brother and husband, effectually ruling her out. With Prince

Charles Edward Stuart's birth on 31 December 1720, Lady Misset found herself in the middle of this storm as the only bedchamber woman to Queen Clementina and also the only person responsible for the upbringing of the Prince of Wales. As Corp observed, 'she was out of her depth, and she knew it'.[168] She wrote to her brother in February 1721 acknowledging the honour she had been given, saying also, 'but when I consider the importance of the task compared to the very little merit that I have, and that I am occupying a post instead of several other people far more worthy than myself, the honour puts me more in a state of embarrassment than of vanity'.[169]

Wogan wrote to James on 20 February that news of the prince's birth had reached Spain. The birth of a successor to the royal Stuart line would have been cause for huge celebration (and relief) for the Jacobites all across Europe:

> I need not mention to your majesty the joy of your loyal subjects in this place, but must do justice to the honest Spaniards, who swear that neither they nor their forefathers have ever been so much put out of their gravity by the birth of any prince of their own. This whole town has been all in a flame for three nights with fireworks, illuminations and artillery. The dames have ventured abroad for the first time to balls and assemblies, and their husbands have for the first time gotten drunk.[170]

He continued that the 'Whiggish consul' there had been provoked to so much anger at this that he had to retire of a fever, and that all the towns of Murcia celebrated the same way.

Two months later, Lady Misset lost her position of honour at the Stuart court in Rome being replaced by Lois Hughes. It appears that the former had let it be known that her loyalty lay with Queen Clementina and not King James and his favourites. James could not tolerate such disrespect towards him at his own court and regarded it as a challenge to his authority. In a missive to Mar, he wrote that 'what is above all requisite is prudence, a reasonable knowledge of the world and a principle of obedience, attachment and submission to me', and that Lois Hughes would fill the post temporarily until a person of suitable rank could be found.[171] Lady Misset was humiliated by her removal especially since it became known in Jacobite circles that she had been disrespectful towards the king.[172] She appealed to both Lieutenant-General Arthur Dillon in Paris who consoled her but warned her to tread carefully. She also wrote to Wogan in Spain for support describing 'the revolution that has occurred here as to my position',[173] after which both Wogan and her husband, Sir John, left Spain for Rome to defend her. There they remained throughout the rest of 1721 until James eventually found a person of suitable rank to look after the young prince. In April 1722 Dorothy Sheldon, Dillon's niece, became Prince Charles's new nurse and Lois Hughes returned to England. James ordered Wogan and the Missets to leave Rome,[174] but provided the men with brigadier's brevets to soften the blow. Queen Clementina despaired to lose Lady Misset, who had been her close companion since 1719. Marjorie Hay, whom she disliked intensely, was now the only woman of status to attend her. The Hays' influence at the court lay behind the dismissal of Lady Misset.[175] Unfortunately for the royal marriage, these events initiated the queen's estrangement from her husband and his favourites. Writing a few years later, she wrote in a letter to her sister that they were continually 'teasing [James] every day to part with his best friends and most faithful subjects' referring to the dismissal of Wogan and the Missets from the court.[176] Wogan wrote to Cardinal Gualtiero from Leghorn on 30 April 1722 to report that the Missets' young daughter, Clementina, had contracted the measles there and they needed to remain there for some time until she had recovered:

> …it is easy to conceive that Madame [Lady Misset] would be inconsolable, if we had the harshness to leave her, or, to put it better, to abandon her here during her daughter's illness, joined to her own indisposition and all other misfortunes. We regard these controversies as real marks of misfortune.[177]

Apparently they did leave her, as in a letter to James later in December of the same year they mention that they needed to send Lady Misset some money to pay for her passage to Madrid which had been impossible to do since the end of April. It is possible that they had orders to return to their posts in Spain. In the aftermath of such humiliation, it must have brought them comfort to have word and support from their cardinal protector as they waited to make their way back to Spain.

Even after this searing experience for Wogan and his companions, they continued to correspond and communicate their loyalty to James in Rome and the king remained well disposed to them. He also continued Lady Misset's pension for many years after her departure from Rome.[178] A warrant listed among the Stuart Papers also shows that James granted Wogan a brevet of brigadier dated 1 April 1722 (while he was still at court) to help him gain the promotion he sought in Spain.[179] However, Wogan had made enemies at the Stuart court in Rome as evidenced from his next letter to James on 19 December, which asked that his liege dismiss 'some misrepresentations that have been made to your Majesty concerning my conduct here and in Italy and can't but hope that your Majesty is by this time persuaded of my innocence', stating his 'utter dislike of cabals of all kinds'. He concluded by appealing to his 'former goodness' towards him.[180] Obviously he knew he had enemies at court but did not know their identity. It is likely that the Hays and Murray played a role in discrediting him. In contrast to the defensive and pleading opening of this letter, the latter half is fascinating as it contains the first reference to Mrs Anne O'Driscoll, a young widow with children from her previous marriage. She had a position at the royal court in Spain as a *camarista* to Queen Elizabeth Farnese. Apparently Wogan had asked James to write a recommendation for her to the Duke of Ormond who could present it to the queen to secure a promotion for her, which he duly did. Anne received a promotion to *Azafata de la Infanta*, a prestigious position of responsibility for one of the young Spanish princesses. The queen made excuses to the duke for not making her *Señora de Honor* saying that she could think of nobody better to have near the princess and that she would soon promote her again.[181] Anne's file at the *Archivo General de Palacio* contains confirmation that her new position commenced on 10 December that year, signed off by the Marqués de Santa Cruz, who would serve as Wogan's commander at Oran years later.[182] Wogan jubilantly thanked James for the brevets of advancement that both he and Misset had received from him, expressing his hopes that they would be promoted soon. They promised to send a gift given to him from the Marqués de Castellar of a hundred pounds of the mildest snuff which they hoped the king would find agreeable.[183]

Cardinal Gualtiero may have smoothed over any lingering ill-feeling the king may have had for Wogan and the Missets. While he waited for confirmation of his promotion, Wogan wrote two letters in April, one from El Escorial and another from Aranjues. He confirms that the cardinal's intervention in support of them on two important matters for which expressed deep gratitude for having 'entirely put our minds to rest on an article which has caused us more pain than all the misfortunes that are ours'.[184]

The Jacobites persisted in their plots to build better alliances and ultimately to regain the three kingdoms for the Stuarts. Since the turn of the century there had been attempts in 1708, 1715 and 1719, all involving military commitments from various foreign powers. Francis Atterbury, Bishop of Rochester and the most influential English Jacobite at court, launched another plot between 1721–1722. He had become disillusioned with the Hanoverian succession and began to organise in favour of James III. In essence, the plan involved contacting senior Jacobites in the British nobility, to coordinate a secret mobilisation date, and to march on London in a great rush of surprise to oust George. At the same time, James III would travel incognito through France with officers and soldiers of the Irish brigade and cross the channel to be collected by his supporters and restored to his thrones.[185] The British government's intelligence network discovered the plot and its surviving records provide a fascinating insight into the Jacobite movement. The level of penetration achieved by George I's agents is astonishing, with detailed information regarding Arthur Dillon's activities in Paris, the Pretender (James III) in Rome, and the Duke of Ormond in Spain. One agent's letter from among the Duke of Newcastle's papers at the

British Library actually states, 'I have enclosed a letter I received from Mr Hay [John Hay at the Stuart court in Rome] which I beg your excellency, after perusing, will return. Lawless's secretary told me that while Hay was employed by the Pretender he should never know the intentions of people inclined to serve him'.[186] The possibility that Hay actually operated as an agent himself is quite explosive given his unrivalled access to James III. It is also shocking that Sir Patrick Lawless fell foul of the British intelligence machine. Lawless, as an old-guard Jacobite, had very close ties to Philip V and a very high-profile diplomatic career. The Wogans are also mentioned among the papers, with reports (corroborated above) of 24 April/5 May 1722 stating that Charles had returned from Rome to Spain.[187] Although the plot had just been foiled, the British remained on high alert to the danger of a military invasion of Britain. Some confusion exists as to the identity of Nicholas Wogan, and the possibility of there being a number of that name. These papers attest that there was one Nicholas Wogan who was heir to Wogan of Rathcoffey in Kildare, and another who was a younger brother of Charles. Both of these hailed from the Rathcoffey area of Kildare, which means that the Nicholas Wogan who appears later in the French military records is yet another Nicholas, from County Galway. In any case, the British government closely watched Nicholas of Rathcoffey, an accomplished captain of a frigate, but made no mention of whether it was an official vessel of the Spanish Navy. He might have been employed as a privateer in the Mediterranean, for a report alluded to his 'earning his bread' and 'repairing his losses' at the expense of Turkish imperialists. They wrote that 'he has taken such affection to the sea that he has attained much perfection on it and pretends to no less than an admiralty. He will have the pleasure of Charles soon in those parts, who was called away to his post'.[188]

British agents kept the authorities fully informed on Nicholas's traffic with his brother, not least the expectation that he and Ormond would head an Irish expedition force for Britain.[189] The reports are full of information regarding activities in Spain's ports, noting comings and goings, the massing of vessels, and the movement of arms. A report from Madrid in June 1722 noted that 12,000 weapons intended for James III's supporters were being stored in Bilbao and that one Captain Morgan, formerly a Whig loyalist, intended to transport these weapons to England with Ormond.[190] They also closely monitored James III's movements. One intelligence report from a British agent in Rome stated that Queen Clementina had departed for the Tuscan coast so that she could try the baths at Lucca; the same letter reports the movements of James but also that it may be a ruse to get him to Spain undetected.[191] As hope faded for this attempt at a restoration, one report states that 'the Jacobites are now retiring to Saint-Germain; the only motion they are making at present is sending Irish priests in disguise into Ireland to raise recruits'.[192] Another report from La Corunna in Galicia, northern Spain, gave minute detail of recruiting activities taking place in Ireland. Initially the agent said that three vessels from Cork and two others landed 450 men to a small port called Lastres. A farmer from Ireland who had become a recruiting agent for James III took responsibility for this large batch of new recruits to the cause.[193] The response to this letter in August sent from Bilbao expressed alarm that such a recruiting drive could take place without the knowledge of George I's agents. Many hundreds more had been landed along the whole Biscay coast and into the ports in Asturias, enough to fill two entire battalions of Sherlock's Regiment. Some of the Irish recruits 'ordered to the Irish Regiments in the King of Spain's service threw down their pay and declared they would serve no other prince than King James for whom they were listed in Ireland'.[194] The agent complained that the arms for Ormond's expedition were being hidden in various places along the coast, but this mattered little because the Jacobites were able to get as many weapons as they needed from England: 'several chests of muskets and other firearms from London, to a considerable quantity, for the rebels and Jacobites in Spain … two chests made in London and marked with J.R. with a crown over it, which half this town have seen'.[195] James III took effective countermeasures with a network of his own agents who 'debauched' the Whig sea captains in the ports of Spain to smuggle goods, recruits and information for his benefit. The same agent wrote of Bilbao that 'there is no town in

Spain so favourable to the Jacobites and their cause as this; the great liberty the country enjoys, the having no public person from Britain, and the great number of Irish papists dwelling here, are very great encouragement to the Jacobites to lay their designs this way. This town though not big is very populous, and one half are Irish papists. The few English merchants that live here are cowed and stand in awe of them to a degree that's ridiculous'.[196] Although the Jacobites were thwarted this time, they stood ready to fight for James.

Chapter 8

Marriage and Children

In January 1724 the correspondence between Wogan and the Jacobite court opened with the surprising news that King Philip V of Spain had abdicated in favour of his son, Louis. Philip was still a young man at 40 and his formidable wife, Queen Elizabeth Farnese, was 31. In his letter of 16 January, Wogan wrote that the queen would only retain a small number of attendants but makes no mention of Anne O'Driscoll, so her post of *Azafata* to the infanta may have continued after this event. Philip's abdication caused a lot of concern for Wogan as it 'occasioned a general consternation, all the strangers, particularly the Italians, know not what ground they stand upon' as they had 'a principal share in all the employments civil and military, and were therefore hated by the Spaniards'. He anticipated that based on the appointments Philip had made for his son, the new government, with the exception of the Marquis of Castellar, might not hold any prospect for the Irish in Spain. Louis I of Spain was recognised as king by those present, who kissed his hand, which Wogan noted 'was the only ceremony practiced in reconnoitring the kings of Castille'.[197] This event caused some confusion in Spain and some questioned its legality since the court had not been consulted and the abdication itself had been witnessed by so few. King Louis I arrived in Madrid with only a very small retinue, not what would have been expected on a new monarch's first arrival to the Capital. Wogan summed up the overall situation: 'Spain is a perfect riddle at home and abroad with respect to their government and the security strangers have in dealing with them'.[198] He remarked also that Philip's first minister, Grimaldo, and the queen had powerful influence over Philip and that access to him was very difficult.

On a more personal level for Wogan, 1724 and 1725 were dominated by the planning and arrangement of his marriage to Mrs Anne O'Driscoll.[199] While the exact relationship is unclear, the match required a papal dispensation, indicating that they were related. Wogan penned letters in October to James III, Cardinal Gualtiero and John Hay to start the process of obtaining the dispensation. Hay's light-hearted reply complimented Wogan on his engagement to 'so fine a lady, whose fame long before has passed the Mediterranean'.[200] He was flattered that Wogan had entrusted him with such business and promised to send on the letters to the king and the cardinal,[201] who both acted swiftly on his behalf. James asked Pope Benedict XIII to help obtain the dispensation and he agreed to waive the 100 crown fee normally charged to obtain this favour. There seems to have been considerable administration required to obtain it, but Hay assured him of the king's good will while also reporting on the queen's pregnancy. Although 'a little out of sorts but nothing extraordinary', he expressed the hope that 'she will send out a duke of York'.[202] Wogan replied from Spain with huge gratitude to both Hay and the king that he hoped Hay could understand his great impatience to have the dispensation. His missive reported the sudden death of King Louis I, compelling Philip V's necessity to resume the throne. With the requirement of reorganising the government and making new appointments, he could not really expect Philip's promise of a promotion to brigadier and a pension of 200 pistoles per year to materialise any time soon.[203] He also wrote that his intended had 'a just demand upon the crown of 12,000 Roman crowns or an equivalent for the sum in confiscated lands', a significant amount indeed which was constantly being deferred.[204] It is likely that this claim related to her previous marriage. There is no record of her having been married in the royal chapel of the Palace of Madrid. One famous O'Driscoll from within Philip V's milieu was Colonel Cornelius O'Driscoll of the Limerick Regiment who had commanded troops for Philip during the War of the Spanish Succession. Under Berwick's command, the Limerick Regiment had originally been in the French service before being transferred to fight on behalf of Philip against the Archduke Charles of Austria in Spain. Born and raised at Saint-Germain, Anne afterwards finished her education in Madrid.[205] Between Paris and Madrid it is possible that she met and married her first husband in those circumstances.[206]

Regarding advancement in Spain, Wogan wrote 'the truth of the case is that delay is the original sin of this court, and though one has promised the justice of one's side the performance is in the anabaptist way, and must in the ordinary course be some years demanding, before the efficacious grace is actually conferred upon. This is pretty tedious work for a sinner'.[207] This was just the beginning for Wogan. Despite the delay he said with hope that the king and queen were very 'matrimonially inclined' and that 'marriage of any lady of their court has ever been a source of graces'. Wogan left it to Hay's better judgement on whether to ask James III to expedite things in Rome on his behalf since he had 'been hitherto but too troublesome' and that it would be 'unpardonable for him to become teasing'.[208] Meanwhile Anne, 'in her cooler blood' had tempered his impatience until Easter, 'so that we may have leisure to solicit our several affairs and sacrifice so much time to the decency of setting up house with something of a comfortable air'.[209] To assist with this he said 'in the meantime I expect handsome furniture for a house from my father in Ireland, who is worth at least £800 a year in beneficial leases, being a younger brother, besides a good sum of money to the fore'.[210] The comment about leases here is fascinating as it demonstrates what had actually occurred in Ireland in the aftermath of the conclusion of the Articles of Limerick in 1691. Catholic landowners could retain land under the penal legislation but could neither buy nor inherit it; but the Irish landowners leased the same ground at a low rate. Over the century this led to the emergence of a type of middle class in Ireland.[211] Furthermore, Wogan's statement confirms that his father was not the 'Wogan of Rathcoffey' referred to in the *Jacobite Correspondence of 1722*, but his brother. So, Charles's cousin, Nicholas, would ultimately inherit the Wogan estate at Rathcoffey. He lamented that all that 'would be of no further use to me' since he could not inherit it anymore; coupled with the fact that his father is 'entirely governed by his present third wife' and that 'he has been and still is an able man in his generation, having been at the trouble of getting 32 children, and 'tis odd enough to see me at forty have a brother of scarce one year old'.[212] He apologised to Hay for going on at length about his personal affairs but explained that 'this plaguing windmill of love is so much in my head that I can rave of nothing else'... but that there was only one way 'I know of getting rid of the whining foolery of it and becoming a reasonable man' but that if he failed in this purpose 'may I then become a madman or a pumpkin for the rest of my days, and this would be entirely deviating from my father's honest endeavours'.[213] Before he posted this letter, another arrived for Anne in her room at the palace with the dispensation enclosed in it.

Hay replied that Wogan would soon receive it and that he expected him to look 'as silly as one commonly does after he has been a month married'.[214] Wogan responded, 'setting out for matrimony with all one's heart is like riding post on a fatiguing journey; the nearer one is the stage, the more one longs to be at it'.[215] After the arrival of the dispensation with a kind note from James, in Spain Wogan put himself at the feet of the king and queen and 'told the king I wanted my woman, and the queen I could live no longer without her', at which the queen laughed aloud and 'raised a universal tittering among all the *Damas* and *Señoras de honor* about her'.[216]

Another month saw further delays to the marriage after the French government sent the Infanta Mariana Victoria back to Spain and cancelled the arranged marriage between her and the young Louis XV. This diverted the attention of the Spanish court. In an attempt to speed things, Anne obtained an audience with the king and queen, which became 'humorous and sprightly, by her majesty's jokes and raillery upon her, in order to raise the king's mirth and provoke him to finish her affair speedily'.[217] The queen did not mind commenting, in spite of 'her grave and matron-like carriage' that Wogan was a good choice, 'that [he] was a pretty fellow...bateing some whimsical turn about [his] nose' with the compliment that Anne had the queen's confidence while her intended spouse enjoyed the king's.[218] Anne replied that his nose would grow more awry if the matter of consent for their marriage was not speedily resolved, at which the queen 'went off agreeably, saying [to the king] in a very humorous manner "depechez les depechez les, Monsieur, ou vous serez peutêtre cause de bien de pêchéz" [hurry them hurry them, sir, or you may encouraging them to sin]'.[219] All assurances aside, Wogan resolved to travel out to Aranjuez if no resolution occurred within the week. Of his own promotion and Anne's promised financial claim or land equivalent, he surmised that a half-grant would enable them to breathe.[220] At the end of the letter Wogan refers to his own life as a sort of Quixotic romance.[221]

His gratitude to both Hay and King James could not have been expressed in more gushing terms, reaffirming his loyalty to James and his willingness to lay down his life for him.[222] He extended similar marks of respect and gratitude to Cardinal Gualtiero for the part he played, writing that 'I receive the blessings you are willing to give to my marriage as a certain presage of my happiness in the future'.[223] However, a month later and he had still not married, but he had repeated assurances from both king and queen of their good will and sincere promises to meet their requests. Wogan also reported that the queen spoke to him of her 'satisfaction and joy at the happy news … of her majesty's [Queen Clementina's] late happy delivery and the birth of a second prince, Henry, Duke of York'.[224] James had asked Hay to acknowledge receipt of a letter from Lady Misset paying kind compliments to James and Clementina upon the birth of the Prince Henry – the king was 'fully persuaded that her expressions on that occasion come from real good wishes for the prosperity of the royal family'.[225] In addition to sincere good wishes from Lady Misset, this letter may also have served as a memorial to the king and queen in Rome so that they might consider her for a new position at court for the care of the new prince, which would have completely rehabilitated her reputation. James III had appointed Hay (Lord Inverness since 1718) as his secretary of state, the highest position of authority under the king at the Stuart court as a replacement for the Duke of Mar. The duke had previously held the position but had since been disgraced in Jacobite circles for his rapprochement with the Hanoverians in London.[226] Wogan wrote of it that 'you have happily detected the person I ever looked on as my enemy, though I know not how I may have deserved it from him'.[227] Wogan erred in that opinion, as Henrietta Tayler found no evidence of enmity towards Wogan in Mar's correspondence, unless Wogan held him responsible for sending James

Murray to conclude the marriage contract in Ohlau in 1718. It is more likely that Hay and the Murrays damaged his prospects, and those of his companions.

Meanwhile Charles and Anne still waited in July when John Hay sent his compliments and those of his lady to the hapless couple. A further delay ensued with the Bishop of Kildare, with whom Wogan and his intended had had to share the dispensation. The bishop had queried the wording of the dispensation and caused this extra delay. Charles commented that Kildare 'must ever be a County absolutely given over to forms and etiquettes'.[228] This dispensation had involved James III, Cardinal Gualtiero, Pope Benedict XIII, the Bishop of Kildare, King Philip V and Queen Elizabeth, the papal nuncio in Madrid and the Archbishop of Toledo.[229] In the meantime, Queen Elizabeth had granted Anne a continuation of her pension even after her departure from court, contrary to a recent 'law of pragmatica against it', while the king granted Wogan a pension of an additional 200 pistoles per year to take effect after the marriage. Apparently, the Bishop of Kildare's issue was that the Archbishop of Toledo (under whose jurisdiction Madrid fell) couldn't sanction it or allow the marriage to proceed.[230] The situation required that the Bishop of Kildare officially give his authority to proceed to a Church official in Spain or at the Stuart court in Rome so that the document could be changed and addressed to the Archbishop of Toledo. This new delay worried Wogan as the king and queen of Spain planned their return at the end of the month for the feast of Saint James, patron saint of Spain, and they expected that they would be married by that stage. Wogan wrote that he went to the nuncio 'in pure vexation of spirit, arising from both love and the pain I was in' to see if he could do anything to help.[231] He said he could not, so the document had to be sent back to either to Ireland or Rome to be changed. Frustrated, he wrote:

> … though nothing on earth can be more sensible to us than your most obliging letters to Mrs O'Driscoll and me … for my part, I don't possess myself in the extreme pain I am in about this unforeseen difficulty and delay… Mrs O'Driscoll is little less mistress of herself, because in the assurance we

> were in of the vicar's ready compliance, we had declared to the court our design of marrying next week, for which reason I must engage both vicar and nuncio to give their Catholic majesties an explanation of the reason of our retardment.[232]

He worried how it might look to the court that yet another delay had occurred given they had been waiting four months to get married.

Wogan implored John Hay to initiate the rapid amendment of the dispensation and its return to him in Madrid, promising that he would repay any cost incurred for this request immediately.[233] The delay and the unhappiness of Anne and Charles moved the king and queen of Spain to take another agreeable action in their favour. Wogan mentions that 'since Sir John Misset and I could not serve agreeably or with honour under Mr Bourke, his majesty has been pleased to change our aggregations to Irlanda's Regiment, in which he has likewise given us companies, with the pay of both employments, of which there is no example in Spain'.[234] This must have been extremely happy news for the two Irishmen, given their acute financial difficulties since their arrival in Spain. The queen instructed Castellar to allow Wogan to stay in Madrid to conclude the marriage, despite orders from King Philip that all officers immediately return to their posts.[235] This concerned Charles though, since he would be obliged to depart soon after finally getting married; he also worried that he would be less use to James III not being in Madrid, and assured Hay of his continued willingness to serve the cause:

> … I have been but too long by necessity a useless servant to his majesty and now that I begin to be tolerably acquainted with this court and might give you some sensible lights into the humours of it, tis a hard case that I should be obliged to leave it.[236]

The new dispensation arrived in Wogan's hands on 18 September and by 21 September it had been seen by the Archbishop of Toledo and passed to the Vicar of Madrid. He reported that 'the lady and I are to pass the examination in a very few days: after which we are keen to be fairly coupled together for life'. He could not foresee bad luck after 'so many powers, ecclesiastical and civil do us the honour to interest themselves so heartily for us'.[237] Immediately after their marriage they intended to 'kiss their Catholic majesties' hands at San Ildefonso'.[238] Wogan's happiness is palpable in his comments to Hay: 'I ever was and ever shall be equally ready to serve his majesty at the expense of the life I have and of any fortune I ever shall have'.[239] While obliged by *de facto* dual loyalties, he beseeched Hay to 'put us at their majesties' feet, till we can have the honour and happiness of kissing their hands, and only theirs and those of their royal issue, in a better country'.[240]

The letter mentions that Charles had written to James Murray under cover of a letter to his brother Nicholas, who resided in Paris at this time. Murray had been ordered to leave Rome in 1720 after loud, persistent and almost universal protestations against him by Jacobites of all ranks across Europe. However, in 1724 James elevated Murray with the title Earl of Dunbar, and backdated it to when he had been at the royal court in 1720. He later named him as governor to Prince Charles Edward. Murray's appointment to this position caused Queen Clementina such stress that it brought the long-simmering differences between James and his queen to a head. Overruled by James on the matter and finding herself without any voice or power, she withdrew from the Stuart court into the Convent of Santa Cecila in Trastevere, Rome. This public relations disaster for the Jacobite cause once again had the troublesome triumvirate (John Hay, Marjorie Hay and James Murray) at its centre. James and Clementina's marriage would never recover.

Regarding Wogan and Anne's marriage, the first record book of the chapel of the Royal Palace in Madrid ceases about 1720 and Book 2 begins in the 1750s, so it cannot be ascertained if they were married there. Earlier marriages of ladies of the queen's household are recorded therein. Thus the record of their marriage could be in one of the dozen or so local churches in Madrid with a likely date between the end of September or the beginning of October.

By December 1725 they established a home quite a distance from Madrid in a tiny town called Mequinenza, situated on the junction of the rivers Segre and Ebro on the border of Aragon and Catalunya. The sedate feel of their new home left a lot to be desired for the newlyweds, and Wogan commented that Anne had 'repented her complaisance more than once since her arrival to this detestable little hole and thought it too big a sacrifice to be made to any man breathing'.[241] Of the town he said that it had 'neither society nor amusement', that everyday items such as bread and wine had to be brought in from outside, that the fog hanging over the valley left them frequently in shade, and the town itself only had eel and partridge to offer them.[242] Anne was pregnant by then and, in spite of the withering description of their new home, they eagerly awaited the prospect of the birth of a Roman senator. Even in this isolated place Wogan continued with intelligence-gathering for James, writing to Hay that he kept a regular correspondence with an intimate friend of Castellar who shared details of all goings on in the Spanish court.[243] He also suggested that with his current connections and good relationships with the king and queen of Spain, he could serve James well in this regard. He also proposed that Ormond could be given a commission 'more agreeable to him', perhaps referring to another invasion attempt, or even for a place to be made for him at the Stuart court, at which his status and prestige would have been most welcome.[244] He reaffirmed his commitment to James and placed himself at his disposal.

It is unknown at present exactly how many children Anne and Charles had. While Winch and Tayler claimed that Anne had three children from her previous marriage, the author could not find any definitive evidence to confirm that number. Charles mentioned in a letter to Ormond in May 1739 that he had a 'numerous family', but all evidence the author could find for some were official records, for others passing mentions in his letters. In April 1726, Wogan reported that Anne was towards her seventh month and asked 'that your majesty, to whom we entirely owe the happiness of being united, should condescend to bear a part in the making of our child a Christian. Your majesty may be pleased at the same time to direct whether we may be honoured with the queen's name too', though he feared that being so far removed from society in Mequinenza, he might not be able to find anybody fit to take the place of his king and queen at the font when the baptismal occasion arrived.[245]

James accepted Wogan's request and considered it a mark of honour.[246] Wogan's letter to Hay of the same date is bursting with information: about Spanish troop movements and military posturing; rumours of war with France or England; the latest gossip in international relations, including the return of the Spanish infanta; on the Austrian succession; French domestic tax policy; the struggle for dominance in overseas trade by the European powers; as well as other items. He also informed that Philip, second Duke of Wharton, had passed nearby on his way east. Wharton once served as lord lieutenant of Ireland and had by this stage made overtures to James III to serve the Jacobite cause.[247] The duke had met with the Spanish ministers and used his clout in James III's favour against their 'common enemy'.[248] While in Spain, Wharton fell in love with and would eventually marry an Irish woman named Maria Theresa O'Neill O'Beirne, the daughter of an Irishman who had died in exile, Henry O'Beirne, a colonel in the Spanish service, by his wife Henrietta, daughter of Henry O'Neill.[249] Maria Theresa was a maid of honour to Queen Elizabeth Farnese and would have been acquainted with both Wogan and Anne O'Driscoll. Regardless, he passed nearby the Wogans and at Lerida, the duke 'dined with the Macdonnells' before he reached Barcelona where he would settle for the remaining years of his life.[250] Wogan mentions the unlikelihood of he and Anne remaining long in Mequinenza, which may indicate that their lodgings there were not part of the above-mentioned land grant to which Anne was entitled. His letter to Hay the next day shared his newly pessimistic outlook for Spain internationally with other news that despite Irish officers in regiments in Spain holding commissions, they could only receive their base pay as reformed officers. This might be connected to the large influx of new Irish recruits and the financial strain of their pay and upkeep. He mentioned that officers in Aragon had been waiting seven months for their pay from the Spanish government; furthermore, vacancies would remain unfilled for the foreseeable future. The last paragraph of the letter relayed the sad news of the death of Clementina, daughter of Sir John and Eleanor Misset: 'Poor little Clementina died here last week of a malignant fever which puts her parents, who doted on her, into perfect desolation'.[251] The child had contracted measles in April 1721, necessitating her mother to remain in Leghorn with her for a substantial period of time afterwards. On 1 May, Wogan reported that 'I much fear Lady Misset will soon follow her daughter, so entirely and unpersuadeably [*sic*] is she abandoned to her grief. Sir John is not much easier, though a good deal stronger'.[252] This harrowing description of a couple dealing with the loss of a child provokes empathy from readers despite the long years since these events occurred. Wogan describes the situation and his own trepidation of being a father thus: 'though I hope soon to be a father, I have no notion of doting on an infant to that unreasonable degree'.[253] Hay responded from Rome, 'I am heartily sorry for the loss Sir John Misset and his lady have had in poor Clementina, and I beg the favour of you to make my compliments of condolence to them'.[254]

Anne gave birth to James Wogan in June 1726.[255] It appears that Anne and Charles moved to Monzón, a large garrison town in the north of Aragon and there they had a second son, whom they named Diego (a form of James in Spanish) in about October 1727.[256] Wogan wrote to James to ask again for the honour of having James and Clementina as godparents, saying that 'he could do your majesty no other service in these distant parts and bad times, than that of begetting new subjects'. Though not reported or alluded to in the Stuart Papers when she was born, they later had a daughter whom they named Clementina. James Wogan would later enter the Spanish military, his service record lists his name as its hispanised version, *Jaime*. He started as a sub-lieutenant with the *Regimeinto de Ultonia* on 8 October 1739, transferring to the Walloon Guards on 20 August 1745, attaining the rank second lieutenant on 26 April 1747. At the time of the creation of the record (end of July 1751) it is stated that James served at Castello dei Ventimigli (Castelbuono) in Sicily in Count Hize's company, then guarding the young Spanish prince. By this time he had served eleven years, nine months and 29 days and it stated 'su pais del Reyno de Irlanda/his country the Kingdom of Ireland'.[257] Don Diego Wogan commenced his service with the Ultonia Regiment in Captain Téidí O'Connor's company, under the command of Colonel Guillermo de Lacy. This record states 'su patria Españia, hijo de Padre Irlandese de distinctión/his country, Spain, son of an Irish father of distinction'.[258] At the time of writing (end of April 1743), Diego had served three years, seven months and ten days. A note on his record states that 'this officer has never presented himself in this regiment, having obtained a royal order to continue his studies in Barcelona and so has never served'.[259] Exactly what Diego was studying there is unknown at present, perhaps the intention was to become a military engineer or a surgeon. Significantly, James listed his country as Ireland but Diego listed his as Spain. Could this be his father's influence, who maybe considered that James might one day come to inherit the lands in Ireland? Clementina Wogan is mentioned in a letter of 23 August 1746 written to James III in the immediate aftermath of the 'Forty-five': 'I had however some little domestic comfort a few days ago, my daughter Clementina having been most graciously received as *camarista*, or maid of honour by the queen dowager (Elizabeth Farnese)'.[260] These three individuals are without question the children of Anne O'Driscoll and Charles Wogan. Other names and references are mentioned in his correspondence, for example on the happy occasion of his promotion to the position of *corrigedor* of San Clemente de la Mancha, Charles wrote to James III reassuring him of his loyalty and stating that 'my daughters are at court' and that their loyalty ran 'in the blood'.[261] Later, on 5 November 1745 when Wogan was reporting on progress relating to the Spanish government's preparations to assist Prince Charles Edward during the 'Forty-five', he mentions that 'my daughter O'Driscoll … has the honour to be in the bed chamber and confidence of the queen'.[262] One other reference to of one of his children is to be found in a document listed on the *Pares* system of Spain where 'Ana O'Driscoll Wogan Delagde *y de* Macarty, *natural de Madrid, para contraer matrimonio*' with Mattias Chevers, a knight of the Order of Santiago, when they were getting married in 1749.[263]

Chapter 9

Spain through Irish Eyes, 1726–1731

After his marriage, over the following few years Wogan's letters to the Stuart court in exile are brimming with the latest rumours in international relations, the movements and disposition of the king and queen of Spain, domestic financial chaos there, apparent military preparations in Spain, and even reports from Ireland. The twenty-six surviving letters between Wogan and the court form the basis for this chapter. The delayed payment for rank and file members of the Spanish military impacted him directly and provided a recurring theme. In an earlier letter to the Stuart court, Wogan mentioned that the Spanish had been put into a disadvantageous position by the British who grew from strength to strength by their diplomacy. He speculated that as long as peace continued and with it that state of affairs, Spain only stood to lose by it.

The delicate game of diplomacy during this period receives an intriguing commentary from Wogan. George I remained steadfast in his preservation of British entente with France, which continued, much to Wogan's ire. Spanish concerns chiefly related to their claim to territory in the Mediterranean, especially Queen Elizabeth Farnese's ducal inheritance of Parma. The queen was eager to secure her ducal territories in northern Italy and, if possible, the Two Sicilies (as Naples and Sicily were then known) for her children. Emperor Charles VI, Britain's ally against his dynastic rival, had benefited from the Treaty of Utrecht which concluded the War of the Spanish Succession, giving him territories in the Mediterranean. Likewise, the Spanish had also been beaten out of Oran in North Africa in 1708 by the Moorish leader Bey Mustapha Ben Youcef Ben Mohamed ben Ishaq el-Mesrati, known to the Spanish as Bey Bigotillos. The Spanish had been the biggest losers of the Treaty of Utrecht, with the loss of Naples, Sicily, Sardinia and Milan, along with the loss of Gibraltar and Port Mahon to the British, though Philip later seized Sardinia in 1717. He considered it a matter of dynastic pride that he reconquer Spain's lost territories. Wogan could not fathom France's intentions, but it can be concluded that they wished to preserve the peace. In the small garrison towns in Spain to which the Irlanda Regiment had been posted, Wogan sent frequent updates to the Stuart court about the outlook from Spain. He found it difficult to separate fact from fiction amidst the wild rumours of the ongoing international negotiations of the great powers. To John Hay he wrote: 'public notions and events seemed to be guided more by whim and accident, though we should lay aside corruption. T'were enough to turn one's head… I conclude now that either I am out of my senses, or the more southerly princes of Europe are mad'.[264] Spain leaned towards war, for which they had been preparing consistently for some time, while the others sought to avoid it. As the negotiations continued, Wogan reported that 'every village is as fertile in invention as the Piazza d'Espagne, every man pretends to know, and makes a windmill of it according to his fancy, till some other Don Quixote beats it down to set up a new one of his own instead'.[265] He frequently referred to international diplomacy in terms of a stage play, with the actual dealing going on 'behind the curtain' and that 'alliances grow up, like mushrooms'.[266] These negotiations sought to settle all differences between all the major powers of Europe and to promote stability. Philip V worked hard with Charles VI towards an arrangement regarding Spanish claims in Italy, which also involved the Imperial succession.[267] Wogan reported that the Spanish king had sent large sums of money to Vienna to help his envoys there to secure their objectives.[268] The Irishman referred to the Treaty of Vienna (1725), into which he hoped the French could be wrested away from their arrangement with Britain.[269] Meanwhile, frustrated with George I's reluctance to give up Gibraltar, a limited war broke out between Spain and Britain which became known as the Anglo-Spanish War (1727–1729). Wogan gave details of the subsequent military actions in a letter to Cardinal Gualtiero, which included British harassment of shipping in the West Indies, including one prize worth nine million *piastres*.[270] He also provided details of the Siege of Gibraltar of 1727, doubting that the 25,000 Spaniards would be enough while the British controlled the harbour. He reported that the British 'brought by force a few herds of sheep, cows and other cattle from the vicinity of their garrison to provide food in case of need, killing and wounding some of the peasants who wanted to resist them'.[271] In the end, British diplomacy successfully isolated Spain from Austrian support, forcing the Spanish to lift their costly siege.

The threat of war kept the Spanish government on high alert, as Wogan observed that they had stationed a large force along the Pyrenees as a deterrent to France, and they continued to move troops around the country for fear of a descent or a bombardment by the British squadron in the Mediterranean. 15,000 men had been sent to Mallorca for its security against such an attack and to fortify the Isle of Cadiz. As it stood, the British had already secured Gibraltar and Port Mahon in Menorca as permanent bases in the Mediterranean at Spain's expense. Philip V could not stand for this. Wogan made frequent references to large-scale military preparations in Spain including the manufacturing of new artillery pieces, all other necessities for war, and the construction of new and formidable warships, hoping to counterbalance British naval might in the area. However, Wogan feared that Spain suffered from a lack of experienced officers and able seamen to crew them.[272] Military posturing played an important role during the international negotiations. The power to intimidate and cow your enemies was significant, as Wogan observed that the wavering king of Portugal had quickly declared neutrality upon arrival of the English squadron to his coasts; that the 'squadron might beat down his town of Zilbonne and his very palace about his ears', and that he 'couldn't be depended on and might cause the Spanish trouble if forced to be their enemy'.[273]

The Spanish state had been financially debilitated by the loss of its territories in the Mediterranean. In an earlier letter to Arthur Dillon,

Wogan reported that senior officials of the Spanish state had complained to Philip of 'the many horrible abuses committed since his coming into the country by the advice and under the administration of foreigners, the violent oppression of the people under heavy and extraordinary taxes, things unheard of in former reigns'.[274] In the same letter he describes the bleak outlook for the Spanish state and that without sufficient funding for the upkeep of the army, it would be neglected and so hand the military advantage to Britain. The result of this, he saw, would be that Britain would become master of trade and that Spain would become a secondary power to them.[275] He noted that the British had offered an arrangement whereby they would secure the Spanish trade from the West Indies on their behalf, pointing to Britain's emerging maritime dominance.[276] His second letter to Dillon indicates the fall of José de Grimaldo, a long-time favourite minister of Philip V, which would clear the way for the rise of the talented José Patiño to secretary of state. Spain's fiscal difficulties had already been felt by the army as Wogan repeatedly describes in his letters to the Stuart court in Rome.

In 1726 he noted that the French had an altogether a different problem. They couldn't raise enough men to manage their Pyrenees border because the peasantry had made so much money from the Mississippi Affair that they couldn't be coaxed into service, even when offered 100 livres a man.[277] Furthermore, the French, like the Spanish, had stopped paying 'court-graces and pensions to officers and colonels … leading to misery there', since they were dependent on those payments as Spanish officers seem often to have been.[278] Wogan gave exact details as to his rate of pay for his ranks of captain and colonel, amounting to 300 pistoles a year, which, to his frustration, was paid irregularly; but more promptly from Madrid 'by the most fatiguing and irksome solicitation there at the war office and treasury'. He remarked that his pay would always be four, but sometimes seven or eight months behind. He invested some money in a mining operation in Aragon to open another stream of income. He wrote of 'a great machine for the purpose arrived from England' and that each investor had hopes to several pistoles per day by it; though he said the mine's reserves had been depleted since the time of Philip II.[279] Anne had received 100 pistoles per year for her former post at the court and another by pension, but the then minister in charge, Juan Guillermo, Duke of Riperdá, had stopped those payments completely for the time-being.[280] Wogan concluded that it would be impossible to do any service for James III if he were based in Madrid on such pay, as he could not even afford a coach or other necessaries of decency and presentability as an official of his exiled liege. Perhaps, he wrote, only if the Duke of Ormond received orders for more important business that he could fulfil some duties if he stayed there without his family.[281] In reference to officials and nobles operating in Madrid he wrote that though 'all their eyes and all their tongues [would be] upon me, because they think this is a province that ought to be reserved to them (as your lordship may judge by their vile treatment even of the duke of Wharton)'.[282] No further elaboration is made on how Wharton was mistreated in Spain. It could possibly refer to Queen Elizabeth's initial obstruction of the duke's marriage to her *camarista*, Ms O'Beirne. On the contrary, the duke had a reputation for having a strong personality and being too fond of his tipple. Wogan concluded that his good relations with the ministers of state and the king and queen would counteract any ill-meant activity he would face in Madrid.[283] James Edgar, King James III's private secretary from 1728, informed Wogan that 'the king is persuaded that you'll lay hold of all opportunities there to promote his interests' and that he would always lay any information he sent before the king.[284] This showed James's continued confidence in Wogan.

This period seems to have been characterised by much uncertainty both in Spain's domestic and international affairs. The shocking return of the Spanish Infanta Mariana Victoria by the French government received some notable commentary from an increasingly Francophobe Wogan. He said that it was less the fact of it happening and more the 'extraordinary and unbecoming manner' in which she was sent back to Spain that caused embarrassment. He opined that Philip should have demanded public satisfaction for it.[285] Infanta Mariana Victoria would later be celebrated with 'royal cavalcade at the Portuguese border' when betrothed to the Portuguese Prince José in 1728.[286] Following this trip to the Portuguese border, the king and queen of Spain travelled to Seville, Cadiz, Grenada and Murcia before returning to Madrid 'at the extraordinary expense of two thousand pistoles per day or probably more for six months' travel for king queen and court'.[287] Wogan surmised that the possible reason for this was a plan by Queen Elizabeth to prevent King Philip from sinking into a renewed bout of depression. The king's mental health caused much anxiety and commentary in contemporary Spain, with the consistent fear that he might abdicate the throne again. A year later Wogan reported to James III that the king had again taken to his bed 'out of a distinct and sudden melancholy' and that the queen tried everything in her power to help her distraught husband.[288] Charles's own arrears of pay had mounted to 800 pistoles (more than three years' pay), but the problem came to a head with 'a universal crying out in Spain' that 'nobody is getting paid, and Madrid is starving'.[289] He wrote that Spanish troops feared that if England and France got the better of Spain in the ongoing negotiations, there would be huge reforms in Spain and widespread disbandment of troops. He continued that the people longed for the old way as under the Austrians, where they had few troops to pay and low taxes on the people, and that if Philip abdicated again the game would be up for all foreign troops in Spain.[290] Despite these difficult circumstances, Wogan could not believe that the Spanish government had agreed to a defensive alliance with Britain and France, who would not be obliged to help them retake their lost possessions in the Mediterranean, noting that he and many others were sick of peace and longed for war, not only for Spain's benefit, but also that it would present opportunities for a restoration of James III.

As regards Britain and France, Wogan's contemporary missive had much to report to Rome. In 1729, he stated that 'England is as sick at heart as France is rotten'.[291] He regarded the French alliance with Britain as an ill-timed and ill-placed alliance amounting to betrayal, especially since James III had been required to leave French territory, thereby badly damaging prospects for a Stuart restoration by military means. Of the French he wrote:

> … notwithstanding all their whim of Salique law, which our kings have deployed and made a nose of wax of, and would have continued to laugh at with scorn to this day, had

> not the unhappy divisions in our royal family withered our laurels and made our rightful conquests abroad ineffectual by the bloody wars we raged at home.[292]

His use of first person plural points to his sense of identification with and membership of a greater British-Irish sense of identity among the Old English of Ireland. During the previous century, Wogan observed that it had been French policy to foment as much unrest in England as possible as a strategy to keep them weak; and lamented, in reference to Anglo-French Wars of the late middle ages, that there was a time when France was totally in the power of England but that the English were foolishly merciful to them. He squarely laid the blame with the French for the fact they'd caused the deaths of '100,000 men of our countries who died bravely without having been any use in the cause they banished themselves … for'.[293] Of England, he correctly observed the growing dominance at sea of the Royal Navy. Quoting Sir Francis Bacon (1561–1626) he wrote:

> … a prince who is master of the sea, if he has not the universal dominion, has at least what is next to it … by keeping his enemies in constant respect of him… This is true in the case of George, but if the others [other powers] know their own strength and his weakness at home, how easy a bargain they might have of him.[294]

This certainly was the case at that moment in history, as the British government frequently used the threat of their naval power to bully the king of Portugal, the northern powers (Sweden and Russia) and the southern ones alike despite the fact that George was 'hated as he is by the vast majority at home'.[295] As regards George I's domestic affairs, he commented that the British state was so deep in debt that it amounted to 'more than the intrinsic value of the whole country'.[296] During the truce and ongoing peace negotiations to end the Anglo-Spanish War, Wogan observed that the 'English will cry like a woman in travail' if forced to hand over Gibraltar and Port Mahon after spending forty years of their 'blood and treasure' to then give them up and purchase a 'wretched peace'. He noted that taxation in Britain 'was at its highest' as if in full-scale war and that the time was ripe 'to throw in a few thousand men and a quantity of arms, the whole kingdom being in the highest discontent and ready to shake off the yoke on the least occasion given'.[297] The British government had been 'forced upon the expedient of lotteries, just as they were in the last years of the great war, when England could no longer furnish the expense by the speedy payment of taxes'. In reference to the tireless and brilliant work of the British intelligence system and George I's envoys and ambassadors, Wogan wrote that 'the English seem to carry witchcraft about them both at home and abroad', later noting that Stanhope had bewitched the court of Spain.[298] In the end, the peace was concluded to the 'several interests of the princes of Christendom', Wogan noting that 'Italy and Flanders are all cut into piece-meal without a blow'.[299]

Reporting to James III, Wogan shared an invasion plan for Ireland based on intelligence he received about its state of security from a group of Irish officers in Spanish service, 'gentlemen of good sense lately returned from Ireland' having spent most of winter of 1728–1729 there attending to their domestic affairs. His report gives a fascinating image of Ireland during the era of Protestant ascendancy. Irish landowners could easily go back and forth from the Continent and continue to manage their business in Ireland. The invasion plan centred on the southern town of Cork in Munster, and the western town of Galway in Connacht. Cork, a wealthy and populous town, was only guarded by a single regiment, and Jacobite supporters in the town greatly outnumbered the garrison. He wrote that they were 'crying out … why some opportunity is not put into their hands to get rid of their tyrants, as every petty justice of peace is'.[300] Of Galway, the gentlemen spies told Wogan that it 'has an old rotten wall and only three companies to garrison it, its people rich and almost all Catholic; behind [the town] an inaccessible country full of ports and landing places … called *Iar-Chonnacht*[301] on which side the bockety old gate was only guarded by a single man'.[302] The overall strength of the British army in Ireland stood at 10,000 men and horse, but Wogan observed that these tended to be widely dispersed throughout the kingdom 'to frighten the people from any notion of rising'.[303] About the standing army, the returned Irish officers reported that they were 'in the most profound indolence and heedlessness as to discipline, guard and everything else but good living'. The barracks and country quarters of the force, both horse and foot, were 'in the most supine neglect and carelessness. Most of the officers pass their time feasting and hunting at the gentlemen's houses in the neighbourhood; the soldiers straggling about among the peasantry with very little care of either horses, arms or duty; that the major part of all wishing, out of wearisomeness of their idle life, to have something to do'.[304] The returned Irish officers apparently travelled freely throughout Munster and Connacht, eating and drinking with whomever they wanted, and were even hosted in some of the barracks themselves, which they noted 'could be surprised by a single officer at the head of eight or ten men'.[305] Since most parish priests in Ireland 'keep a list of their parishioners of bodily strength and spirit' they could 'serve as masters to direct them to any proposed rendezvous point', and they exercised 'absolute dominion' over the Catholic population in Ireland.[306] Despite penal legislation against Catholicism in Ireland, according to this source the laws were unsuccessful, or at least not very rigorously applied in Munster and Connacht. Wogan claimed that the 'Church Protestants were uneasy in Ireland but mostly were principled Tories' and that they might actually be counted on to support a Jacobite insurrection there. He wrote:

> … many gentlemen of figure and fortune in those provinces had reluctantly converted to Protestantism to retain their lands in Ireland, Catholics being largely barred from landownership… These have horses and arms and no small sway in the country, being looked at by the poor peasants as their only protectors against the insolence of their masters, and would be charmed at any occasion to shake off the yoke from their consciences and inclinations too.[307]

A force of 2000 sent to these parts of Ireland would be met with pathetic resistance, according to Wogan, and at the same time would receive the widespread support of the vast majority of the people, were a main landing to be made there. The forces in Ireland would be tied up and unable to reinforce the army in Britain where other landings could be made. The difficulty, he later observed, would be the logistics of drawing together the dispersed Jacobite forces throughout Europe who were loyal to James without raising the alarm. Given the formidable British intelligence network, he mused that he could not see this happening, and that the best chance they had of success recently was the attempt of 1720/22.[308] Wogan's plan would never be put into action.[309]

The active defensive posturing of the Spanish army during the period kept Wogan on the move as evidenced by his letters to the Stuart court. From Mequinenza he moved to Monzón; from there to the town of Jaca, in the snows at the feet of the Pyrenees; the Aragonese capital, Zaragoza; and finally, to Morella in the Kingdom of Valencia in the south east. In Morella the Irlanda Regiment settled on the top of a mountain and he observed 'tis my lot to pass the summers in the hottest and the winters in the coldest regions of Spain'. Even though many think it's always warm, 'tis certain that upper Silesia, the most bitter air I ever felt, is scarce comparable to this; while people are at the same time scorching with heat in the plains below us, where they scarce ever know anything of winter but the name'.[310] He gives us many glimpses of other events in his correspondence during these years, including Queen Clementina's and King James's loss of their third child, which Clementina apparently carried very close to full term.[311] Though explained in greater detail in his later correspondence, he had a falling out with Sir John Misset. There are no details on the subject of the quarrel at the time, but Wogan wrote to Hay about it in Rome who felt obliged to show it to James III who asked Ormond to set the matter straight:

> I did not take notice to you of what you mentioned of Sir John, because I thought a measure marking might have been the case, which time would have set right again, I find now your differences have gone further, which I can't but be surprised at, considering all the obligations which Sir John owes you… I was sorry to be obliged to show your

> letter to the king... His majesty has actually by this post written to the duke of Ormond ... to set the matter right by representing the distinction H.M. made between you and Sir John, which is no prejudice done him.

The king also wrote to Castellar by the same post concerning the matter of their promotion in Spain; though it is unclear if this was the sole cause of the argument.[312] Subsequent correspondence from Wogan does not contain the usual postscript stating that Sir John and Lady Misset extend their regards, which might indicate that they were out of contact and that the friendship between the two had been irreparably damaged.

In 1729, Wogan sent James 'an account of service and loyalty to the crown' of the Wogan family since the twelfth century. He asked Murray to present it to the king, while at the same time making an unmentioned request of the king. Wogan may have asked James to send him the royal patent of knight-baronet from 1719 or may have asked to be elevated to a higher noble rank. Whatever the request, both the letter to Murray and the Wogan family history does not appear to be in the Stuart Papers.[313] Wogan included in his request 'that very few of the unennobled families in the three kingdoms can make so circumstantial and well-grounded a pretention to the favours of the crown it has served almost to its utter extinction in every respect'.[314] Whatever his request, James gave him a very polite refusal stating that it wouldn't be any use to him in Spain and might actually cause him 'inconveniences' there.[315] Despite this, the king wholeheartedly agreed to assist in another request of Charles on behalf of his brother, James. James Wogan had entered the Church and 'studied in Paris with distinction ... having defended theses in Latin, Greek and Hebrew in the Sorbonne' and now sought a position. A century earlier, Irishmen had apparently been barred by Cardinal Richelieu after he had been 'piqued by a satire which some Irishmen' produced about him in Paris.[316] This obstacle to James Wogan's progress had just been removed and his brother was now working to secure him additional funding to finish his studies, having been maintained 'thitherto on a pension from his uncle, the bishop of Kildare' created for his relatives who wished to study and enter the Church which only covered him for the duration of his studies. Wogan added that his father 'though very good in business, follows the example of other fathers and relatives in Ireland who no longer trouble themselves for the maintenance of their own children'.[317] This interesting observation tells us a lot – Irish noble and gentry families basically could not support their children and looked for ways to have them provided for. The Church guaranteed them an education and later a decent position and livelihood.[318] In any case, both James III and the cardinal successfully assisted him, and Father James Wogan would go on to receive a position in Lille, later becoming professor of philosophy of the College of Navarre and the College of the Lombards (the Irish College).[319]

Wogan's correspondence also provides insight into his Jacobite network in Spain. During these years he mentions prominent Jacobites such as Sir George Keith, tenth Earl Marischal, and a Brigadier Campbell.[320] He reported his friend Davy Erskine's promotion to lieutenant-colonelship of Berwick's Limerick Regiment. In the same letter he said that he had forgiven the Duke of Berwick 'for the very wrongful insinuations he was pleased to give of me to my master in those days, in order to gain his point for Mr. Burke in his majesty's opinion'.[321] Burke was chosen for a position in the Limerick Regiment over Wogan and Misset, who resented it and transferred to Irlanda afterwards. Berwick is also mentioned as having suffered a reversal of fortune after the death of King Louis I; having had huge influence at the new king's court, he 'forced himself upon all the Irish regiments as director and arbiter general of the Irish brigade'.[322] Wogan noted the duke's sidelining after Philip resumed the crown, but it is unclear whether Berwick continued in the position mentioned above. In the same letter, and while describing Spanish troop movements, Wogan mentions Count Dermot O'Mahony, son of the infamous Count Daniel O'Mahony who won an almost impossible victory for the French while in command of a battalion of Dillon's Regiment at Cremona in 1702.[323] As speculation grew in 1731 around a major invasion by Spanish forces, shrouded in mystery, Wogan thanked King James on behalf of Brigadier Daniel O'Sullivan, Count Berehaven,[324] 'for the gracious letter he was pleased to honour him with' adding that 'Brigadier [Randal]

Macdonnell begs you'll speak to Sir William Ellis about the picture', referring to a request to receive portraits of the Prince of Wales and the Duke of York from Rome.[325] Wogan himself had received a stamp with the impression of Prince Charles and marvelled at the likeness, saying that the lower half of his face was like his father's but the upper more like Clementina. Such items provided a much-needed morale boost for James's supporters across Europe, especially for those like Wogan who found themselves out of pocket.[326] Wogan and James continued to communicate in the warmest terms through these years. In response to another new year's blessing from Wogan (which he rarely missed), James replied, 'I have been long acquainted with your zeal for me, and can never forget the proofs you have given me of it, I hope better days may yet soon come in which we may be all at our own homes again and I shall be able to be as kind to my faithful servants as they deserve. The queen returns your compliments, as we both do to your lady'.[327] On receiving this letter from James, Wogan wrote to Edgar 'this letter has been much the more consoling to me … chiefly on account of his majesty's most kind and comforting expressions which shall ever be lodged near my heart'.[328] Nothing could do more to raise the spirits of James's Irish knight in Spain.

Chapter 10

The Spanish Conquest of Oran, 1732

Spain's ongoing military preparations for war in the Maghreb over the previous years soon bore fruit. In April 1732 the *Regimiento d'Irlanda* took up positions in Valencia and Wogan wrote to Edgar in Rome that neither the troops nor the officers knew exactly where they would be disembarking; some speculated Italy, though more thought Oran on the Barbary coast of modern-day Algeria the most likely destination. Luis Reggio Branciforte y Colonna (the fourth prince of Campoflorido), one of the commanders of the expeditionary force, had granted Wogan the use of his residence in Valencia while it lay unused enabling him to 'leave my wife and family in this fine house and garden'.[329] He described how the preparations for the expedition continued 'with great alacrity and expense' and that the amount of transports were 'in greater quantity … in every respect than has been perhaps seen in the world in a like case. Meal, biscuit, wine, water, tents, fascines, ladders, grenades, powder, ball and even wool sacks for sieges on rocky ground'.[330] Clearly Philip V spared no expense as he aimed to rebuild Spanish power. Officers flocked to Alicante which was the rendezvous point for the expedition and Wogan expected that Oran would be the ultimate destination, however this would be 'only a bite' and that Spanish forces would be directed elsewhere quickly afterwards, though he questioned the wisdom of sending a large force outside Spain with a high chance of war in Europe.[331] The portraits of Prince Charles and his brother Henry requested by Wogan duly arrived in Valencia a couple of weeks later as final preparations for the expedition were made:

> I had no sooner appeared at our General Campoflorido's, that he embraced me and told me with a great deal of joy that he had got the pictures, which he ran himself to fetch me. I had the little box instantly opened and showed them to him, upon which we went into the prince's apartment, where both he, the ladies and our many general officers could not cease admiring the beauty and promising air of our princes.[332]

He observed in frustration how most of the other powers and peoples of Europe apparently supported the Stuarts and the Jacobites but that none of them were willing to give them the help they needed: 'they neither will do the thing themselves, nor suffer any other to carry away the honour of it from them'. He added rather chillingly that 'this will draw a vengeance upon them all in the last, and since they envy one another the glory, the Almighty will bring it about to their confusion'.[333]

James had written to the Spanish minister, Castellar, in Wogan's favour to help him obtain command of the Irlanda Regiment. For his part, Charles wrote 'my getting this regiment is so much my due, that it can do no man any wrong, though it may do a displeasure to others who pretend to it'. He described how Berwick had used his influence against him, causing him to wait for years in what he described as 'a double and very disagreeable apprenticeship in the station of colonel *agregado*'. He mentions Sir John Misset for the first time in years, in reference to how Sir John felt the better qualified to be appointed colonel of Irlanda. Indeed, Misset's Spanish service record reads like a thundering rollcall of Louis XIV's battles during the War of the Spanish Succession, including Luzzara, Casano, Cremona, San Sebastian, Turin, Landau, Lerida and Alicánte among others.[334]

It states that he had been wounded seven times during his career in Dillon's Regiment in the French service. He had both a colonel's and brigadier's brevet from James III, but still served ten years later as a mere captain of a company. His value would soon be recognised. Being much more experienced and Wogan's elder, it is understandable that

The ruins of Rathcoffey Castle, Kildare, the ancestral family estate of the Wogans. Charles was a member of a junior branch of the family on lands close by to the south of the main estate at Rathcoffey. (Photograph by Mr Ed Hannon, Visions of the Past Blog; online.)

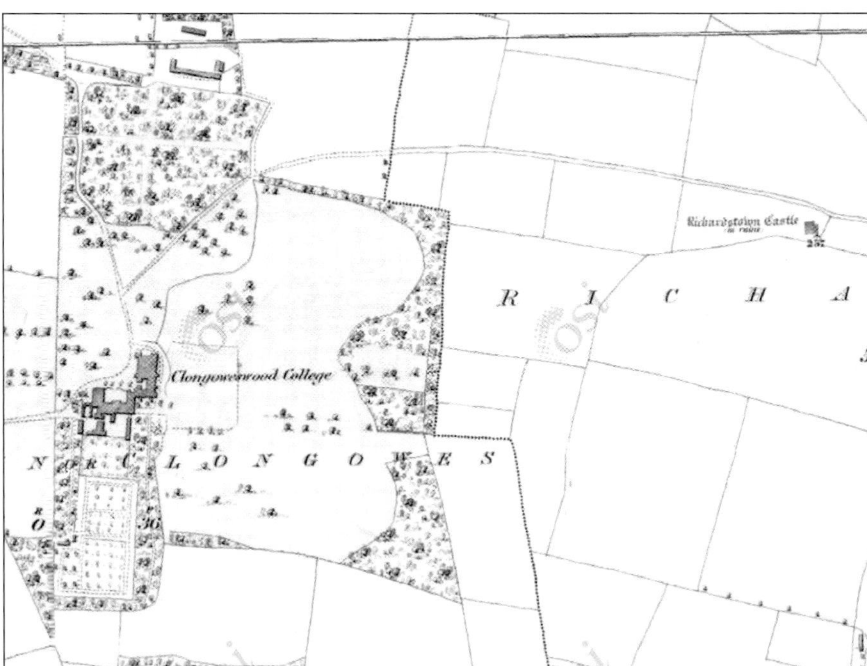

Richardstown Castle, shown on the Ordnance Survey of Ireland. (Irish Townland and Historical Map Viewer (online), made available by Tailte Éireann.)

Left: View of the rebels as they were brought pinioned to London. (National Library of Scotland, Jacobite Broadsides; public domain image, Creative Commons License CC-BY 4.0. Blaikie.SNPG.18.18.)

Below: The inner court of Newgate Prison in the eighteenth century, from a contemporary print. This is exactly what the interior of the prison would have looked like while the Wogan brothers and other Jacobite prisoners from Preston awaited arraignment and trial. (Wellcome Trust.)

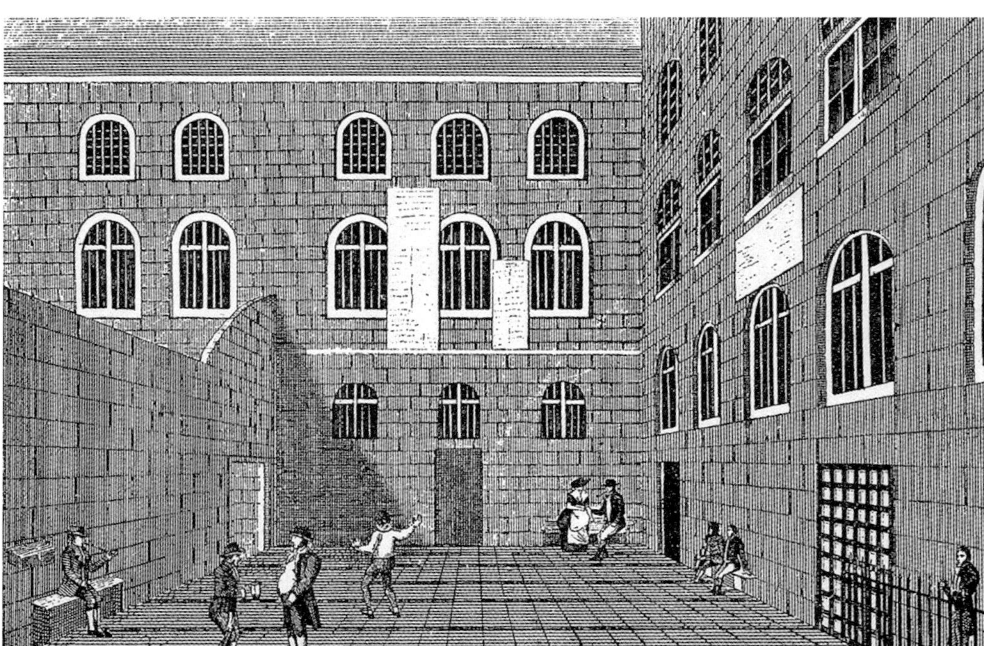

Portrait of Colonel Nicholas Wogan, Circle of Garret Morphy, 1720, oil on canvas. This portrait is very similar to that of his brother, Charles, including a similar red jacket and white undershirt. Nicholas's daughter, Frances, married John Talbot of Malahide in 1735. Nicholas died in 1757. The partition of his lands is fully detailed in the Registry of Deeds. Rathcoffey House and demesne was willed to Frances who moved permanently to Malahide in 1769 bringing with her many of the Wogan heirlooms including the family paintings. The author is most grateful to Seamus Cullen whose expertise on the Wogans and the history of Clane is extensive. (Photo © National Gallery of Ireland, housed and displayed at Malahide Castle, North Dublin.)

Veduta frontale del Palazzo Ducale di Urbino, 2012. (Photograph by Fabio Demitri; public domain image from Wikimedia Commons, Creative Commons Attribution-Share Alike 4.0 Intl. license.)

A copperplate engraving from 1693 showing (from left): Konstanty Władysław, Jakub Ludwik, depicted in the framed portrait is King Jan III, Aleksander Benedykt, Queen Maria Kazimiera and Teresa Kunegunda. (National Library of Poland, Warsaw; Benoît Farjat, after Henri Gascar – Ioannes III Rex Poloniae Invictissimus etc. 1693.)

Above: A view of the Sobieski royal palace at Ohlau during the eighteenth century, taken from *Topographia oder Prodromus Delineati Principatus Lignicensis Bregensis, et Wolaviensis.* (Friedrich Bernhard Werner, *Schloss in Ohlau.*)

Right: Portrait of James Butler, second duke of Ormond, by John Smith (1703–1742), ink on paper. (Original stored at Rijksmuseum in Netherlands; public domain image, Creative Commons CC0 1.0 Universal Public Domain Dedication.)

Below: View of Imperial and Royal Provincial Capital Innsbruck and surroundings: detail Innsbruck, viewing south, nineteenth century, by an unknown author. (Public domain image.)

Uniforme et drapeau du régiment de Dillon en 1689, by Claude-Antoine Littret de Montigny. This is the uniform worn by officers of Dillon's Regiment. Major Sir Richard Gaydon, Captain Sir John Misset, Captain Sir Luke O'Toole were listed therein. After their successful rescue of Princess Clementina, they were requested to wear their official uniforms at a religious ceremony dedicated to Clementina's rescue party. The Irish regiments in Spain also wore the red coats of the Stuarts symbolising the strong ideological resilience of Jacobitism among the Wild Geese. (Image from *Vue extraite de l'ouvrage de Claude-Antoine Littret de Montigny: Uniformes militaires, où se trouvent gravés en taille-douce les uniformes de la Maison militaire du Roi, publié en 1772*; held at Bibliothèque Nationale de France.)

Queen Clementina, by Francesco Trevisani, 1719, oil on copper (private collection). The three original versions of the portrait are lost, but this copy was painted at the time for Lord Richard Howard. There are two bust copies by Antonio David in private collections, and two full sized copies made from the original in the Palazzo del Rè by William Mosman in 1733, one of which is in the Scottish National Portrait Gallery. The portrait was not engraved. (Private collection.)

Veduta dei Palazzi di Campidoglio in Roma, by De Vegni, A., 1845. On 15 June 1719, Wogan, Gaydon, Misset and O'Toole were led up Campidoglio to the ancient Capitol to the sound of Litui and Tubae, ancient musical instruments of Rome. A public assembly of Roman nobles, patricians and citizens were in attendance to witness their being made Roman Senators, the highest civil mark of distinction it was possible for Pope Clement XI to confer. They were the first Irishmen in history to receive this honour. (Public domain image via Wikimedia Commons.)

The Solemnisation of the Marriage of King James III and Queen Clementina at Montefiascone on 1 September 1719, by Agostino Masucci, oil on canvas. There is a small copy of this picture in the sacristy of the cathedral at Montefiascone. The painting was also engraved twice by Antonio Friz, and one of his engravings (much inferior to the other) is reproduced in Sharp, *The Engraved Record*, p.214. It is not possible to establish with certainty the identities of the people shown in the picture, apart from Marjory Hay, the king and the queen, Father John Brown (in profile immediately above the queen) and Sebastiano Bonaventura (the presiding bishop). The gentlemen kneeling behind the king are presumably (left to right) John Hay, Charles Wogan and Colonel John O'Brien (all of whom signed the marriage certificate), and the gentleman pointing on the right is presumably James Murray (who had married Clementina by proxy and who also signed the certificate). Murray and O'Brien were the only ones still at the Stuart court when the picture was painted in 1735. (National Galleries Scotland.)

La familia de Felipe V, by Louis-Michel van Loo, 1743, oil on canvas. The king and his second wife, Isabel de Farnesio, appear in the centre of the composition, surrounded by their descendants, the future Ferdinand VI – son of the sovereign's first marriage – and Charles III, both with their respective wives and all the other members of the royal family who were alive at the time. In the family-dynastic assembly, curious and contrasting attitudes can be observed: the exhaustion of Philip V compared to the dominant and authoritarian plenitude of his second wife, Isabel de Farnesio; the presence that pretends to be elegant and turns out to be awkward of the Prince of Asturias, future Ferdinand VI; the somewhat oblivious confidence of Charles III, then King of Naples and the sweetness of his wife, the grace of the girls in the foreground, the frieze of faces of Spanish princes, destined to play an important role in the problematic years that followed, etc. (Museo del Prado, Spain, via Wikimedia Commons.)

Vista del Palacio Real de Aranjuez, by Francesco Battaloili, 1756, oil on canvas. View of the Palace of Aranjuez made on the occasion of the celebration of the name day of King Ferdinand VI (1713–1759) in 1756. This work was part of a set of views of the palace and the celebrations that took place there. This palace was more frequently used by Philip V during Wogan's years in Spain because the Royal Palace of Madrid was significantly damaged in a fire in 1734. (Museo del Prado, Spain, via Wikimedia Commons.)

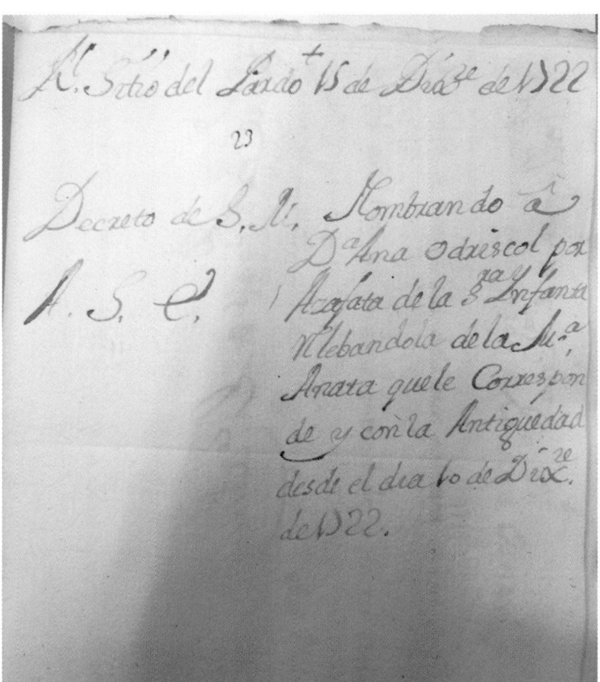

R.l Sitio del Pardo 15 de Diz.e de 1722

23

Decreto de S. M. Nombrando â
D.a Ana Odriscol por
A. S. C. Azafata de la S.ra Infanta
Ylebandola de la M.a
Anata que le Correspon
de y con la Antiguedad
desde el dia 10 de Diz.e
de 1722.

Employment details of Ms Anne O'Driscoll naming her Azafata to the Spanish Infanta (royal princess) in 1722. (Patrimonio Nacional – Archivo General de Palacio, Sección: Personal, Fondo: Odriscol, Ana, Caja 16813, Expediente No. 3.)

Nouveau plan de Gibraltar, by Jean Covens and Corneille Mortier, 1727. This is a contemporary ink etching depicting Gibraltar as it was during the early years of its occupation by Britain. The Kingdom of Spain attempted to recapture it by military force, but the British garrison and its formidable naval squadron defeated them. (Public domain image.)

Portrait of Prince Henry Benedict Clement Stuart, on the left, (1725–1807), later Cardinal York – and on the right, Prince Charles Edward Stuart wearing the *cordon bleu* and star of the Order of the Garter. Wogan and his Jacobite milieu received a twin portrait of the Stuart princes similar to this in the lead up to the Spanish reconquest of Oran 1732. Items like these offered a much-needed morale boost and played a crucial role in sustaining Jacobite hopes of a restoration. (National Library of Scotland; public domain image, Creative Commons Attribution 4.0 International License.)

Sale del Puerto de Alicante, by José Ferrer de Couto, 1854, ink on paper. This is a depiction of the Spanish flotilla which left Alicante on 15 June 1732. More than 500 vessels transported a large Spanish force to recapture Oran. The force included a battalion of troops each from Irlanda and Ultonia. (Ferrer de Cuoto, J., *Historia de la Marina Real Española: desde el descubrimiento de las américas hasta el combate de Trafalgar*, Madrid, 1865; public domain image.)

Oran, Santa Cruz, vue depuis le centre ville (Front de Mer), as photographed in 2005. This stout defensive castle directly overlooked the city of Oran. Bigotillos recaptured Oran for the Regency of Algiers in 1708 by first capturing this crucial hilltop fortress and bombarding the city afterwards. He would attempt the same tactics in 1732. (Mecifi; public domain image.)

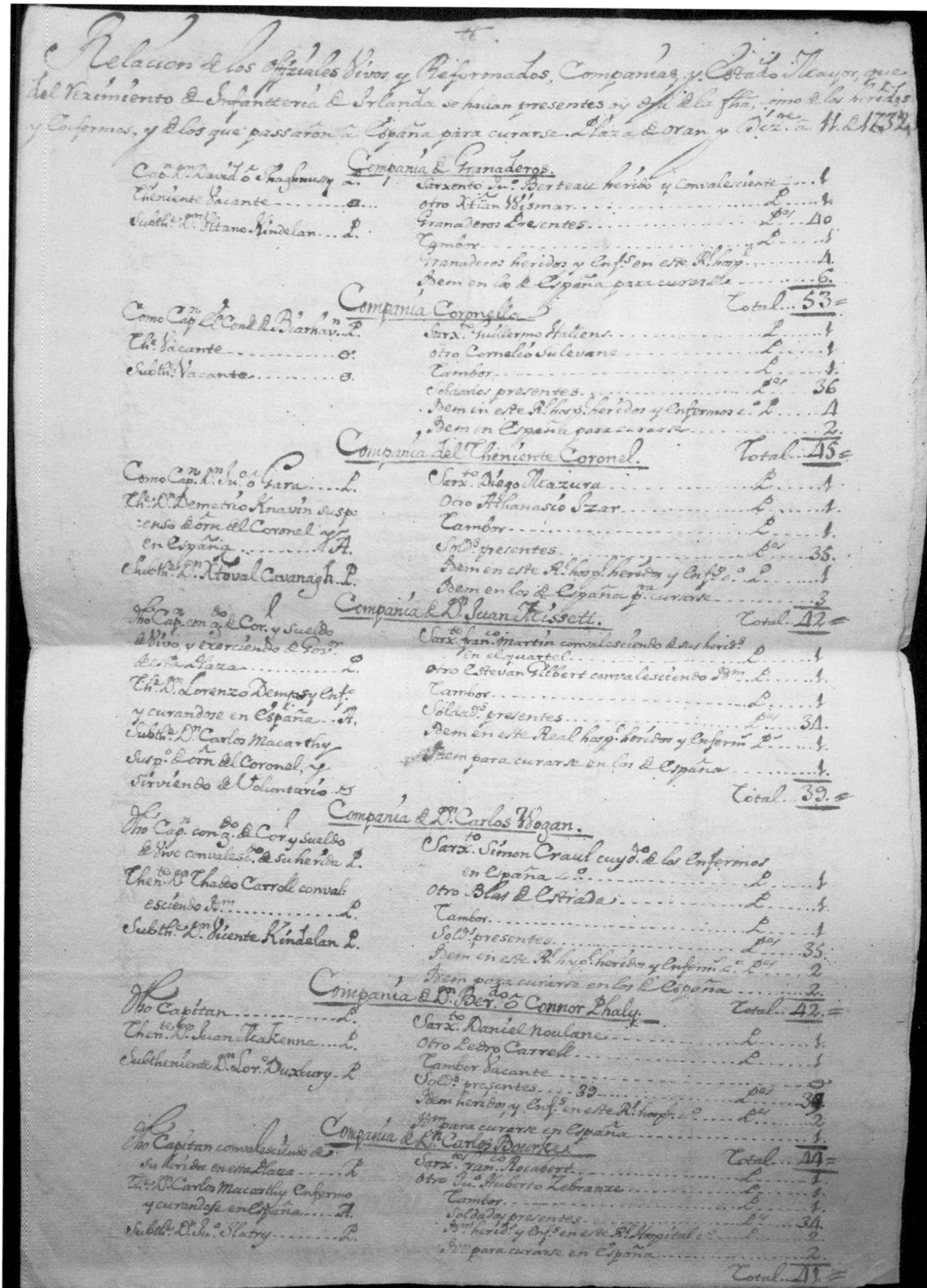

Relacion de los Offiziales Vivos, y Reformados, Compañias y Estado Mayor, que del Regimiento de Infanteria de Irlanda se hallan presentes en este dia de la fecha, como de los heridos y enfermos, y de los que passaron a España para curarse. Plaza de Oran y Dez.re 11 de 1732.

Compañia de Granaderos

Cap.n D.n David O'Shaghnussy ... P.
Theniente Vacante ... o.
Subth.te D.n Gaetano Kindelan ... P.

Sarxento Jn.o Berteau herido y convaleciente ... P ... 1
Otro Xtian Wismar ... P ... 1
Granaderos Presentes ... P.es ... 40
Tambor ... P ... 1
Granaderos heridos y enf.s en este R.l hosp. ... 4
Ydem en los de España para curarse ... 6
Total ... 53

Compañia Coronella

Como Cap.n el Coronel D. Biarnau ... P.
Th.e Vacante ... o.
Subth.e Vacante ... o.

Sarx.to Guillermo Haliens ... P ... 1
Otro Cornelio Sulevane ... P ... 1
Tambor ... P ... 1
Soldados presentes ... P.es ... 36
Ydem en este R.l hosp. heridos y enfermos ... P ... 4
Ydem en España para curarse ... 2
Total ... 45

Compañia del Theniente Coronel

Como Cap.n D. Ju.o O'Gara ... P.
Th.e D. Demetrio Knavin susp.enso de orn. del Coronel y en España ... A.
Subth.e D.n Xtoval Cavanagh ... P.

Sarx.to Diego Mazura ... P ... 1
Otro Athanasio Izar ... P ... 1
Tambor ... P ... 1
Sold.s presentes ... P.es ... 35
Ydem en este R.l hosp. heridos y enf.s ... P ... 1
Ydem en los de España p. curarse ... 3
Total ... 42

Compañia de D.n Juan Missett

Dho Cap.n con grado de Cor. y sueldo de vivo, y exerciendo de Gov.r de esta Plaza ... P.
Th.e D.n Lorenzo Dempsy enf.o y curandose en España ... A.
Subth.e D.n Carlos Macarthy susp.o de orn. del Coronel, y sirviendo de Voluntario ... o

Sarx.to Fran. Martin convaleciendo de sus heridas en el quartel ... P ... 1
Otro Estevan Gilbert convaleciendo ... P ... 1
Tambor ... P ... 1
Soldados presentes ... P.es ... 31
Ydem en este Real hosp. heridos y enferm. ... P ... 1
Ydem para curarse en los de España ... 1
Total ... 39

Compañia de D.n Carlos Wogan

Dho Cap.n con grado de Cor. y sueldo de vivo convaleciente de su herida ... P.
Then.te D.n Thadeo Carroll convaleciendo ... P.
Subth.te D.n Vicente Kindelan ... P.

Sarx.to Simon Craul cuyd.o de los enfermos en España ... P ... 1
Otro Blas de Estrada ... P ... 1
Tambor ... P ... 1
Sold.s presentes ... P.es ... 35
Ydem en este R.l hosp. heridos y enferm. ... P.es ... 2
Ydem para curarse en los de España ... 2
Total ... 42

Compañia de D.n Ber.do O'Connor Phaly

Dho Capitan ... P.
Then.te D.n Juan Makenna ... P.
Subtheniente D.n Lor.o Duxbury ... P

Sarx.to Daniel Noulane ... P ... 1
Otro Pedro Carrell ... P ... 1
Tambor Vacante ... o
Sold.s presentes ... P.es ... 39
Ydem heridos y enf.s en este R.l hosp. ... P.es ... 2
Ydem para curarse en España ... 1
Total ... 44

Compañia de D.n Carlos Bourke

Dho Capitan convaleciendo de su herida en esta Plaza ... P
Th.e D.n Carlos Macarthy enfermo y curandose en España ... A.
Subth.e D.n Ju.o Slatry ... P.

Sarx.to Fran.co Rocabert ... P ... 1
Otro Ju.o Huberto Lebranze ... P ... 1
Tambor ... P ... 1
Soldados presentes ... P.es ... 34
Ydem heridos y enf.s en este R.l Hospital ... 2
Ydem para curarse en España ... 2
Total ... 41

List of the living and reformed officers, companies and staff of the *Regimiento de Irlanda* who are present and present, as well as the wounded and confirmed, and those who will go to Spain for treatment. Oran Square and December 11, 1732, [translated]. This document shows a list of companies of the Irlanda regiment in December 1732, including Wogan & Misset's companies. (Original photograph taken with the permission of the staff of Archivo General de Simancas, Spain: AGS, SGU, Legajo 4728.)

Above left: Portrait of Philip Wharton, 1st Duke of Wharton (1698–1731), eighteenth-century engraving. (Public domain image.)

Above right: Portrait of Jonathan Swift (1667–1745), by Charles Jervas, 1710, oil on canvas 745 x 610mm. Swift was Dean of Saint Patrick's Cathedral in Dublin and is famous for his political essays and satires. He is well known for his authorship of Gulliver's Travels. He kept contact with members of the Jacobite community. (Courtesy of Bodleian Libraries, under Creative Commons License Oxford, Bodleian Library LP 246.)

Below: Town Hall of San Clemente, province of Cuenca, Castilla-La Mancha. (Photo published by user Josemanuel, 2005, Wikipedia Commons, public domain image.)

View of the Monastery of San Lorenzo del Escorial, by Michel Ange Houasse, 1722, oil on canvas. The exertions of securing aid from the Spanish government to be sent to Prince Charles Edward in Scotland during the 'Forty-five' caused Wogan to fall quite ill. On the orders of Philip V and Queen Elizabeth, he was ordered to stay at El Escorial in order to make a full recovery. (Housed at the Museo del Prado, Madrid.)

Portrait of Farnielli 1734, by Bartolomeo Nazari, oil on canvas. Carlo Broschi (1705-1782), known to all as Farinelli, was the most famous singer in Europe during his career. This portrait is held at the Royal College of Music, London. (This photograph was taken by Didier Descouens on 4 May 2019 and is licensed under the Creative Commons Attribution-Share Alike 4.0 International license, via Wikipedia Commons.)

Cathedral of the Holy Cross and Santa Eulalia, Barcelona, 2016. This is a recent photograph taken of Barcelona's cathedral in which Sir Charles Wogan was buried in July 1754. (Ad Meskens.)

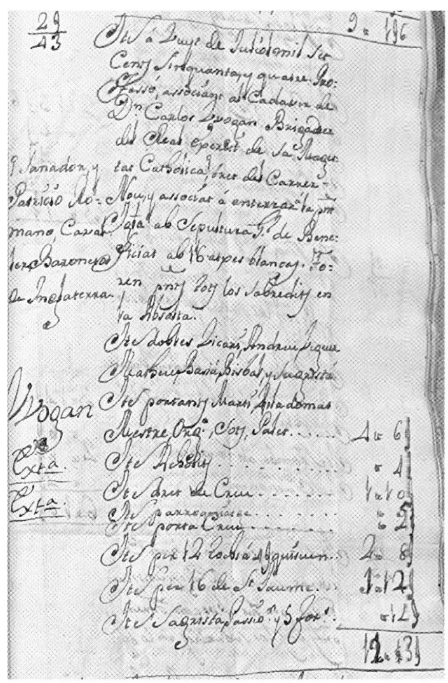

Entry regarding Wogan's death and interment, 7 July 1754. This entry in the record book of Barcelona Cathedral gives Wogan's rank as Brigadier and identifies him in the margin as 'Senator and Patrician of Rome, Knight and Baronet of England'. (With heartfelt thanks to Ms. Lisset Jara, who kindly offered to assist with this part of the research after the author had spent a fruitless week at the notary archive of Barcelona sifting through wills and testaments. Arxiu de la Catedral de Barcelona, Libre de Obits, Tomo XXXIII, desde 1754–1759, f.35., Photo credit to Ms. Jara, 2023.)

Sir John would have been irritated and disappointed that he had been passed over for promotion. Wogan's sole experience seems to have been the Battle of Preston in 1715, and his main justification for this promotion centred on his role in the rescue of Queen Clementina in 1719. It annoyed Wogan to hear that Colonel Daniel O'Sullivan, Count Berehaven, had also applied for the post even though he already had a post with another regiment, because the Irlanda position paid better.[335] In a service with very low numbers of promotions, one could imagine that every vacancy caused a bit of strife between those vying for it, and resentment towards the one who finally got it. It appears that the position was officially left vacant until 1735, but Berehaven may have been given the role of acting-commander.

On 15 June 1732, a single cannon rang out across the Bay of Alicante and the flotilla of over 600 ships set off in perfect order heading south for North Africa. Don José Carrillo de Albornoz, Duke of Montemar, commanded all Spanish forces, while Don Francisco Javier Cornejo took charge of the Navy.[336] An eye witness wrote of it, 'the Mediterranean Sea never witnessed such a variety of banners together'.[337] King Philip asked for public prayers to be offered up for success against their old foes, the Moors.[338] Spanish soldier and poet, Eugenio Gerardo Lobo, composed the following about the expedition…

Ve, lucido escuadrón, ve, fuerte armada,
Del monarca de España empeño augusto,
Y el pendón infeliz del moro adusto,
Se luna llore en ti siempre eclipsada.[339]
[Go, brilliant squadron, go, strong army,
From the August monarch of Spain pledged,
And the unhappy banner of the grim Moor,
The moon cries in you always eclipsed]

The Ottoman/Moorish ruler, Bey Bigotillos, seized upon the turmoil in Spain during the War of the Spanish Succession to wrest back control of Spanish-controlled territory in Algeria. It appears that political control lay in the hands of local strongmen and their heirs who worked together in a loose confederation in the western-most reaches of the Ottoman Empire. Acting in close concert with the bey in neighbouring Algiers, the combined Moorish land and sea forces successfully blockaded the Spanish garrison in Oran. Bigotillos took control of the strategically crucial hills west of Oran which overlooked the town, forcing the garrison to surrender after sustained bombardment. After the Spanish withdrawal in 1708, Bigotillos had ruled Oran until the Spanish returned in 1732.

The Spanish force that sailed from the Bay of Alicante consisted of 23,100 infantry, supported by a cavalry force of 1673, along with engineers, medical staff and every conceivable type of supply. It included approximately 1000 Irish troops, with one battalion each of the regiments of *Irlanda* and *Ultonia*. By 6:00 pm on 28 June the fleet dropped anchor opposite the *Playa de las Aguadas*, a few kilometres from the fortified city of Mers el-Kebir, itself only a short march to Oran. At dawn the Spanish forces began to disembark in good order. It appears that the secrecy of their plans had paid off because they took the Moorish forces completely by surprise. The only major engagement took place outside Mers el-Kebir where Montemar estimated Bigotillos lost 1500 men. The Spanish marched for Oran and found the city's defensive fortifications and big guns abandoned. Bigotillos had decided to immediately evacuate the city, perhaps feeling that he could not hold it given the size and firepower of the Spanish force. Despite this, Montemar estimated the enemy forces at 25,000 men with 5000 Turkish troops and 1000 horses, with the bey's son reinforcing him. If true, the decision to withdraw seems guided more by panic than sense since Oran is defended by strong fortifications which would have bought time for reinforcements to arrive from Algiers. In any case, on 1 July the Spanish occupied Oran and the nearby fortress of Mers el-Kebir capitulated the following day. The Spanish found three months' supplies in Oran and the bey's palace untouched. In the chaotic retreat, the French and British consuls had been abused and robbed, for which they intended to seek compensation in Algiers.[340] The French consul there welcomed the Spanish at the open gates.

The documents pertaining to the Oran expedition in the *Archivo General de Simancas* provide minute detail about all aspects of the campaign. One document provides a list of all officers embarking for Oran and the payments to which their families would be entitled if they died while on duty there; Wogan's family would receive 480 pistoles in the event of his death.[341] Montemar's seventy-page account of the early days of the reconquest tell us that local men and women arrived at the city almost immediately looking for work there, along with traders of cattle and all kinds of wares.[342] The engineers immediately set about the task of repairing and strengthening Oran's fortification system under the direction of the head engineer, a Mr Moreau, with the troops and *trabajadores* (workers) doing the work on rotation each day.[343] The city is bordered to the north by the sea where its harbour is guarded by the fortress of *Rosalquivir*. The castle of *San Phelipe* guarded Oran's southerly approaches. Hills rise immediately west of the city upon which sits the fortress of *Santa Cruz* which dominates the skyline to this day; these hills had proved critical to the defence of the city in 1708 and would do so again soon. Montemar included an order of battle should Bigotillos return and take the field against them, listing the Irish troops of *Irlanda* and *Ultonia* in the centre of the Spanish line with Irishman Don Reynaldo Macdonell named as *Mariscala de Campo*.[344] Moorish troops continued to skirmish around the environs of Oran and on one such occasion an officer of the Walloon Guards, Don Carlos Van der Cruyzen, pursued a group of enemy troops away from the prepared Spanish defences. They drew him into an ambush where they shot his horse out from underneath him and afterwards beheaded him.[345]

A substantial amount of the documents from the Oran *legajos* relate to supply of the garrison by sea, with immediate requests for livestock and rations. Efforts to make the garrison more self-sufficient were taken with the establishment of a bread factory and joinery in the city.[346] From mid-July, the garrison made arrangements to evacuate the seriously wounded by sea to Alicante, Malaga and Cartagena; Don Zenón de Somodevilla, Marqués de la Ensenada, took responsibility for one such operation in July.[347] There are frequent mentions of English and Irish sea captains who made supply runs to Oran, including captains Ramsey, Fanning, Talbot and O'Sullivan. Considerable preparations were made for the establishment, supply and staffing of a hospital in Oran. They would later call for an additional two doctors, six surgeons, six adjutant *botanicos* and six confessors. The extensive supply list includes a call for beds and mattresses and various quantities of medical supplies including fourteen types of leaf, seven of flowers, eight of fruits, twenty-eight of seeds, vegetables, herbs, minerals, oils, wine, aguardiente (strong alcohol) and even four vipers.[348] It gives the reader a fascinating glimpse into medical treatment in the eighteenth century. A Téidí O'Connell is named in one document as having been appointed to a position as a doctor at the hospital in Oran; another lists an individual of the same name captured in transit from Spain with his entire family and taken prisoner to Algiers.[349] This became a concern for the Spanish authorities since the necessity of shipping supplies made both the garrison and the vessels vulnerable to attack by Moorish ships. The crossing took roughly fifteen days depending on the port of departure.[350] The Bey of Algiers had already taken measures to recruit additional mercenaries from the Levant to harass the Spanish at sea and cut off the garrison in Oran, while Bey Bigotillos increased his attacks on the Spanish near the city in preparation for an attempt to retake it.

By August the Spanish had established their civil administration as the local merchants expressed their desire for things to return to normality.[351] The expedition leader, Montemar, returned to Spain with the majority of the troops, leaving about 6000 men to defend the city, which included Wogan and the Irish troops. It has been remarked by Sanchez Doncel that Montemar could have pressed the advantage offered by having such formidable naval and land forces and marched to take Algiers for Spain as well.[352] Bigotillos, whose camp was reported to be within five leagues of Oran, observed the departure of the majority of the Spanish force and immediately increased his raids and attacks.[353] The key mountain-top fortress of Santa Cruz became of the object of increased attacks as he aimed to isolate the defenders by constantly interrupting supply and relief efforts from Oran.[354] The oppressive summer heat had a demoralising effect on the Spanish garrison, the Marqués de Santa Cruz, the new commander, observed. He complained to Patiño that he had been left too few men to rapidly complete the necessary improvements to fortifications around Oran.[355] The work continued through the intense heat of August into September, amid reports that a Moorish force had ejected twenty Spanish grenadiers who had been occupying a forward defensive position to protect construction workers at the castle of San Phelipe. It also states that Colonel John Misset personally led a sally from the castle with a detachment of grenadiers of the Henaut Regiment, along with the twenty men who had retreated, and immediately recaptured the lost post. They then pursued the Moorish force, who were driven off with the loss of thirty men. The report also mentions that the Spanish force returned with four heads, the Moorish troops not having time to remove the corpses of their fallen comrades.[356] Santa Cruz ordered that active defensive tactics be put into operation around Oran. He ordered that 400 *piquetes*, a highly mobile and lightly armed type of soldier, were to be kept at the ready each night to respond rapidly to any attacks against the defences.[357] Each of the defensive forts were commanded 'by a man of valour and experience'.[358] This included Colonel John Misset who was duly recognised for his quality and experience by being promoted by Santa Cruz to the position of 'Governor and Colonel with pay for life of the Plaza of Oran'.[359] The castle of San Phelipe also fell under his command. Philip V and his ministers acknowledged the promotion with two payments of thirty *dublones* for his expenses while carrying out the Royal Service.[360] With his forts and castles sufficiently manned and controlled by good commanders, Santa Cruz deployed 300 *Miquelets* recruited from Catalonia to engage the Moors with guerilla tactics in the surrounding areas.[361] As the best in their class of irregular troop and while fighting for the Carlists during the War of the Spanish Succession, *Miquelets* had proven themselves worthy opponents.[362] These troops performed excellently at Oran, raiding Moorish camps and harassing them on the march. They acted in concert with a detachment of cavalry under the command of Don Phelipe Ramirez and Don Diego Merino who would become the bane of Bigotillos over the following number of months, observing the bey's troop movements, harassing them when possible, and raiding his camps.[363]

As hostilities picked up, intelligence gathering and reporting became a key strategic boon for both sides. Deserters, captured soldiers and workers or slaves provided an invaluable source of information on enemy troop movements and tactics, allowing both sides to adjust their tactics or get wind of upcoming attacks and prepare accordingly. The cavalry commander, Ramirez, captured one such deserter who told him that Bigotillos had assembled a large force of Moorish troops with Turkish and Arab troops in support and was expecting more reinforcements from Algiers.[364] Santa Cruz expressed his concern as some Spanish troops had deserted and taken to marauding around the surrounding countryside;[365] such recaptured faced the noose.[366] He feared they could be forced to give the enemy information about his fortifications and troop strength. On 13 September Count Berehaven, described as 'el coronel de Irlanda', had to relieve another Spanish forward defensive position with a detachment of grenadiers and *piquetes* which had fallen under attack by Moorish troops. Berehaven captured a spy during the action who told Santa Cruz that Bigotillos kept his force on the move, waiting for the opportune moment to attack, all the while adding to his forces to which he had recently recruited 200 camel-riders. The bey tested the defences with probing attacks and continued to attack workers carrying out repairs and improvements to Oran's defences as well as disrupting supply runs.

In late September, he attacked the mountain-top stronghold of Santa Cruz, apparently with all his might. Both Wogan and his commander would later report that the force could have been in excess of 20,000 men, comprised of local Moorish troops supported by Turkish soldiers and troops from the Arab states, recruits and mercenaries from the African interior, and from the city-states of the Levant.[367] A truly cosmopolitan empire, matching the Spanish forces which comprised Spanish, Flemish, Swiss and Irish troops. The line of the curtain wall of *El Castillo de Santa Cruz* rises out of the mountaintop, surrounded on three sides by steep slopes. A steep pathway joining it with Oran to the north-east, or along the crest of the mountain tops to its south-west, provided the only approach. The Spanish garrison of 150 men came under bombardment at San Phelipe and Santa Cruz from Bigotillos' artillery on 27 September. The Moorish force attacked the walls and gates of Santa Cruz and swept around it to cut it off from relief and resupply from Oran. From there, the Spanish could see three Moorish batteries and trenches on three sides of Santa Cruz.[368] By 29 September the besiegers had suffered huge casualties as they began to open a mine at the foot of its walls under constant artillery fire, musket-shot and hand grenades. They erected a timber shield there for their protection while they worked. The commander asked for relief from Oran the following day, unable to expel the enemy from their position. Relief efforts foundered over the following days and the Moorish troops detonated a mine under the wall on the morning of 1 October, opening a wide breach. They rushed at the breach but the besieged Spanish troops repelled them with heavy casualties. Another relief effort from Oran was thwarted and the Spanish troops suffered heavy losses after the Moors charged the retreating force.[369] The Marqués de Santa Cruz wrote to Patiño on the same day asking for reinforcements to be sent, adding that a substantial number of his men had been wounded or suffered from combat fatigue.[370] Emboldened, the Moors tightened the siege. The Marqués wrote that on 3 October the Spanish had repositioned some of their artillery to open fire on the Moorish troops, which they did to devastating effect, taking further casualties and expending large amounts of munitions during the six-hour fight.[371] Santa Cruz recognised the seriousness of the situation he faced and prepared to take decisive action to relieve the hilltop castle of Santa Cruz.

Before dawn the following day, 4 October, he prepared a mixed force of 1200 grenadiers, fusiliers and cavalry from nine regiments along with the necessary supplies. He placed them under the command of Colonel Charles Wogan. Just before dawn, the marqués sent a small force to harass a Moorish forward position in front of San Phelipe which drew a large number of enemy forces away from Santa Cruz to counter. This opened the opportunity for Wogan to lead out the force, which established a line of troops extending from Oran up the hillside to Santa Cruz to protect the vital supplies being moved up to the castle. As the light increased, Colonel Misset informed the marqués from San Phelipe that Bigotillos had realised what was happening. The bey engaged the Spanish with all his troops to break their line in what became a ferocious engagement which lasted for three and a half hours.[372] Santa Cruz reported to Patiño 'I never saw nor hope to see a fire as equal and vigorous for as long a space of time as the king's troops did; and that the enemy had not been lax is seen from the attached list of 544 men killed or wounded, without a single combatant having ceded a foot of land to the enemy' while exposed to attacks from both infantry and cavalry.[373] The relief effort succeeded. The supplies reached the castle of Santa Cruz and the Spanish forces completed the difficult task of retiring to Oran while under constant fire. The list of those wounded on 4 October mentioned by the marqués contains numbers of killed and wounded totalling 544. Wogan received a bad wound to the upper part of one of his legs during the fighting.[374] The Irlanda Regiment listed a total of fifty-three wounded including Wogan, one captain, one sub-lieutenant, two sergeants, forty soldiers and one drummer. Seven had been killed in action. A message came to Oran from Seville on 13 October stating that 'the king has seen with particular satisfaction the valour with which our troops have fought, and the disposition given for the prompt relief of the castle of Santa Cruz, whose achievement makes less noticeable the loss we had in this action'.[375]

Wogan wrote to Campoflorido about the collapse of enemy morale after the battle on 4 October: 'we know from deserters and spies that every day they are on the eve of mutiny'.[376] Large numbers had deserted the camp at night 'through their well-known ravines and rough roads' forcing the bey to post cavalry detachments behind the camp to prevent them from leaving.[377] Many of his troops were outraged and called for his head because he had 'flattered them with vain hopes of taking Oran quickly, from the small, diminished Christian garrison'.[378] At the camp of the son of the *dey* [king] 'the Turks, sometimes, in their greatest mutiny, do not stop threatening the Algerian himself, as an accomplice to the lies of the other'.[379] Bigotillos had ordered increased bombardment of both Santa Cruz and San Phelipe to try to raise morale but his fire proved ineffective and largely symbolic.

At sea, the Moors put out a formidable squadron of nine ships which the Spanish first spotted off *Cabo San Antonio* between Valencia and Alicánte and again off *Cabo San Martín* in Ibiza. Their positioning indicates a plan to intercept ships destined for Oran, which they frequently did. The Spanish shipped supplies and men by convoy under inadequate guard. The tone of alarm in letters from Oran increased since the garrison had taken such casualties, so the supply mission by sea assumed an even greater importance, a fact not lost on the Moors. The English Captain Ramsey's vessel had been obliged to surrender to the Moorish squadron because it had only a single frigate escort. Prince Campoflorido insisted to Patiño that all ships travel by convoy 'so that his majesty's service is not disgraced by having to submit and lose ships to the Moors'.[380] A similar report concerning a ship named *El Leon*, captained by Diego Talbot, stated that the Moors were disembarking and raiding more frequently and that soldiers of the regiments of *Ultonia*, *Aragon* and *Flanders* had been taken prisoner to Algiers after the vessel surrendered to the Moorish squadron.[381]

On 13 November Wogan wrote to Campoflorido with further information on the enemy. His report noted the withdrawal of Turkish troops from the area of Santa Cruz after three companies of grenadiers sallied out of the breach in the walls directly at them and scattered them. He suspected that they had withdrawn most of their equipment and abandoned their camp to prepare for an upcoming assault on San Phelipe. Of the remaining forces available to Bigotillos, the 'Moors and the Arabs, who were their greatest force, have been so chastened and terrified by the ravage they suffered on Saint Francis' Day (4 October), that they have fled the field unanimously and left the Turks'.[382] Of the Turks, the Irishman remarked 'the Turks ... are very tenacious, and after they have put up their banners, they never remove them until they completely despair of their situation'.[383] He gave good news of developments at sea though: 'our ships, having joined with the two from Malta, have attacked the Algerian fleet, sank two of their ships and captured two others. The rest of the Algerian fleet have been saved by a precipitous flight'.[384] Wogan was right about the land forces however, they gathered outside San Phelipe and the Spanish engaged them in what became a decisive six-hour battle on 21 November. The Moorish forces were routed with many losses, their trenches destroyed and their guns captured. However, the Marqués de Santa Cruz died during the fighting. Due to his earlier wound, it is unlikely Wogan took part in this battle and he never mentioned it afterwards. Colonel John Misset kept vital communication lines open between San Phelipe and Spanish forces during the battle.[385] Irish troops played their part on the day, with the troops of the *Regimiento Ultonia* coming in for particular praise along with their commander, Don Guillermo de Lacy.[386] Spanish Oran remained secure for the foreseeable future. Of Bey Bigotillos it is known that he had been treated with contempt by the Dey of Algiers for his loss and failure to recapture Oran.[387] His forces had suffered staggering losses and afterwards, although he continued to attack Oran and its castles, he would never recover. In December Phelipe Ramirez and Diego Merino surprised his camp and sacked it, causing a chaotic rout and forcing Bigotillos to flee.[388] A captured slave informed the Spanish that he had been forced to set up a new camp fourteen leagues to the east.[389] He died later in 1733 after a short illness at one of his camps, and his son took up the fight to regain Oran from Spain.

Chapter 11

Wogan, Wharton, and Swift

Around the time of his tour of duty in Oran, Wogan corresponded with Dean Jonathan Swift. Analysis of his correspondence with Swift has already been done,[390] although the emphasis here is on Wogan's life, with the added dimension of Wharton's relationship with the two. Dean Jonathan Swift was born in Ireland of Protestant English parents. He graduated from Trinity College Dublin and became an Anglican minister. He made a reputation for himself in London as a political satirist but is best known today as a defender of Irish economic and legislative independence and as author of *Gulliver's Travels*, *The Drapier Letters* and other publications. He has been described as the progenitor of Anglo-Irish literature and of the modern, Protestant expression of a nascent Irish nationalism. Swift's political leanings have long been the subject of scholarly debate, though Ó Ciardha observes that according to his writings his allegiance aligned closer to high-Tory than Jacobite.[391] Though publicly he denied any support for James III, Swift remained in contact with many individuals connected with the Jacobite cause including the Duke of Ormond, Viscount Bolingbroke, Robert Harley, and Robert Leslie, among others.[392] Wogan sent an anonymous package to Swift, containing a history of his own life, a dedicatory epistle, a poetic translation of the penitential psalms and some Latin poems, all contained within a purse of green velvet with golden draw strings. In addition, and much to the Swift's satisfaction, he sent a consignment of Spanish wine.[393] The exact timing of when the correspondence started is difficult to ascertain, although in the epistolary dedication containing a sort of history of his life, Wogan mentions the battle in which he commanded on 4 October 1732. However, Swift's acknowledgement of the packet's receipt confirms the same contents but it is dated July 1732, and he states therein that he had received it two months previously; either Wogan had not left for Oran yet or a mistake in transcription occurred. The original documents are not accessible for research purposes, it is only possible for a researcher to peruse a printed transcription of them. Furthermore, Wogan's reply to Swift, dated February 1732 mentions that he is about to embark for Oran. Either the correspondence happened before he sent his works to Swift or they came in two separate posts.

A perusal of the thirty-five-page dedicatory epistle sent by Wogan to Swift along with his literary work, illuminates his sentiments regarding the malice he incurred from his enemies in the aftermath of his rescue of Princess Clementina:

> … the generality of human kind can look up with wonder and admiration to persons placed in a rank far above them, especially where their dignity is brightened up by the lustre of some heroic deed, or shining quality. But great and surprising actions, done by a private man, though they may have a momentary glare at their first appearance, never fail of being attested with more envy, than acclamation in the inmost recesses of all hearts...[394]

Wogan continues:

> But, among the narrow and lower geniuses, those impressions are either wiped off, or in great measure defaced by the secret intervention of malice. It gives them pain that any man but such as they are bound to admire should execute things, of which they, in their own conscience, hold themselves incapable in all other cases.[395]

One detects the distinctive crack of grapeshot from Wogan, with regard to his enemies at the Stuart court and at the Spanish court. He further expands his point by referring to historical cases where valorous men showed spirit and ingenuity in their missions only to be diminished by their jealous comrades for their own advancement. He cites the historical cases of Cortés and Narvaer, the latter achieving notoriety at the former's expense of Cortés in the aftermath of their conquest of Mexico. He uses the case of Henry Crofton (whom he refers to as 'my old friend') and General Marques de Bay, where the former's heroic cavalry charge led to a crushing defeat for the Anglo-Portuguese forces at the battle of La Gudina in 1707, however de Bay usurped the full glory at Crofton's expense.[396] He writes also of favourites poisoning their masters.[397] Wogan concludes on this point by using the classical historical case of *Scipio Africanus*, 'in the final words of Scipio the African in the Roman Senate, when the sentence of banishment was read to him: "Let us ascend to the temple of Jupiter, and give thanks to the Gods, this is the anniversary of that day, on which I gained the victory of Zama"'.[398]

Wogan's own views on the proliferation of gazettes reflected Swift's view that the freedom of the press, while essential, actually undermined knowledge and understanding by creating a multiplicity of opposing and contradicting views.[399] It is likely that he had read some of Swift's publications.

In reaching out to Swift, Wogan attempted to circumvent the perceived injustices done him by sending his writings for consideration and publication so that his name and deeds would not be forgotten. He also wished to belong to what he considered to be worthy society in his Anglo-Irish world. Wogan gives a further glimpse into his sense of identity where, in his epistle to Swift, he refers to Britain and Ireland as 'our islands'. This is also seen in his letters to the Stuart court in the context of his family's loyalty to the English Crown down the generations, where he mentioned the Gaelic Irish resistance to the English Crown 'the barbarous…old enemies'.[400] It is possible that Wogan shared Swift's sense of dual-identity between British/English and Irish. Carroll's preceptive discourse analysis of various accounts of the rescue of Queen Clementina identifies a strong sense of Catholic Jacobite identity, but a very reserved sense of Irish identity; in fact, he only refers to himself as 'a gentleman of Ireland' in his *Female Fortitude* of 1722, and as 'an Irish Catholic' later in 1744 when referring to the reason he was prevented from concluding the marriage arrangements with the Sobieskis.[401] Possible reasons for this are offered below. To Swift, he presents himself as a citizen of the world who fortune and life had drawn into adventure since early in his life.[402] The epistle ranged from discussion on literary matters to religion, forms of government, history and current affairs. It also contains comments on contemporary Spain regarding the surviving memory and practice of certain aspects of Moorish culture.[403] He mentions a practice he refers to as a 'purging of papers' whereby any papers not considered essential were required to be burned before his regiment was redeployed elsewhere; it appears Wogan burned the vast majority of his rhymes, poems and other compositions and sent only the contents of the packet to Swift.[404] Wogan makes clear mention in this document of having battled the Moors on 4 October 1732 and that he might be redeployed elsewhere. His tour of duty in Oran ended in March 1733 and he returned to Spain.

The Wogan-Swift correspondence is reproduced in full in Winch's *The Rescue* from Sir Walter Scott's original unabridged version and includes Scott's notes. Swift replied to Wogan, having discovered his identity by his own means, and complemented him on the quality of his work. He commended Wogan on his writings, noting that it was unusual to find such quality from 'a soldier, an exile and a native of Ireland'.[405] Swift highly praised the Irish serving in the military establishments of continental European powers. He confirmed what Wogan had written to him, that the English could not afford a good word for the Irish in their writings or other representations. Regarding the Irish peasantry, he made a comparison between their English counterparts, casting the Irish favourably as possessing more wit and good sense. This view, he contrasted sharply with the sustained historical and contemporary English portrayals of the Irish as ignorant brutes. Regarding the Irish he wrote that despite their good sense of humour:

> … the millions of oppressions they lie under, the tyranny of their landlords, the ridiculous zeal of their priests, and the general misery of the whole nation, have been enough to dampen the best spirits under the sun.[406]

Swift also praised Wogan for his treatment of the seven penitential psalms that still require proper assessment in their own right.[407] He disclaimed any qualification as a judge for his work, calling himself 'a man of rhymes, and that upon trifles – never having written serious couplets in his life, yet never any without a moral view'.[408] He also showed the works to some of his friends who were equally impressed, although they doubted that he would find a publisher given Dublin's cooler political climate. Swift wrote a defence of satire as a style and introduced Wogan to the members of his literary network (the famous Scriblerus club, which included Alexander Pope, John Gay, John Arbuthnot and Dr Edward Young), and defended Gay's *The Beggar's Opera* (1728) against Wogan's ambiguous feelings regarding its representations. He promised to send Wogan some portable versions of the works of Pope, Gay and Young, suitable to take with him on his marches. Ó Ciardha notes that he also sent two copies of his own work, which the latter forwarded to James III.[409]

Wogan sent a charged fifty-page response to Swift. As Miller observed, Swift's 'expression of surprise at receiving such a letter from a native of Ireland had obviously drawn blood'.[410] Its content, like the original epistolary introduction, ranges across many subjects, providing a rare surviving historiographical insight from a member of the Irish gentry and what had happened since the time of the War of the Three Kingdoms (1639–1653). Of Ireland he wrote that those who went into exile gave themselves up:

> … with great gaiety of spirit to the slaughter in foreign and ungrateful service and … the rest who have been content to stay at home, are reduced to the wretched condition of the Spartan Helot. They serve their inhuman lordlings, who are the more severe upon them; because they dare not yet look upon the country as their own.[411]

He commented that there had been very few people with any ability to write a history of the events from the Irish perspective and what few there had been were dismissed or drowned out by the opposition. On this point he continued at length about his perceived discrimination by the English against the Irish, and that the notion had taken root in England that the Irish deserved all the cruelty and misfortune which their rulers had visited upon them. This idea, conveyed in English-written histories across Europe, had gained credit because it had not been refuted in time.[412] Thus 'whatever is taken from them either at home or abroad is lawful prize'[413] and 'their constant misfortunes have given a sort of sanction to all this imposture and iniquity'.[414] He wrote perhaps too freely with Swift and continued to criticise the English by writing that the Irish have found 'the English language as backwards as the English nation, to do them common justice. Their enemies have spared them the labour with a vengeance'.[415] The newly arrived community of English Cromwellian settlers came in for criticism as well,[416] and he decried their obsession with negative examples of Irish difference to curry favour with the English, which he referred to as 'Teaguism', received with pleasure by the 'honest generation of numbskulls, the mobs of England[417]... The English and their adherents in Ireland have long been in a confederacy ... to tarnish or suppress all the renown accruing to that nation'.[418] However genuinely Wogan held his opinion about what he was writing, his views were probably not well received by Swift.[419]

He moderated his sentiments by laying the blame for Ireland's fall on Oliver Cromwell and Edward Hyde, first Earl of Clarendon. For Clarendon in particular he reserved his most aggressive criticism. He held him responsible for the Act of Settlement (1662), which confirmed the confiscation of Irish lands in favour of Cromwell's opportunistic adventurers and in consequence dubbed him the father of whiggism.[420] Clarendon saw that 'the government of England has been reduced to a democracy' and that he had been the architect of contemporary British politics which screened the king from any censure from the people because the parliament defended him and protected him; thus, George could blame his parliament for his lack of faith in international relations. As things stood:

> ... Clarendon's anti-monarchial scheme is like to continue for ever the surest support of tyranny. The whigs must be in

> majority in the parliament. They alone can be bribed to sell or subdue the people; and the king of Great Britain must be a downright fool, or a madman, not to be on a surer foot of reputation, as well as power, than any other sovereign... He may be at the head of different alliances at the same time, as well as different churches; and has a more undisputed right to personal infallibility than the pope.[421]

Wogan also surmised that the contemporary British/Irish power-structure would result in a growing desire for separatism among the 'Irish whigs' who would eventually go the same way that Portugal did from Spain in the previous century. Of Tories in general he wrote that they 'never expose his life or his fortune, by rising to the sublime pitch of cavalier ... he may drink, and prate, and protest, to get a name among the vulgar; but Clarendon's usage of the loyalists after the restoration is a sufficient warning to him to keep his own house, and to live within the verges of the laws in being'.[422] Nobody escaped Wogan's criticism.

He mentions having had many discussions with older Jacobites in exile who had participated in the war campaign in Ireland against William of Orange, stating that they should have accepted the liberal terms William offered before the Battle of Aughrim.[423] This tells us that the exiled Jacobite community discussed these events abroad. French self-interested duplicity and half-hearted military aid for Ireland, and her final abandonment to her fate also attracted Wogan's ire.

After his emotional outpouring he qualified his message with the phrases 'my patience is exhausted', and 'I own I am a little mad'. From his and his family's perspective, however, they had lost much in the period he discusses and had lived among many other exiles in a similar situation. Furthermore, he had remained in contact with Ireland through his continental network and his relatives at home, so he fully understood the conditions there. He keenly felt the injustice of what had happened in Ireland after the Wars of the Three Kingdoms and the War of the Two Kings and expressed himself forthrightly to Dean Swift.

Wogan presented his views on religion in which he described himself as an old-fashioned, tolerant Catholic. He wrote that the 'modern

Christians are too hard for me'; this could have been a comment about the hard version of Catholicism he encountered in contemporary Spain. He concluded that if he had no religion at all to begin with, he would not choose to follow one because of 'the vile and cruel rogueries I have seen them misapplied to. Most of them, for want of authority, are lost in freethinking; others by arrogating too much authority, vanish into superstition'.[424] To Swift he could offer him nothing in return for helping him to publish his work except:

> … some heads of the Saracens of Oran which I shall be ordered to cut off because they will not become Christians, I must be their executioner in my own defence; for, with all my spleen and vexation of spirit, I am the most inoffensive creature in the world, in regard of religion. I would not shed an ounce of blood in anger or enmity, or wrong any man living of a cracked sixpence to make all the world Catholics… I am all for the primitive church, in which people made proof of their religion only at their own expense. But I laugh with great contempt at those who will force others to heaven their way, in spite of charity.[425]

These moderate terms of religion with which Wogan characterised himself would have been welcome to Swift. Keith-Schuchard observed that rather than being offended by Wogan's long aggrieved letter, Swift might have been influenced by its contents. She writes that he would have welcomed it when engaged in a pamphlet battle against Whig efforts to remove the Test Act. Swift penned an ironic review of Irish history posing as an anonymous Roman Catholic under the title *Reasons Humbly Offered* (1733)[426] and defended the contemporary and historical actions of Catholics who had held to their principles against the puritans who murdered their king.[427]

He beseeched Swift to get his work published, thereby securing his place in his literary society. Wogan also recounts his time spent at Newgate prison in the aftermath of the Jacobite uprising of 1715/16. Having paid his entry fee into Newgate, he would now do the same to enter the dean's literary society with a consignment of fine Spanish wine.[428] It is clear that Wogan desired to branch out and become a part of a literary community in which he could participate:

> As I have no friend of genius or freedom of thought enough to comprehend these notions, they had rotted in my breast if I had not come out with them.[429]

In another statement on his disposition regarding his exile, he writes to Swift:

> The cheerfulness of my temper is, in great measure, sunk under a long and hopeless exile, which has given it a serious, or, if you will, a supercilious turn. I lash the world with indignation and grief in the strain of a Jeremy.[430]

The latter quote sheds light on Wogan's wider resignation of hope for a Stuart restoration to the three kingdoms.

In 1735 Swift wrote a short reply to Wogan's long letter and while he enclosed the works he had promised him, he apologised that it had not been possible to publish any of his material. He praised Wogan for the quality of his work, that had 'entertained some very ingenious friends, as well as myself'.[431] The dean tried to find Wogan's brother to ask him to review the work but had been unsuccessful, writing that he was probably keeping a low profile on account of his religion, 'although the court has thought it better in point of politics (and, to keep the good will of Cardinal Fleury), to make the Catholics here much more easy than their ill-willers, of no religion, approve of in their hearts'.[432] This refers to the British government's delicate game of relaxing the application of penal legislation in Ireland in order to keep the French in alliance with them. It may also indicate that the French government understood the situation facing Catholics in Ireland and had used their influence to gain a moderate improvement for those living there. A couple of curious comments are contained in the letter. Swift expressed his thanks and desire for more Spanish wine.[433] Towards the end of the letter he asks

Wogan to help him get a good shipment of wine sent from Spain and adds 'and if you were not a person of too considerable a rank (and now become half a Spaniard), I would try to make you condescend so low as to order some merchants there to consign to some of ours, directed to me, some good quantity of wine that you approve of'.[434] Regardless of what Swift may have made of Wogan's long letter, he did not (or could not) permit him to join his polite literary society; nor did he pursue the task of publishing Wogan's work.

Keith-Schuchard draws on existing evidence connecting Wogan, Swift, the Earl of Rosse and the Duke of Wharton. It sheds fascinating light on Swift's milieu, his writings and his relationship with exiled Jacobites like Wharton which is outside the scope of this book. Keith-Schuchard also examined the evidence available in the writings of Wogan, Swift and Wharton to conclude that all were involved with the freemasons.[435] It seems that Wogan befriended Wharton who was living his latter years in exile in Spain. Indeed, the duke introduced Wogan's work on the psalms in *The Wogan Manuscript*, dedicating it thus 'to my friend Sir Charles Wogan, baronet, on his excellent poeticall [*sic*] comment on the seaven [*sic*] penitential psalms.' He ended the poetic opening with the lines:

> These lines, my friend (late in exile found)
> Test of the union, must with yours be bound:
> That both may share a happier fate than ours,
> Welcome at home, whoever guard the doors.
>
> …
>
> … your laurels, as your bays, ever green,
> Great in your verse, as on the martial scene,
> Whose essay was to free a captive queen.[436]

Keith-Schuchard's text selects specific words and phrases associated with Jacobitism, for example describing a person as 'honest' to mean that they supported James III as the only legitimate king of the three kingdoms. Furthermore, it is likely that Wogan and Wharton were members of the quasi-masonic chivalric Order of Toboso, established in Spain by the Episcopalian Masons, the Earl Marischal Keith and Reverend Ezekiel Hamilton.[437] The Order pays tribute to Miguel de Cervantes's romance-epic *Don Quixote*, whose innocently deluded main character had an imaginary love named Dulcinea del Toboso who spurred him along in his adventures in knight-errantry across the sleepy Manchegan plains. Both Wharton and Wogan make Toboson-style self-identifications in their letters and writings, mentioning either knight-errantry itself or referring to themselves as Don Quixote.[438] It is clear that Wogan maintained regular contact with the duke and developed a good relationship with him in his final years. Having lived a rakish life, Wharton converted to Catholicism in Spain and made serious efforts to reform himself.[439] Wogan observed his physical deterioration and desire to make peace with God before he died. The only surviving piece of writing addressed from one to the other is Wharton's aforementioned poetic tribute.[440] Such social and fraternal institutions added further ideological sustenance for the Jacobite exiles as they waited for a Jacobite restoration of James III and the return of their estates.[441]

Chapter 12

Long Night, Brilliant Dawn

The years 1733 to 1744 are, in essence, a long interlude in Charles Wogan's fortunes. Contemporary relevant sources are almost entirely confined to the Stuart Papers. Unfortunately, a number of letters from Wogan are missing, as receipts for letters are acknowledged both by James Edgar and James III but Wogan's original letters are not among the Stuart Papers. For instance, on 13 February 1733 James III writes to Wogan acknowledging receipt of two letters from him thanking him for his accounts of the action in Oran. The same letters contain the final mention of Queen Clementina before her death shortly afterwards with the following post-script, 'the queen thanks you for your compliments and returns them in the kindest manner'.[442] By March 1733, Wogan wrote to Edgar that he had 'returned to Christendom after my summer and winter campaigns, extremely fatiguing and every day exposed to new dangers and the frequent alerts of a barbarous enemy'.[443] He wrote that the Spanish government reneged on his promotion in Oran 'because of a trick that has been played me', claiming that all Spain was aware of his exploits in Oran except the royal court in Madrid.[444] The gazettes published in Spain were mistaken in some details but mentioned him by name. He had promised to send James III a gift of a captured Moorish gun, taken as a prize on the field, but explained to Edgar that 'few of the Moors or Turks had left their arms or their friends behind them on the field'.[445] He did eventually get one and sent it to James III who acknowledged receipt of the Moorish gun 'which has at last come to my hand, and it is indeed a very curious piece'.[446]

By October, Wogan had begun to despair of his promotion after he had written to James of his disappointment and would soon travel to Madrid to press his claim there.[447] James offered to help, as usual, but could do little outside of writing letters to his own agents and supporters to put in a good word for him. He did mention that he had been working hard to secure a good position for Charles's brother, 'Dr Wogan, of whom I have heard such favourable accounts that I shall probably sooner or later give him my nomination for some Irish bishopric, of which I think him the more worthy that his modesty makes him decline that dignity for the present'.[448] James ends his letter by reminding Charles of the regard he had for the Wogans and his fond wish to give them better marks of it. All of James's letters to his beleaguered knight in Spain are couched in similar terms of respect and friendship.[449]

Queen Maria Clementina Sobieska Stuart died in January 1735 at the age of 33. The dispute between herself and James III begun in 1725 had never fully healed after she had returned to the Stuart court from her retreat at the convent of Santa Cecilia. It is clear that from the time of her triumphant arrival in Rome in 1719, Clementina had suffered a deterioration in her mental health as a result of her treatment by the king's favourites, John Hay, his sister Marjory, and James Murray, who held too much sway over James III and made him all the more uncompromising in his treatment of his royal consort. Clementina wrote to Queen Elizabeth Farnese of Spain before, during and after her retreat to the convent. The content of her letters and the desperate scrawl of her writing show her severe emotional and psychological distress. She dedicated the rest of her life to her children and to her Catholic religion. Of the latter, she had always been closely observant of Catholic doctrine and had practiced fasting and self-denial. In Wogan's account of her rescue written in 1744 there are references to her fainting from hunger. After her return to the Stuart court, she had become reclusive in the Palazzo del Ré. She devoted herself more and more to harsh forms of self-denial and even, it appears, wore a cilice.[450] She became anorexic and died in January 1735.[451] Wogan wrote to Edgar that he had heard the news of 'the queen's never enough to be lamented death. Though we could expect no long lease of that mortified and self-denying sort of life her majesty had led'. He offered the consolation that her marriage had produced an enlargement of the Stuart royal family and that her children were a credit to her since they were 'objects of highest admiration and applause' in Europe.[452] He hoped that the king was coping with the loss 'in the midst of so deep an affliction, that has put his spirit and his resignation under the severest trial they ever have endured'. He concluded that God had already provided for a succession and when the time came he would surely finish the work by restoring the Stuarts.

Regarding contemporary Spanish affairs during this period, Wogan wrote much of Don José Patiño, the Spanish premier minister, in his letters to the Stuart court. He wrote to Edgar that, 'he sees into the machinery of the English court' at a time when there was continued international turmoil and the looming threat of war. He added that:

> Patiño, who with all his ill fame, as a trickster, is certainly the ablest and the haughtiest minister in Europe … and deals accordingly with England in particular, which he has hitherto overruled and twisted to all [his] measures, that were for his purpose without ever giving England the least advantage or even doing her, or his promises in regard of her, common justice. He entertains Mr Keene (the British Ambassador) and jokes with him more familiarly than with any of the foreign ministers: but when he speaks in his master's name, tis true he does not swear so heartily, but he is higher again, than ever Alberoni was and much more inextricable into the bargain, to the degree that neither Keene, not any of 'em know from one moment to the other what to make of him.[453]

He concluded his letter that he hoped to obtain his promotion by April 1733 at the latest since the Spanish military had so few brigadiers, but he feared that the positions might be given to 'the favourite boys who ran post with good or bad news from Oran or Italy. I doubt they'll hardly think it safe or advisable to trust brigades in actual service to those callow youths'.[454]

In December 1735, Wogan informed Edgar that he had abandoned his attempts to secure his promotion at the Spanish court after two years of fruitless effort, and retired to Barcelona. He apologised for the delay in responding, writing that 'the perplexity and agitation of spirit I have been in for some months past, as well as the hurry of travelling with my family', had been the cause.[455] His 'bustling hitherto has been useless' to him and 'could not be continued by me any longer, according to the rules of honour. You know 'tis natural for a man to grow weary of labour in vain; but when there's any unbecoming circumstance attached to that labour, 'tis madness to persist in it'.[456] It had finally become apparent to Wogan that Patiño had never had any intention of promoting him. Of the minister he remarked that his 'disingenuity towards me I had no reason to suspect, because I neither could then, nor can yet discover any end he could have in it of consequence enough to engage him to the fatigue of playing double with me, that neither could nor had any sort of design to hurt him'.[457] Having reviewed all his correspondence it appears that Wogan's promotion was affected by a combination of the ill-offices potentially of both the first and second dukes of Berwick y Liria and their pervasive influence at the Spanish court from the 1720s onwards; Wogan's own blunders with minsters which are reported in the Stuart Papers in 1720 and again in 1732; and by the fact that he was a well-known, notorious and resourceful Jacobite. On the latter point he would later write that he could not be promoted to any position of civil or military authority in Spain owing to the interference of 'the government of England, to which I am, upon many accounts, so obnoxious'.[458] This source of frustration for Wogan's fortune was very powerful, given the far-seeing eyes and reach of contemporary whiggery. In his disillusionment, Wogan decided to retire from the court and become absentee from his military post, and from public life, writing to Edgar 'in regard of the party I have taken, which is that of retiring and becoming an idler for the rest of my days in this place'.[459] James III immediately wrote to Wogan expressing concern for his low morale, and maybe for the loss of his services in Spain: 'I am at the same time fully persuaded that none [depression] you can be in will alter your zeal and attachment to my service in which I hope you will have opportunity to act successfully in. I will always do what I can for you and your lady'.[460]

Wogan wrote to Edgar one year later and the tone of his letter is quite different from others, indicating a kind of depression in him. He described how his mind, 'showered with disappointments is very ill qualified for entertaining a correspondence' and this life of retirement 'to which I have been forced by caprice of the late minister, because I showed a manifest repugnance to serve under a person I had ever been in right of commanding has rendered me so mopeish and stupid that … I have not the least curiosity about news or anything … except where there may be some appearance of advantage for our master's affairs'.[461] He qualified the last statement with the remark that, 'In respect of these, my zeal has often led me into great mistakes, by engaging me to judge at the aims of princes from my own point of view'. That he had found himself 'always the dupe' and decided to withdraw instead of being drawn by them into a 'fool's paradise'. He concluded that he had grown sceptical of all of them and decided to leave it to fate instead of exerting himself in their regard, possibly indicating a resignation to the defeat of the Jacobite cause. He reported that Patiño had 'died in a blaze of glory, with extraordinary honours and encomiums heaped upon him and his carcass while it was above ground'. On the subject of the Spain that the minister had left behind he painted a bleak financial picture. He mentions that another impending and costly expedition larger than Oran, 'whereby the funds of the time to come must be anticipated to supply the want of the present, that are already swallowed up'.[462] The same secrecy shrouded the destination of the new expedition as it had before Oran, but he remarked that some astrologers of policy had pointed at Dalmatia, Algiers, or Port Mahon, sarcastically adding 'nay some have marked it for Brazil, and before the winter is over, tis to be hoped China and the grand Mongol's dominions may not be forgot… Perhaps our view is, by the alarm of such a bug-bear, to obtain what we look for, without aiming at any mark at all'.[463] He kept his friendships and contacts at the Stuart court by asking after them during his letters, including hearty compliments to Lord Dunbar, Thomas Sheridan, Jack O'Brien and Lords and Ladies Derwentwater and Nithsdale. On wishing his king a happy new year, he hoped for a restoration so that he could escape 'the oppression I lye under' and from the 'unbecoming way of life I have been obliged to embrace... notwithstanding my own merit and sense. But I am a plant it seems, that can't thrive but in the soil that's natural to it'.[464]

The following year he would have an unusual reason to write to James when he appealed to the king to use his influence to help 'a countrywoman of yours, the countess of Boustlers, daughter to the late General Wauchope, whose wretched condition Lord Inverness has judged proper that I should have the honour to lay before your majesty'.[465] The countess had been reduced to dire straits by her husband who only sent her a very small allowance to live on while in Barcelona. Wogan surmised that the man had assumed that because she would not know anyone there, that she would not be able to get any assistance, almost as if he had hoped to discard her there. He requested that James III write to Father Clarke, the Jesuit confessor to King Philip V, to use his influence to help the countess.[466] He described her family as being 'of known worth and honour' who were always loyal to the Stuarts.[467] He hoped that the king's letter 'cannot fail of having an excellent effect upon him [her husband], and of putting an end to that absolute slight and tyranny he has used her with hitherto'.[468] In response, James expressed his concern at not having heard from him for quite a while, but also his discomfort in interfering in what was essentially an issue between husband and wife. His position doubtlessly reflected his own experiences when Clementina had withdrawn from him in 1725, leaving him open to huge criticism and interference from many people. He wrote to the second Duke of Berwick to do what he could to help the countess and extended his humble respects to 'my lady Wogan and you my dear Sir, all health and happiness, and a speedy deliverance out of the lazy-indolence you are in at present'.[469] Wogan asked the king whether he could prevail over the duke to use his influence in Spain to help him, writing that 'he certainly owes me that good office, by way of reparation'.[470] Later in the year Wogan wrote that the situation with the countess had been resolved satisfactorily[471] and that the countess was 'extremely sensible by the share your majesty takes in her'.[472]

Despite reporting that he had retired, Wogan continued to unsuccessfully apply for vacant military and civil government positions. He wrote to Father Clarke to use his influence with King Philip in his favour but remarked that the Irish priest was not very active or effective in that regard. Montemar, the military commander of the Oran expedition, remained well-disposed to the Jacobite cause and to Wogan but his 'military luck has not followed him to court; he went thither with a conquering air; but the grass has been cut under his feet ... by the vermin Patiño had left in several offices of state' who had secured the king's ear for themselves. Finally, the queen's influence had been managed by the same favourites. He commented that one Sir John Hely, 'who had been laid aside for many years, has obtained the government of Valencia, by the merit of what La Quadra (the first officer now of the state)' had been able to obtain for him and with whom he has been good friends for twenty years.[473] This last comment should have indicated to Wogan that even with allies, promotion could take many years. He further commented on how the long-standing, dire financial situation facing the kingdom of Spain manifested itself with delayed payment of all civil and military officials. His own pay had been twenty months in arrears at that point and of Spanish debt he wrote the state 'can never get clear of in all probability, and never will certainly while Spain maintains two kings',[474] a reference to the accession of Philip V's eldest son Charles, Duke of Parma and Piacenza, in 1734 to the Kingdom of the Two Sicilies. Clearly Spain groaned under the weight of supporting Charles as well as the kingdom of Spain. Wogan noted that the Spanish depended on shipments of gold from the Americas but feared that it would be preyed upon by the British at sea in retaliation for Spanish seizures of British shipping in the West Indies.[475]

Matters came to a head in Spain in 1739 when Wogan reported to Ormond that things 'are come to such a cruel extremity in this unhappy government by the ill economy of the ministers, the dilapidation of the funds upon the support of our new acquisitions, and the prodigious arrears due to the court, civil and military lists, that the desperate disease could have no other, than a desperate cure'. With no means to subsist and no credit available to the Kingdom of Spain 'we are thrown from the frying pan we have been in these last years, into the fire'.[476] He lamented that all pensions, *sueldo-vives*, *sobre-sueldos*, double-employments, gratifications, and assignations of the Crown had been cancelled by the new minister of state in a drastic action to try to rescue the kingdom from financial ruin. No private credit could be had because no future payment could be made and most officials in civil and military employment had their pay reduced to a 'ship's ration'.[477] Regarding his own pay, he wrote, 'Thus from 34 pistoles per month, I am reduced to less than ten, which is my bare pay of colonel reformed. My pay of captain, my full pay of colonel, and my pension are all equally struck off, and I am left, with my numerous family after 20 years' service, in a much worse condition, than when I began it, with the sole comfort of thinking that (after I and mine have perished for want here) the world and particularly our three nations will remember how much I have contributed to the blessings they enjoy'.[478] He wrote to Ormond, not to worry the king, but to ask the duke that he might make use of him at the court in Madrid after Patiño's demise. He did write to James III a few months later with good information regarding the diplomatic situation unfolding between Britain and Spain, suggesting that James empower him to represent him in Madrid 'to keep up the fire already kindled there'.[479] The British ambassador, Sir Benjamin Keene, had been recalled but Wogan had learned that he had secured his lodgings in Madrid for the next year and had removed none of his furniture, obviously expecting to return soon.[480] These rumblings indicated the opening phases of the War of Austrian Succession. James III decided against sending Wogan to Madrid and instead sent Ormond to exploit the breach between Britain and Spain in his favour.[481] The duke had the status and experience for the job and carried more weight than Wogan. In November 1740, Edgar wrote that the king had been made aware of the hard situation facing the Wogans in Barcelona, writing that the king 'directs me to send you the enclosed bill for 60 pistoles and in making you his kind compliments, to tell you that he is sorry his own circumstances don't allow him to give you such relief and assistance as you want ... but given the present turn of fortune he hopes to soon have it in his power to be as kind to you as you deserve of him, which will give you the additional satisfaction of living at ease, and independent of all the world, but H.M.'s bounty'.[482] In January 1741, the king himself wrote to Wogan acknowledging a letter in which the Irishman expressed his gratitude, 'I am sorry my own circumstances did not allow me to make it greater' and that he hoped soon to be able 'to be as kind to you as I desire, and as you deserve so well of me'. James III had many exiled adherents over the years who faced difficult circumstances and he could not help them all. The fact that he financially assisted Wogan with the equivalent of more than six months' pay is a very significant mark of the good will he had towards him.

In June 1741 the response came from Wogan: a detailed account of the various setbacks he and Sir John Misset had faced since they had arrived in Spain. The letter gives clear, illuminating insight into the experience of the Irishmen. The rift between Wogan and Misset, which occurred in 1726, can partly be explained by the contents of this letter. Sir John went to Madrid in 1726 to solicit for promotion. The king promised it to him upon audience and he went to Castellar the next day; however, Castellar had just received word from Rome about Clementina's withdrawal into the convent and of the severe rift between herself and James III. Castellar received Misset 'like a dog in a nine pin alley' and 'ordered him to return immediately to his regiment, and think himself happy in keeping what he had got, for that neither he nor I were ever to raise our heads higher in this service – he came back thunderstruck, and I was little better at the recital'.[483] Given the queen of Spain's relationship with Clementina, it might be postulated that Castellar's poor treatment of Misset on this occasion might have been at her request. As for command of the *Regimiento d'Irlanda*, Wogan lost out and the court took no notice of his memorials.[484] Though Misset became governor of Oran in 1732, Wogan wrote that 'Sir John laboured in vain … seeing he could neither get an advancement, nor even, his patent of governor from the king, died there in a little time of pure grief and vexation' in 1733.[485] Though he was badly reduced in his circumstances, he conceded that many of his companions were far worse off than he. What affected him much worse was:

> … the slur upon my character, that grieves me to the soul. People generally, except in their own case, judge of a man's

> merit by his fortune. The retrenchments here are a general calamity … though nobody suffered as much as me since most of my pay were in pensions and gratifications … but what must those that know my services here, ministers, Spaniards, country-men, think of the utter neglect and slight I am treated with at court? The former can't but conclude that I am guilty of some hidden crime, or misbehaviour, that has drawn the royal disregard and disgrace upon me.

He continued that his countrymen 'must imagine since Irishmen are as well treated here, with respect to rewards and advancement, as the natives, that it must be known to this court that I have some way or other deserved to be in disgrace with your majesty'. Having held the rank of brigadier from James III since 1722, he had remained captain of a company with a colonel's pay. He felt that his community in Spain deduced that 'some fatality hangs over me that must have its rise in some misbehaviour of mine, with respect to our common sovereign'. After fifteen years of waiting and exercising restraint in sharing his grievances with James, and now faced with extreme financial difficulty and the 'dumb censure of friends and strangers, I own my spirit is oppressed within me, and obliges me to have recourse to your majesty who I ever found a father, for the only expedient' he had left. Wogan requested a royal patent of major-general from James.[486] He concluded that though he would prefer to leave Spain, it would satisfy him to see his character and good name restored there before that should happen; and that it would 'disabuse his countrymen of all the sinister judgements they make about me', with respect to James III. He asked his king's forgiveness for his long letter of grievance, writing that it was made 'in the fullness of my heart, which pines for the honour and happiness of serving its own master and to show marks of its zeal'. He sent the letter using Ormond's cover in case it fell into the wrong hands and his situation became public knowledge. The king's response came immediately, 'I am sensible that it cannot but occasion many melancholy reflections in you, but, all circumstances considered, I own I cannot think your honour is longways concerned, which ought to be of some comfort to you. I enclose the commission you asked for'.[487]

Through this long period of frustration and distress for Wogan and his family in Spain, he could rely on the good will of his king and community. With his hopes of justice and promotion extinguished, his twin belief in divine justice and his ultimate deliverance from their exile and difficult circumstances sustained him. Furthermore, it can clearly be seen that Jacobitism acted as a sustaining ideology from which exiles like Wogan could draw strength to continue, and especially so in Wogan's circumstances because he could keep in touch with his contacts at the Stuart court in exile in Rome. In this context, even letters of best wishes for the new year exchanged between the Jacobite community gave a very welcome boost and a sense of shared experience during their long exile. They deeply lamented the death of the queen in 1735 while at the same time reporting with pride the progress of the young Stuart princes.[488] James could only encourage his Irish knight to perform what services he could for the cause. He finally obliged Wogan with the brevet of major-general in 1741, and a few years later his services in Spain would finally be recognised. In the meantime, the death of Wogan's friend, Colonel John O'Brien, at the Stuart court[489] was offset by the elevation of Wogan's daughter in-law to a new position as *camarista* to Queen Elizabeth Farnese.[490] The king continued to write to members of the Spanish court in Wogan's favour to secure him a position.[491]

Wogan kept himself busy in the interim between receiving the brevet from James III and his next piece of good news. In 1743 he drafted an official proposal for a major trade agreement to be established between the Kingdom of Spain and Great Britain. The plan is available to read in full at Cambridge University Library. Wogan penned the document in 1743 and its title is *Plan de la Compagnie Royale Americaine*. Analysis of its content is outside the remit of his biography. The eleven-page preamble is followed by *Projet d'Accommodement entre l'Espagne et l'Angleterre: Contenant un Plan general de Commerceentre le vieux et le nouveau Monde, à l'Exclusion de toute Contrebande, et au Profit de tout l'Univers*. Primarily, the plan involved the establishment of a new *Compagnie Royale Americaine*, with which all maritime powers of Europe would be invited to trade under the protection of Philip V of Spain. They would enjoy free trade with all Spanish territories in the

Americas and the East and West Indies. The plan had seventy-one points and was signed by Wogan at San Lorenzo on 30 September 1743. It is clear that his proposal was received and discussed, for at the back of the document Wogan handled objections that had been raised. In the end, the plan was not adopted by the Spanish government.

On 28 November 1744, after twenty-two years in the Spanish service, at long last Charles became *corrigedor* of the Spanish province of La Mancha.[492] The position gave him much satisfaction, given his frequent references to Don Quixote and the gleeful comparison he made between the adventures of the Don and those of his own life. His letter to his friend, James Edgar, is written with a tone of elation which had long been absent from his letters to the Stuart court in Rome and the best part of it is worth reproducing here:

> You'll be surprised, without doubt, at the date of this letter from the very capital of Don Quixote's country. You are to know then that the 28th of last month I was solemnly installed *Corrigedor*, or supreme magistrate of this country in a chair of state with a white wand in my right hand, and among a number of Dons, that carried the very air and mien of their famous ancestor. There was one in particular of the face, figure and gait exactly of the much renowned hero, with a red wig on. There wanted nothing, but the lance and Mambrino's helmet (which to be sure he keeps among the archives of his family) to make him the complete copy that ever was made from such an original. For my part, if I had not clapped a padlock on my mouth and forced my countenance into seriousness, that was far from my heart, I should have burst out into laughter and ruined myself by the loss of my new title, that is worth me about 500 pistoles a year, with much authority, a little chariot to the take the air in, a decent and easy living in a very cheap country.[493]

This giddy letter reads like a tonic after the long dark of his depression and frustration in Spain. The relief of being paid well, being able to look after his children properly and to live like a gentleman must have felt so good. He wrote to James III in a more formal tone that 'though I have in a manner laid down my sword by taking up with a civil employment (as governor of this country, so celebrated for the life and labours of the famed Don Quixote) 'tis but to snatch it up again with the greater eagerness whenever your majesty shall be pleased to honour me with your commands'.[494] He continued that 'providence designed me from my birth for a knight-errant; and, since it has, in fact, made me the most remarkable one in Europe by the importance and singularity of my adventures, it seems (not by caprice or chance) but in pure justice to my merit in that calling, to have preferred me in my advanced age to this post, which lays the renowned Toboso itself, and all the Dulcineas thereto belonging, as well as the greater part of the ever famous La Mancha under my jurisdiction'.[495]

Wogan's promotion could be explained by developments in international affairs over the preceding years. The Kingdom of Spain had gone to open war with Britain since 1739, so the influence of British envoys at the court of Madrid was much less significant than in preceding years.[496] Even so, Wogan now governed a quiet and peaceful province of central Spain, which made the setting for Cervantes' *Don Quixote* the more humorous. Therefore, Wogan's promotion would have caused little distress to the British since he could only make limited mischief from his new home in San Clemente de La Mancha. He reassured James of his loyalty writing, 'in case I should die here in my post, I beg your majesty may be persuaded I have no ambition to lay my bones near my noble predecessor Don Quixote's. I should have a better estate at home; than ever his fathers enjoyed; and a tomb too, where no man of honour need be ashamed to lie. Thus I entreat your majesty not to forget me here, whenever kind providence gives a call, I am but five and twenty when any occasion can offer to serve your majesty with that sprightly zeal and inviolable duty, that must ever distinguish me'.[497] He also affirmed the steadfast loyalty of his children to the cause with the postscript, 'my son, who is here with me, begs to be put at your majesty's feet. My daughters are at court. I can answer for their zeal too. It runs in the blood'.[498]

His friends in Rome replied expressing their happiness for him on the promotion. Edgar wished that it may long continue and increase 'until the happy time comes that you can boldly change it for a country more natural to you'.[499] On the prospect of a Stuart restoration he wrote, 'I would fain hope that that long wished for time cannot now be far off, for indeed I don't see how the present war can well end for the advantage both of France and Spain but by our royal family's being settled at home'.[500] The king also wrote to Wogan congratulating him on his new position and expressed similar hopes of a restoration with the assistance of France and Spain. Opportunity to that effect was about to knock, and the king ended his letter to Wogan with his familiar goodness, 'be always assured of the continuance of my friendship and kindness which will never fail you'.[501]

Chapter 13

The Forty-Five

As the War of Austrian Succession raged in Europe, the Jacobite community watched with interest. Britain's assiduous diplomatic game had finally crumbled after so many successful years, as they now battled the combined might of France, Spain, Prussia, Bavaria, Sweden and other allies. The Irlanda Regiment of the Spanish army, in which Wogan had been an officer, achieved notoriety in a battle at Velletri in Tuscany in 1744. Over 200 soldiers and 40 officers of Irlanda, including its commander, were killed in action defending Philip V's son, Charles (the future Charles III of Spain) from being captured.[502] Upon hearing of their heroics, the Spanish king bestowed Irlanda with the additional motto of 'In Omnem Terram Exhivit Sonus Eorum' ('their sound went forth into all the earth').[503] The forces of the opposition were those of the Holy Roman Empire, Hanover, the Dutch Republic, and Russia, among other allies. Imperial succession and the validity of the Pragmatic Sanction[504] were at stake, as both sides fought to gain the maximum advantage from the candidates they supported: the British-supported candidate, Maria Theresa, daughter of Charles VI; or the Franco-Spanish candidate, Charles Albert, the Elector of Bavaria. With so many British troops committed on the Continent, the 25-year-old Prince Charles Edward Stuart seized the opportunity, in summer 1745, to restore his father to his ancestral kingdoms. On 11 May 1745, the Irish troops in the French service had just rescued victory from their English opponents at the Battle of Fontenoy of which the French commander, Maréchal de Saxe, had despaired.[505] Considered a good omen, the young prince sailed on 15 July for the West Highlands of Scotland. Only one ship arrived after they had been intercepted by the British Royal Navy; which forced the other ship that carried all the military supplies and volunteers to return to port. Prince Charles arrived in Eriskay on 23 July accompanied by the 'seven men of Moidart'. Before he left, he had sent instructions to Wogan to secure aid from the Spanish court.

Letters dated 8 June only reached Wogan on 26 July and included a personal billet from the prince empowering him to solicit arms, munitions, supplies, financial aid and soldiers of the Hispano-Irish brigade to be sent to Scotland with all haste. By that stage, Prince Charles had already assembled an army with the Highland clan leaders in Scotland. Wogan departed the same night from his new residence in San Clemente for Madrid and arrived there three days later only to find that Mr Stafford, the prince's representative, had been waiting for an audience for fifty days. This proved a portent of what was to follow, but Wogan nevertheless got things moving more quickly after he arrived. Though the Spanish royal family considered the prince's action rash, sudden and very dangerous, the queen gave him the title of 'young hero' and spoke of him 'as her nephew and favourite'.[506] Philip V felt the need to consult his nephew, Louis XV of France, about how best to support Prince Charles and immediately dispatched a courier. Stafford stood aside to allow Wogan to take charge of the solicitation on behalf of Prince Charles Edward.[507] Wogan wrote to James III that 'I had Mr Kelly's instructions, and my noble prince's billet to me already translated into French to be shown to their majesties by Villarias [minister of state] along with the originals, to serve for my credentials'.

The next night he visited Villarias who told him their 'majesties seemed very satisfied at the choice his royal highness was pleased to make of me for the conductor and manager of the enterprise of succours here; their majesties laughed heartily at the prince's kind expressions to me, which were all in the style of the ancient chivalry, as to the successor of Don Quixote in the government of his native country'. The king and queen marvelled at the prince's gaiety of spirit given the difficulties he found himself in. As it had done thirty years beforehand, Bourbon Spain undertook the provision of crucial financial aid, armaments, supplies and personnel for the Jacobites:

> … a hundred thousand crowns were ordered to be furnished and ten thousand arms, distributed in 4 small frigates, two to be armed immediately at La Corunna and two at San Sebastian … each frigate, besides its proportion of money and arms, was to put onboard 500 quintals of powder and 600 of ball and lead and some Irish officer on board, such as I should appoint.[508]

When the *Elizabeth*, one of the prince's two ships that sailed from France, returned with all its money and stores on board, the Spanish government balked at dispatching the promised aid until they could independently verify that the prince *was* in fact in Scotland and where exactly they could land the supplies. Wogan pleaded to send the supplies, but they would not, and things remained in that poised state for a month. When various Spanish ministers (and some exiled Jacobites in Avignon) wrote letters characterising the prince's actions as rash, he unburdened himself to James III that this 'fired my blood to such a degree and filled my head with such dismal ideas of the prince's being abandoned … that I was seized with a violent fever and jaundice so as not to be yet in a condition to get out of my room'.[509]

Wogan's indisposition continued for many weeks 'attended with several relapses of fever and jaundice'.[510] He added that 'the fruit of my endeavours here towards obtaining necessary succours of arms and ammunition for my noble prince, which at length are happily procured in a measure corresponding to the generosity of their catholic majesties, and far above my expectation, considering the exhausted situation in respect of money and stores that this government is reduced to'.[511] Wogan would travel with the last of four frigates sent from La Corunna and San Sebastian by trusted captains and commanders chosen by him. The 100,000 crowns and the arms and ammunition were distributed between each of the vessels and they were sent individually for greater speed and stealth. Despite his illness he continued to solicit further aid and secured bayonets for the muskets that had been already sent. One noteworthy comment in his letter regarded his status in Britain and Ireland, revealing a potential anxiety he had of travelling there to join Prince Charles Edward, 'I am attainted by act of parliament in England these almost 30 years, which renders me incapable, as yet, of my inheritance at home. But I hope in God, that his divine majesty will soon break all these bonds of iniquity'.[512] In the end, he was ordered to receive medical treatment and rest at El Escorial and did not travel with the last of the four frigates as scheduled.

Meanwhile in Scotland, Charles Edward had raised the Stuart royal standard at Glenfinnan on 19 August and gathered more supporters and good advisers to his side. They took Perth on 4 September and marched unopposed into Edinburgh on 17 September, the Whig government's garrison confining itself to the castle. The Jacobite army waited there for news of aid from France and Spain, not least the prospect of regular French troops being sent across the channel to swell their ranks with professionally trained soldiers. An elated Wogan wrote to James III from his cell at El Escorial how the prince had captured Scotland 'by the force and happiness of his own genius and the grandeur and vigour of his spirit' and 'all this executed, and your majesty proclaimed and acknowledged, as only sovereign over all Scotland in less than two months' time, without any foreign assistance, or any officer of note, outdoes the glory of your famous ancestor Robert Bruce, et est mirabile in oculis nostris'.[513] Wogan received frequent visits from his daughter and by his friend Augustin Montiano, deputy to the Marqués de Villarias, the minister of state. The king and queen had their own physician perform medical treatment to recover his health.[514] He expressed sober concern for the prince when Crown forces would eventually be sent against him:

> … she [England], alas, is kept in chains by the power of the usurper both at home and abroad, a parliament at his devotion; a bank ready to answer all his demands; fleets, armies and foreign troops at his call; generals, arms and forces, all trained up to the war. These are dreadful resources in actual possession; whereas we have none but in prospect, except the same omnipotent hand of God, a just cause and our native but undisciplined valour.[515]

He also mentioned that the French had cantoned the Irish brigade in Ostende and the Flemish coast in anticipation of their being sent to Scotland, though he doubted French sincerity, stating that they were just posturing and had no real intention of sending them.[516]

The king and queen of Spain continued to follow with keen interest all news about the prince, dubbed Galien in their correspondence about him.[517] Wogan fuelled the queen's interest by hinting that her youngest unmarried daughter, the Infanta Maria Antonia, might be a good match for Prince Charles. Wogan also spoke to Mrs Lacy, the queen's favourite *governante*, and her favourite *camarista*, Miss O'Moore, to fuel interest in the idea. Montiano, who had two daughters with the princess, also encouraged them to do the same, while Wogan's daughter O'Driscoll fuelled the queen's interest in the proposal. Of the Spanish princess he said, 'she is one of the charmingest brunettes in Europe, of the finest size and shape, dances and sings in perfection, has a vast deal of wit and vivacity, an excellent education, and more charms in my opinion, than the celebrated *dauphine* with her great white long face'. Of the French royal family he rather unkindly wrote that 'by some extraordinary humour running in their blood, that fills them with blotches … that get through the skin and cover them, from time to time, like lepers'.[518] He asked that his letter to Prince Charles be forwarded to James III, via Paris, to ensure it got to him, adding in concern, 'so that I might not suffer in his opinion', regarding the slow progress of Spanish aid.[519]

Throughout October, Prince Charles Edward had argued the case with his Highland supporters and his advisers for invading England without delay. The Highlanders were reluctant to do so without the promised French troops. Furthermore, tensions had arisen over the young prince's demeanour which had been overruling and autocratic since his arrival. A council had been established as a mechanism to moderate the prince's decision-making which he deeply resented. When a French envoy arrived confirming the French government's intentions of sending their troops, they decided to invade England. They did so on 8 November, taking Carlisle, Preston and Manchester in quick succession. The Jacobite army lacked cavalry and artillery which left them vulnerable, but could march at high speed. When they reached Derby, just over 200 kilometres from London, a large majority of the council decided to retreat to Scotland. With neither sign nor signal of a French landing, they had not received the significant support and extra recruits they had anticipated in England, and more importantly the English commander at Newcastle had moved his forces south to link up with those of the young Duke of Cumberland en route from London. Of the military aid sent from Spain, Wogan confirmed to Prince Charles Edward that the first ship had been taken by a Bristol privateer and Stafford was imprisoned in Newgate.[520] Another of the four frigates from Spain had tried to sail through a Biscay storm for ten days but eventually had to return to port in Galicia. Of the two other ships that left, he knew one had landed on the Isle of Barra and hoped that the other had also arrived.[521]

Wogan set out plans to the Spanish government for when he himself would travel to join the prince. He negotiated with Montiano, 'the officers from the Irish brigade, some sergeants and drummers which I offered to conduct and land in Wales, where I proposed to make a number of men and discipline them for the prince's service, as well as the rest of his low land troops'. Of the highlanders, he decided it best to leave them 'to their own way of fighting and breaking the enemy by pouring in upon 'em with their usual cry and impetuosity'.[522] Wogan also might have had the added advantage of ancestral and family networks in Wales which he could use to the advantage of the good cause. He sent a six-point plan to the Spanish government listing ways to help the prince but also how they could use the situation to their own advantage:

1. All the battalions of the Irish brigade, much reduced and so only 200 men apiece, be sent to Wales and Cornwall to have their numbers brought up with fresh recruits from there. Once the prince had retaken the kingdoms, they'd be sent back to Spain at full strength.
2. If the first would not be possible, then Wogan's pick of officers should be sent to La Corunna to travel to Wales to join HRH in England, with grenadiers' sabres and pistols for the cavalry, which they could put together using the workhorses from the mines around Newcastle-Upon-Tyne.

3. To ban any shipping from England, Scotland and Ireland who do not fly the prince's colours, or allowing only those who carry patents and passports from the prince himself. This would throw huge confusion upon the mercantile class in those kingdoms who have long been wanting to trade freely with Spain.
4. The governors of all port towns of Spain should issue a declaration that all privateers and merchants resident there should carry arms, munitions, stores and powder to Scotland to be sold to the prince's forces there.
5. With all this confusion, it would provide a great opportunity to blockade Gibraltar since the British navy was otherwise engaged.[523]

Wogan intended to stay in Spain until he recovered and until the king gave him the troops and officers he requested before travelling to Wales or Scotland. He noted Spanish jealousy of the prince's correspondence with Paris, that they looked on it as a mark of contempt of them for their taking so long. He wrote to the prince that despite his best efforts to move things along 'everything lags exceedingly sore'.[524] The Spanish had not committed to sending any of their Irish troops but gave tacit permission to Irish officers who wished to go to Scotland from their posts in Italy; however, they would not advance them the pay they needed to get there. He asked the prince for fresh orders so that he could put more pressure on the king and queen in Spain to send more aid and also asked that he write dispatches to the Spanish court to boost activity there in his favour. If he did not receive further orders, then he would travel from Spain to join him at the beginning of February 1746.[525] He hoped that the people of England 'may behave as heartily and zealously as those of Scotland have done, and as those of Ireland would do, if they could be withdrawn from the slavery of their tyrant-lords at home; or had the wherewithal to join Your Royal Highness's banners from their service abroad'.[526] He did not know that the Jacobite army had retreated to Scotland by the date of his letter.

Wogan wrote to his old friend James Edgar in Rome, lamenting that for many years all they had were their hopes but now, 'thank God, we have the acquisition of one of our three kingdoms' and hoped to soon secure the other two… May heaven soon bring its own work to perfection and put a happy end to what it has blessed with such prosperous and surprising beginnings, that we may have the satisfaction of seeing each other at home after so tedious and irksome a banishment'.[527] As Frank D'Arcy observed, 'it must have felt like the last chance in a lifetime of Jacobite hoping'.[528] Even the ever-stoical James III's letter of January 1746 expected to hear any day of the duke, his son's arrival in England at the head of the French troops. He surmised that 'on that event, humanly, all depends, without foreign assistance the Prince at long run cannot succeed… In this situation you see all our hopes are in France, who has heartily espoused my interest; anything the court of Spain might be willing to do would probably be useless by coming too late'.[529] On 7 February he instructed Wogan to travel to Paris with his party of officers from Spain where Sir George Walters was expecting him. James doubted that the Spanish aid would be of much use to the prince but expressed his gratitude for the money they sent. As regards the Irish officers with Wogan, he considered it a signal of good will from the Spanish government that they had sent them but that as matters then stood with the prince retreating throughout Scotland before formidable Crown forces, they might not be of great use to him. One other remark from the king in this letter stands out where he wrote, 'The few Irish officers willing to join the prince on this occasion will probably prove of little use to him at the end and will I fear be inconvenienced themselves by their zeal in joining him, and therefore all things considered, I have been far from encouraging of late any of those officers to do so'. This may have been James's indirect way of telling Wogan that if he did not travel to Scotland he would not suffer in the king's opinion. James understood that Wogan would face the prospect of execution if captured in Scotland. Furthermore, having witnessed how difficult it had been for his Irish knight to obtain a measure of comfort in his exile, perhaps he did not want to see him lose everything again. He concluded that only the French court could effectively assist the prince, although he appreciated the zeal of Charles and his son, James.[530] On 25 April he again wrote to Wogan stating that he had received his letter of 4 April expressing regret that his son's illness had hindered their departure from Paris. The king instructed him to consult the Duke of York and Colonel O'Brien about what action would be best to take with the officers he had taken with him to Paris. He reiterated that single officers can be of little use to the prince without troops to command and also that some officers who had travelled to Paris to join him had returned to Italy. He concluded that Wogan should do whatever he decided was best for the cause and that 'the steps you have already taken, will in all cases have an equal merit with me'.[531] Neither of them knew at this stage that Prince Charles Edward's army had been decisively defeated at the Battle of Culloden.

Prince Charles Edward had crossed back into Scotland with his army on 20 December and after augmenting their forces with new recruits and some arrivals from the Continent, their forces stood at 8000. The Duke of Cumberland pursued them, retaking Carlisle in the last days of December 1745. The Jacobite army besieged Stirling Castle, defeating an attempt to relieve the fortress by Crown forces on 17 January, but without heavy artillery they withdrew later in the month with the arrival of the Duke of Cumberland's army. The Jacobites retreated up the eastern coast to Inverness with the duke's army in pursuit. The latter entered Aberdeen and was resupplied by sea there, while both armies waited for better weather to resume hostilities. Cumberland left Aberdeen on 8 April and the Jacobites decided that due to dwindling supplies they should offer battle. On 16 April, a combination of factors led to the decisive defeat of Prince Charles Edward's smaller army, including a lack of artillery and cavalry, a poor choice of battlefield, coupled with the exhaustion and inexperience of Jacobite troops. Between one and two thousand Jacobite soldiers were killed or wounded with the duke's forces suffering very few casualties by comparison.

Wogan and his son had followed the orders of James III and joined the Duke of York at Arras to wait for an opportunity to join Prince Charles Edward.[532] After Culloden however, any hope of the insurrection's success diminished rapidly. The promised French aid did not materialise and the prince ordered his forces to disperse on 20 April until he could return with regular French troops at his back.

The prince expressed his fury at the French court, writing that he was 'now resolved to act in concert with his friends in England, and no longer serve as a scarecrow...'.These last words seem to sum up the situation very faithfully. In short, the cabinet of Versailles had simply made use of the prince to attract the attention and the forces of England elsewhere.[533] Wogan wrote to James III from Paris on 13 July 1746: 'tis with a sorrowful heart I do myself the honour to inform your majesty of my departure this day for Madrid, there being no further encouragement for the affair I came about, and having received orders from the court of Spain to return to my employment there'.[534] The response came a month later stating, 'how sensible I am of your zeal on this unfortunate occasion, if providence has disposed matters as that you could not be more useful to us, your good will is the same and will always have equal merit with me'; adding that he hoped Wogan would be satisfied with the new government in Madrid.[535] James alluded to the death of King Philip V and the accession to the Spanish throne of his son in 1746, King Ferdinand VI and his royal consort, Barbara de Braganza of Portugal. To Edgar, Wogan wrote: 'I have no other party to take now but to return to my government of La Mancha and pass my time there, as you may believe, not very agreeably'.[536] He and his son James stopped in Navarre on the road between Paris and Madrid to await further orders from the Duke of York, whose company they had just left. He recalled how his son had made an impassioned appeal to a group of Spanish ministers to assist Prince Charles in his escape from Scotland. The appeal was applauded and related to the king who soon afterwards decided to send a financial subsidy to help bring the prince to safety.[537]

Prince Charles Edward's supporters returned home and before long he found himself with fewer and fewer people to accompany him. His circumstances during this period caused great anxiety among the Jacobites – a £30,000 bounty was offered for his capture, bringing a substantial risk of betrayal, and the 'Butcher' Cumberland's forces pursued him relentlessly through the heather. His travels through Scotland also entered into folk memory, with many poems and songs written about him to commemorate his flight. In Blaikie's *Itinerary of Prince Charles Edward Stuart from his landing in Scotland July 1745 to his departure in September 1746*, published in 1897, many first-hand narratives and accounts are assembled which shed substantial light on his disposition. He had already shown signs of alcohol abuse during the campaign in Scotland and some parts of Blaikie's *Itinerary* indicate an erratic emotional state.[538] The frustration and disappointment of the 'Forty-five' exacerbated this and in years to come he would succumb to alcoholism. He was hunted by British forces for five months through the Highlands and islands until, in September 1746, he was rescued by Richard Warren, of Corduff in Dublin, to whom James III awarded a knight-baronetcy for bringing the prince to safety. Any suggestion that the British government allowed him to escape can be dismissed by the contents of a letter to the Duke of Newcastle, 'nothing is to me more convincing proof of the disaffection of that part of the country than that of His [Prince Charles] lying so long concealed amongst those people, and that he should be able to elude our narrowest and most exact searches, and at last make his escape notwithstanding the greatest reward offered to apprehend him'.[539] The prince arrived safely in France on 10 October 1746.

While the prince evaded capture, Wogan wrote to James III from Madrid on his return there, 'to make the best of a bad market, pursuant to earnest desires, or rather orders from the duke of York, since all hopes of our affairs were blasted by the ill wind that blew from France'.[540] He would later expand this criticism in his letters to Richard Warren. He also relayed James III's satisfaction that the new king and queen treated the queen dowager, Elizabeth Farnese, with dignity and respect and that all the same pro-Stuart ministers held the same positions they enjoyed under the old regime.[541] He continued to solicit aid for Scotland from the new king and queen to the prince in Scotland but as before, they would not commit to sending anything until they had confirmation that he was still there. Though he returned to La Mancha with a heavy heart, he had received 'a little domestic comfort a few days ago, my daughter Clementina having been most graciously received as *camarista* or maid of honour to the queen dowager'.[542] He wrote to Thomas Sheridan[543] on 15 September of his anxiety for the prince's safety and assuring him of the continuance of the Spanish subsidy to secure his safe passage back to

France. Wogan had mixed feelings about his own current situation while the prince remained in danger, 'I am here at full ease at my government … I should be charmed to be with him and share his danger or serve him in his flight'.[544] By December, news had reached him of the prince's safe conduct to France and he wrote to the Duke of York, 'I beg leave to wish you joy with a cheerful heart upon the happy and almost hopeless return of your royal brother'.[545] To James III he held out the hope that heaven had not taken such pains to save the prince that it would not eventually bring about a restoration in good time.[546] A response came from the king in February 1747, thanking him for his expressions of zeal and attachment, observing that the reprisals against supporters of the Jacobite cause had been so cruel that it 'should naturally make our countrymen more forward than ever to shake off the yoke'.[547] He wished Wogan content in his 'retreat' in San Clemente, adding that 'you may soon be called out of it to better purpose and with more success than you were lately, but wherever you are my constant kindness will ever attend you'.[548] Upon analysis of the above quotation it is possible to imagine James's relief that Wogan had not lost his position in Spain on account of involvement in the 'Forty-five' and his regret that Wogan could not secure rapid assistance from the Spanish government, or to join the prince in Scotland and achieve the long-desired Stuart restoration. In Wogan's defence, he faced formidable logistical difficulties. As Hugh Law so accurately put it, 'though there were renewed promises and evidence of sincere good-will, nothing he could do prevailed against the invincible lethargy of Spanish administration'.[549]

Richard Warren had fought on the battlefield with Dillon's Regiment at Fontenoy in 1745, embarking soon afterwards to join Prince Charles Edward in Scotland. The prince quickly recognised his competence, promoting him to colonel, and sending him back to France to secure funding and troops for the insurrection. After Culloden dashed these hopes, he volunteered to bring the prince to safety. He successfully did so and had been honoured by James III with a knight-baronetcy. Louis XV of France also promoted him. The last available correspondence from Charles Wogan relating to the 'Forty-five' was written to Warren early in 1747. In January that year Wogan acknowledged receipt of a letter from

Warren dated 29 November. He refers to Warren as 'my dear Boy' which seems very familiar. It is likely that they met while in Paris before the latter set out to rescue the prince. Of Warren's gallant actions he wrote:

> The blow was valiantly executed, and I would gladly have given half the days that remain to me to be part of the expedition. Be sure that if I had known, or even simply foreseen, that such a decision was going to be taken by this rascal of a French ministry, at the moment when I left Paris, neither the orders of my masters in this court, which I had already been asked several times to report, nor any other earthly consideration would have prevented me from staying to join you.[550]

He blasted the French ministry for their failure to support Prince Charles Edward, writing, 'the honest Lord Clancarty and I were so stunned with the insipidity and indolence which seemed to reign in this ministry' that they left Paris in a rage. He continued that, 'my opinion was then and still is, to my great chagrin, that the French ministry has never been and never will be so serious and bold as to attempt an invasion of England which, however, so often, and so successfully, has invaded France'.[551] He concluded that if the restoration were to come about by the actions of France that it would be, as the Spanish said in those days, the result of a *milagro patente* (a miracle). The contents of this letter echo his correspondence with Swift years before – that it was ever in France's interest to keep Britain divided and weakened so that they could accomplish their goals on the Continent. Wogan enclosed two letters to the prince in the same packet.

Unfortunately, only a small part of Warren's response to Wogan is included in the publication available in the BNF. Warren wrote that Prince Charles Edward had already left Paris in secret and that nobody knew his whereabouts at that time (7 February 1747). It appears the prince went to Madrid, abandoning in frustration his hopes that the French government would send troops with him back to Scotland before the conclusion of peace negotiations.[552] Wogan reported that the prince had arrived in Madrid in his response on 13 April 1747. His presence there, however, caused concern to his Spanish hosts. He wrote, 'our timorous court in Spain desired his speedy departure for fear that the dispositions of our enemies would come to cool at the conferences of Breda,[553] being able to take offense at the fact that we seemed to take the Prince under our protection … and that they would no longer add credence to our love of peace, of which they, however, have greater need than we do'.[554] Wogan reminisced of his having made merry with Warren's father on one occasion in London years before then, the last time Wogan was in London was in 1716, possibly after he escaped from Newgate. He may also have been there in secret during the organisation of the Atterbury Plot, but never mentioned that in any of his many letters. He hoped that the same songs were still enjoyed in 'old Corduff, which I hope your father still enjoys, [and] old Racoffy, which I have lost through the follies of my youth'.[555] Wogan expected to inherit the estate of Rathcoffey but could not now because of his 1716 attainder. The Wogan-Warren correspondence ends there, although there could be much more. Warren left Paris soon afterwards to join Maréchal de Saxe as his *aide-de-camp* in Flanders and went on to have a very successful military career in France.[556]

In yet another surprising and fascinating aside in one of Wogan's letters, he wrote that he left Madrid without permission to go with his son and pay court to Prince Charles Edward for two days in Guadalajara, only a short distance from the Capital. It appears he escaped the ire of the Spanish minister to whom he was reporting at the time through his friendship with Carlo Broschi, known as Farinelli, one of the most famous and delightful singers in Europe and possibly in the history of opera. Farinelli had performed throughout Europe for the highest in all its societies. Accepting a royal invitation to Spain in 1737, he impressed King Philip and Queen Elizabeth so much that he became a favourite, gained permanent employment, and never sang in public again.[557] He befriended Wogan and expressed his sympathy for the Jacobite cause. He used his talents to help Wogan on this occasion, the Irishman writing that 'such is the power of music which can reach [even] rocks and bend the gnarled oak, Farinelli … who, by his romances, has had a prodigious ascendancy at this court, has shown himself to be my friend and has so fascinated the minister with his song that his indignation towards me has been calmed'.[558]

Wogan might have had very real private apprehensions for joining Prince Charles Edward, including his likely execution in the event of his capture and also the fear of losing his new employment in Spain. As a man of advancing years, being then 62, his thoughts were probably turning to his children and what property he might be able to leave them after his death. These thoughts may have entered his head during the period, but his intense meaningful activity at the court of Spain to secure military aid for the prince caused him a debilitating illness which, according to his own testimony, almost cost him his life. The agonising waiting both in Spain and France while following the rumours of the prince's progress must have been very difficult. James III's comments about his not encouraging any more officers to travel to Scotland speaks volumes of his expectations of French aid, without which he correctly foresaw the doom of the 'Forty-five' and a repeat of his own experiences in 1708 and 1715. Prince Charles Edward never recovered from his defeat in Scotland.

Chapter 14

Twilight Years

After the intense flurry of activity of his involvement in the 'Forty-five', Wogan returned to his government in San Clemente de la Mancha. Between 1747 and 1754, the year of his death, there are nineteen letters in the Stuart Papers concerning him. Unfortunately, many of his own letters to the Stuart court are missing from the collection, as well as some letters to his son, James. His correspondence suggests that his position as the civil governor of La Mancha lasted for a three-year period after which he was obliged to apply for other positions. Edgar reported to Wogan in July 1747 that Dunbar (James Murray) had retired to Avignon to live with his sister, leaving very few acquaintances at the Stuart court.[559] The same letter gives the news that the Duke of York had been made a cardinal by Pope Benedict XIV the previous month. This did not preclude him from marrying and continuing the Stuart royal line as the cardinalate was a conferred rank; but the following year he took holy orders, to the dismay of his brother Prince Charles Edward.

There is a gap of two years before Edgar's next letter of 21 January 1749 in which he acknowledged Wogan's letter to him the previous December, thanking him, as ever, for his good wishes for the new year. Edgar expressed joy that Wogan enjoyed a visitor to Spain who was famous all over contemporary Europe and that he was 'glad to see he has some influence upon you, and adds a little to your natural vivacity and jollity, long may that temper continue'.[560] He expressed concern to Wogan about the activities of Prince Charles Edward but remarked that 'he is safe and in good health at Avignon, and I wish with all my heart the French may allow him to stay there'.[561] This refers to the French government's obligation as part of the Treaty of Aix-la-Chapelle of October 1748 to enforce the banishment of Prince Charles Edward from the territory of the kingdom of France, as had happened to his father in 1717. He resided in Avignon among a strong Jacobite community.[562] In the same post, a letter from James III thanked him for his new year wishes; but also the remark that he was 'truly sorry for the disappointments you mention to have met with in the settling of the private affairs of your family at home, for my sincere regard and value for you will always make me take a share in everything that relates to you'.[563] Without Wogan's letter it is impossible to know whether the king was talking about his family affairs in Spain or Ireland. If the latter, it might relate to the inheritance of lands there. A whole year went by before Edgar acknowledged two letters regarding Father Edie.[564] This was the same priest who had taken the Countess de Boustlers under his protection after she had been left destitute by her husband in Barcelona many years before. Wogan had asked for letters of recommendation from high-ranking Jesuits in Rome to be written in Edie's favour, as it appears the priest had been banished from his own parish.[565]

Wogan again requested that the patent of knight-baronet, which James III had created him in 1719, be sent to him in Barcelona in December 1749. It is curious that he did not have it, but maybe he never took it with him when he left Rome, assuming that it would be safe at the Stuart court. In any case, the king wrote to him in February 1750 that 'I should be very glad to gratify you in that and all other respects, but this is really not a time for granting such sort of empty favours, and as a few days ago I actually refused one of the same kind to a gentleman considerable in his country and who joined the prince in person when he was in Scotland. So that my rule of not granting such favours just at this time is general and without exception … do not be less persuaded for that of the justice I do to your merits towards me, and of the particular value and regard I shall always have for you'.[566] The reference to the request as of granting 'empty favours' is significant in that it might indicate James III's acceptance that he would never be restored to the three kingdoms. Furthermore, the mention of his refusal to grant a similar favour to a man who had in fact joined Prince Charles Edward in Scotland could well have been meant to indicate his displeasure at Wogan's failure to join the prince in Scotland. However, James had previously assured Wogan that whatever action he considered correct for the cause, there would be no ill-consequences. In any case, James felt he could not oblige in sending Wogan a copy of the already existing patent. Perhaps he finally felt the keen hopelessness of his case and the pointlessness of his royal honours. The cordial correspondence between James III and Wogan over the thirty-year period since 1719 indicate a bond between the two, along with the fact that Wogan's frequent requests to the king were almost always happily obliged.[567]

Finally, in September 1750, two full letters from Wogan to Edgar arrived at the Stuart court which survive today, with their customary minute detail of the comings and goings. He thanked Edgar and the king for a letter of recommendation sent in his favour to Cardinal Valenti Gonzaga[568] adding that 'according to accounts from my son, who is now at his station at this court with his company of the Walloon guards, where he is second lieutenant, his eminence has complied with in the best and most feeling terms to our minister, marqués de la Ensenada'.[569] He expressed his gratitude in the following bright terms: 'I have the happiness to be entirely convinced that no prince has ever showed such an unwearied continuance of royal bounty in equal circumstances to any subject; long grown useless and insignificant, as I have the misfortune to be'. It appears that Wogan had governed for three years in San Clemente and was then returned to the long and frustrating process of procuring promotion in Spain. He had applied in May 1750 at Aranjuez and the minister had given him his 'aggregation to Barcelona of colonel en pied (with the exclusion of that of captain, which was joined to my former one by Campillo in King Philip's time) according to a fixed plan this minister has formed extending to all the system of military government, exclusive equally of double salaries as of double employments which he has made a standing rule and will not break it regardless of any solicitation'.[570] He corresponded with Don Miguel Taxardo, first officer to Ensenada at the war office, with whom he had a good relationship. He was aware of Wogan's long wait for military promotion and that he was still a colonel after thirty-one years of service. Wogan pushed for a promotion to major-general. He wrote that King Philip had promoted him brigadier in 1746 when he set out from Madrid with fifty Irish officers to Dunkirk to join the prince. It seems that the promotion did not result in better pay for Wogan. Taxardo appreciated the various *passe-droits* played on Wogan and desired to help him. He informed Wogan that he could not undo the new system that had just been established, but that if he received a similar recommendation from the cardinal and his patent of major-general, it would be easier to perform under the new rules. Wogan's seniority in the service would be an added advantage. He could also procure him a military government, although they were subject to the same new rules as civil governments and liable to *residencias* every third year according to the law.[571] In frustration Wogan wrote, 'I renounce 'em and all the fatigue of process that attend 'em. I am come hither with a resolution to die in peace, and would choose rather to live upon the stinted bread of 18 *pistoles* a month, that my present aggregation gives me, than enjoy treble revenue, with my head battered at every turn with lawsuits and animosities and brangles without head or tail, and often without honesty or common sense'.

At the same time, he again beseeched James III to re-issue the patent of major-general that James had sent him in 1741. He sent the original ahead to Prince Charles Edward in Scotland in 1746 in anticipation of his travelling there, and also to prevent the same patents from being used against him should he be captured. The patents were lost or destroyed when the insurrection failed. He concluded the letter with a very telling and very touching comment that, 'I shall die here, when God pleases, with less temporal honour or justice from this court, if I remain as I am, and if I have the transient honour I deserve here, what will it avail me at that hour but the comfort of leaving something to my children'. This had obviously been his motivation for asking James to send him the patent for his knight-baronetcy, so that he could pass that honourable title to his eldest son, James.

Ten days later he wrote another letter to Edgar in a tone of excitement and urgency. The letter stated that both the minister of war, the Marqués de Ensenada, and his first officer, Taxardo, had confirmed to him that on receipt of the above-mentioned documents, Wogan would get a much more honourable and beneficial employment. He mentioned the power of the *empeño*, which was a kind of obliging letter of recommendation in an applicant's favour, written by a high-ranking, honourable member of the Spanish court. He enclosed a letter of his son's, asking that they 'forgive him some faults in the orthography and expression, because the uncouthness of writing on a guard-table and in the midst of soldiers does not admit of the same facilities for writing as in a closet'.[572] Wogan then mentioned once again the famous singer resident at the Spanish court, Farinelli. It appears that he hadn't forgotten Wogan and had taken his son under his wing at the Spanish court. Wogan deemed his 'the best *empeño* in Spain, and more almighty, as he [his son] terms it, with the minister himself than with Taxardo, he is in fact, the premier resort of this court'. He also was very discreet about it and never let on that he had anything to do with the promotions, thereby he 'keeps himself artfully under the curtain; to keep himself free from censure of doing or seeming to do anything at court'. The English composer and music historian, Charles Burney, wrote of Farinelli thus: 'Of almost all other great singers, we hear of their intoxication by praise and prosperity, and of their caprice, insolence, and absurdities, at some time or other; but of Farinelli, superior to them all in talents, fame and fortune, the records of folly among the spoilt children of Apollo, furnish not one disgraceful anecdote'.[573] Whenever a person declared an interest in a position, he gave a favourable note in the person's favour and 'freely lets the other have the honour of the success'. He had the power to make or break a person in relation to promotion by how he spoke about him in public, and if he heard that a person he had helped had been publicly giving credit to Farinelli, the singer would turn against him to protect himself lest it come to the knowledge of the court that he had such influence on political appointments. 'Such is the real genius and artifice to keep himself safe, and without danger of losing the ground he has got here. He has taken a great liking to my son, whom he reserves in time for his protection.' He ends his letter by asking James to resend the patent of major-general and the *empeño* to the minister being sure it would 'take me out of the dirt and do honour and justice to his own [James III] commission, which I unhappily lost upon a good occasion, if it had been better timed'.[574]

The warrant/writ for Wogan's patent of Major-General is among the Stuart Papers, showing that James once again obliged his Irish knight in his hour of need. The document lists Wogan's honours and ranks: 'Sir Charles Wogan, knight & baronet, brigadier general of the King's forces – a major general'. The entry on the main page reads: 'The commission is dated and signed at Rome 24 July 1741. Renewed of the same date and sent to him 10 November 1750'.[575]

In May 1751, Edgar wrote to Wogan thanking him for his letter of acknowledgement and gratitude for what he and the king had done for him. Nothing in the wording of Edgar's letter indicates the type of position Wogan obtained, but his application was successful and he received a new position and military promotion in Spain.[576] Wogan was attached to the 'Barcelona Headquarters' in 1750 and served as acting governor of Barcelona in subsequent years before his death.[577] O'Kelly de Galway included in his *Mémoire historique* a transcription of a document in Spanish which included the exact wording: 'attachment to the General Staff of the City of Barcelona … Brigadier Don Carlos Woghan [*sic*] – as graduate Brigadier'.[578] The king asked Edgar to express his delight that he could assist him and to communicate the 'constant regard and value' that he had for him.[579] Always with an eye on international affairs, Edgar remarked that the recent death of the King of Sweden, as well as the eldest Prince of Hanover could bode well for the Jacobite cause, adding that should the Duke of Hanover himself, who was in bad health, also die, the outlook would be even better for a restoration.[580] On this hopeful note, the last piece of surviving correspondence between the Stuart court in Rome and Charles Wogan ends.

Four letters from his son James Wogan are extant among the Stuart Papers; however, Tayler quoted a letter written by James Wogan to the Stuart court on 15 December 1753 on behalf of he and his father: 'Sa situation et ses infirmities l'empeche de s'en acquitter luy meme/His situation and his infirmities prevent him from doing it himself'.[581] Age had finally caught up with the illustrious knight. Charles's death was acknowledged in a letter dated 10 September 1754 from Edgar to James Wogan as having occurred in July 1754.[582] Surviving records housed at the archive of the Catedral de Barcelona indicate that his body was received at the cathedral on 7 July 1754, suggesting that he had died the preceding day or on that date.[583] Above his name on the left margin it reads: 'sanador y patricio romano, cavalero-barono de Inglaterra/ patrician and senator of Rome, knight-baronet of England'. The main entry states that he was a 'brigadier of the army of his Catholic majesty' suggesting that this was his highest rank before his death, despite his hopes of promotion to major general and the civil position he had obtained a few years prior. His exact burial place is not known, but it could be either in the crypt of the cathedral or in a separate lot used as a cemetery in contemporary Barcelona which has since been built over.[584] No record of his last will and testament survives in the archive of the Colegio Notarial de Cataluña in Barcelona.[585] Edgar assured the young chevalier that he had laid the letter before the king who 'was pleased to express a sensible concern for the loss he has sustained by his death', followed by a note of encouragement to follow his father's principles with regard to loyalty to the Stuarts. Edgar's personal note in the same letter is revealing of how close-knit the exiled Jacobite community had become: 'I was very sensibly touched when I read your letter, for I had a true and sincere esteem for your worthy father, and that will make me glad of occasions where I can be useful to you'.[586] All four of James Wogan's letters are written in French, perhaps indicating a discomfort in writing in the English language; after all, he had been born and raised in Spain. It would be odd though, if he had not learned to write in English given his parents' origins.

James Wogan accepted Edgar's open offer of assistance and in a letter dated 12 April 1755 he requested a letter of recommendation from James III to Richard Wall, secretary of state to King Charles III of Spain. Wall's parents were from Kilmallock in County Limerick. Wogan hoped that 'this mark of [James III's] protection can contribute much to my advancement, since Mr Wall is a great friend of my colonel, the count of Priégo'. He continued: 'I flatter myself that your good offices will make my pretensions suffice; I have in the world no other appanage than the sword'. He mentioned his late father, 'in whose footsteps I would like to follow, and to sacrifice myself for the interests of his majesty'.[587] The next letter, written in December 1755, is little more than a happy new year message, which had been typical of his father throughout all of his years in exile in Spain. No mention is made of his father in the letter. The second, of 14 December 1757, wished all the royal family best wishes for the new year with his prayer of a restoration to the kingdoms. He confirms the death 'of my uncle Mr Nicholas Wogan of Rathcoffey' adding that 'I was hoping to have a part in his last wishes, but … he forgot me at the time of his death as he did while he was alive; his memory would have done me good'.[588] He remarked that he was en route to Madrid and his letter contains the familiar refrain of a financial difficulty in Spain.

His final letter of 11 February 1758 contains a few fascinating details. For example, he thanks Edgar for writing to him and 'of showing me the desire that you have to see me near his majesty'. Edgar might have encouraged the young Chevalier Wogan to travel to Rome. The knight continued by elaborating on his current circumstances:

> I have resolved to explain to you clearly my present situation, the death of my late Father, the last honours that he was just giving you in his memory, and some debts that I had to pay, bothered me considerably; to leave for Madrid in a month and find myself very embarrassed to seem decent; in these humiliating circumstances I … beg [you] to kindly ask in my favour the generosity of the king our master, assured as I am that his great goodness, will deign to make me receive some money to enable me to undertake my journey, and to discharge the debts which I have seen myself obliged to contract for the reasons which I have deduced.[589]

James Wogan wrote that the cardinal Duke of York might think favourably on the question of sending him some money for his expenses, stating 'I had the honour to pay him court and I sincerely hope that it will be in my power to show my attachment to the whole royal family; I desire no other happiness'. The letter contains a reference to Lady Misset as well. James Wogan reassured that in case Edgar's letters arrive and the young chevalier had already left, 'Lady Misset will take care of everything' and that when he told her he was writing to Edgar, she asked him to write that she had not answered his last so as not to end up sending him too many letters. It is heartening to know that the exiled Jacobite community continued to look after each other after all their years in exile. James Wogan and his siblings had lost both their parents, so one could imagine that the elderly Lady Misset, an old friend of their father, would have become a kind of family matriarch for them in Barcelona. The last letter from James Wogan to Edgar is signed 'Le Chevalier Wogan', indicating that James inherited the knight-baronetcy from his father.[590]

Epilogue

This book is the result of years of work. It was a pleasure to travel to the various archives in some of the most beautiful cities in the world. To do so without institutional affiliation and the advantages that can bring meant it has been a very expensive enterprise. The purpose of this short epilogue is to help any future scholars who wish to take up the scent and uncover more material on Sir Charles Wogan, and those in his network, which has yet eluded historians.

While completing this project it has occurred to me that however complete a picture we can make of a life such as that of Sir Charles Wogan, it would be almost impossible to locate all the letters he ever wrote. The Stuart court in exile was the nexus for all the Irish Jacobite exiles and among the Stuart and Cumberland papers we can find correspondence from many in Sir Charles's personal network from which can be gleaned much of their own personal circumstances and their motivation for writing to the court. Between and among the exiles, however, there must surely have been many more letters transacted on an equally broad range of topics. Sir Charles referred to his keeping a personal archive in one of his letters. His children would have inherited all his papers. According to files at the National Archive of Ireland, a member of the Bey family of Paris, claiming to be descended from Sir Charles, offered a copy of the original patent creating Wogan a knight-baronet to the Irish embassy in Paris in the 1950s. This might point to the existence of a family archive which could contain Wogan's personal archive somewhere in Paris today. The Irish embassy in Paris said that the best way to track down living relatives would be to visit the French national office for recording births, deaths and marriages.

As was shown above, Wogan sent James III a full genealogy of the Wogan family, but that document, along with some of his letters, are missing from the Stuart Papers. It is possible that in the interim between the death of James III in 1766 and the transferral of the Stuart Papers to England in the nineteenth century, that individual private collectors could have purchased some of the papers. The author of the book titled *Mémoire historique et généalogique sur la famille de Wogan, avec une relation inédite de l'évasion de la princesse Marie-Clémentine Sobieska, femme de Jacques III, roi de la Grande-Bretagne et d'Irlande (1719)*, Count Alphonse O'Kelly de Galway, was based in Belgium when he published it in 1896. In order to complete this very detailed work, which included some of Charles Wogan's personal papers, he must have had access to or ownership of them. The material O'Kelly de Galway gathered for that project could well be among a family archive either in Belgium or in Ireland today, or in a local archive. They are not in the National Archives of Belgian. Correspondence between Wogan and Prince James Louis Sobieski from the time of the Sobieski-Stuart match are probably to be found among the Sobieski Papers housed at the National Archive of Belarus in Minsk. Correspondence between Wogan and members of the Irish clergy in Europe, and between he and his friends and relatives could equally be located in surviving Irish colleges or local archives such as that of the Archive Départmental de Vannes and Morbihan, which contain the copious correspondence of Sir Richard Warren and among which are some of Wogan's letters. In Spain, there will undoubtedly be more letters between Sir Charles and various Spanish ministers such as José Patiño, whose correspondence is housed at the Archivo Nacional Historico in Madrid. To future scholars these clues might save time and money.

For many people living in Ireland, the eighteenth century seems to elicit very little to mind other than the monolithic and bleak phrase 'Penal Laws'. It is as if that was all we need to know about it, that Ireland was a difficult place to live for approximately eighty percent of people living there who were Roman Catholics, Protestant Dissenters or Presbyterians. Yet, the men and women who left Ireland to seek their fortunes across a range of professions in Europe or farther afield again are largely absent from memory. Sir Charles Wogan's life is but one example of how colourful, exciting, and full of possibility this period was for the Wild Geese, some of whom, as has been mentioned above, rose to the highest offices in their host countries and achieved the highest marks of distinction. A desire to study the Wild Geese may, as Daniel Szechi writes, have been affected by the still-pervasive nationalist republican ideology in Ireland which could conceivably cause a difficulty when explaining the steadfast loyalty among the majority of Irish people of that time to an English king. This particular niche of historiography does offer the chance to show a more encompassing range of Irish experience which might stand to the inhabitants of the island as the two largest communities on the island edge into further cooperation together. It also offers the chance to understand the Irish experience of migration at that time and the challenges they faced in their host societies, which Ireland has itself become to many migrants from around the world. Sir Charles Wogan was a survivor, a mercurial character who could adjust himself to different audiences at different moments as he sought to gain the maximum advantage for himself and his family during his long exile. He desired that his story might be told, and it is a great pleasure to have facilitated its telling.

Bibliography

Primary Sources

'Francesco Bianchini to James III', 16 June 1719, Archivio Segreto Vaticano, Segretaria di Stato, Inghilterra, 1700–1745, 21.

'Socorro al rey Jacobo sobre el socorro doda a dicho rey 1711–1715' (Aid for King James … regarding aid given to that king 1711–1715) Archivo Nacional Historico (Madrid).

Arxiu de la Catedral de Barcelona, *Libre de Obits, Tomo XXXIII, desde 1754–1759.*

Autos generales de la residencia que en la villa de San Clemente (Cuenca) tomó Carlos Wogan a Salvador Antonio Barnuevo, corregidor de ella, y demás ministros que debieron darla. Archivo Histórico Nacional, Consejos, 31801, Exp. 3. Available at https://pares.mcu.es/ParesBusquedas20/catalogo/show/6473322?nm. (Document describing Wogan's employment as Governor of La Mancha province.)

Calendar of Stuart Papers, Historical Manuscript Commission, Vols. II, VI, VI and VII., passim.

Contrôles des officiers 1706–1710, Service Historique de la Défense, Chateuax de Vincennes, Maison du Roi, troupes à pied, Gardes françaises, gardes Suisses et infanterie, Gardes françaises gardes suisse, regiments d'infanterie (ancienes regiments). Microfilm GRyB78, housed at the Chateaux de Vincennes. (French army regimental officer lists.)

Diario del Expedicion de Oran de Montemar, Archivo General de Simancas, SGU, LEG 482 SUP. (A vast collection of hand-written reports from Oran dispatched to Madrid.)

Harris Library, Preston, Community History Pamphlet Collection, Item Number LE75 LET, Anonymous, 'A Letter about the occurrences in the way to, and at Preston, by a gentleman who was an eyewitness to the said transactions'.

Jacobite Correspondence 1722, British Library, British Museum, Stowe M.S. 250. (Intercepted correspondence and reports from spies operating abroad.)

Newcastle Papers, Vol. LVI. British Museum. Add. Ms. 32741, 245.

Odriscol Wogan, Ana, AHN, Consejos, ES. 28079, OM-Casamiento_Santiago, Exp. 10319, accessed on Pares system at https://pares.mcu.es/ParesBusquedas20/catalogo/description/1724364?nm.

Odriscol, Ana, Archivo General de Palacio, ES. 28079/AGP, Personal, Caja 16813 Exp. 03.

Papers of Cardinal Gualtiero, British Library, Brit. Mus. Add. Ms. 20310.

Patent creating Charles Wogan a knight-baronet, National Library of Ireland, MS 8340.

Poems of Love and Gallantry, Written in the Marshalsea and Newgate by Several of the Preston Prisoners, (London, 1716).

Reasons Humbly Offered to the Parliament of Ireland for Repealing the Sacramental Test, in Favour of the Catholicks, Otherwise Called Roman Catholicks, and By their Ill-Willers, Papists, Drawn Partly from their Arguments as they are Catholicks, and Partly from Argument common of their Brethren the Common Dissenters, (1733).

Royal Archive: *Stuart Papers*, Main Series, Vol. 233, Manuscript papers.

Schedule of deeds relating to the Wogan property, dated 11 July 1802, Bodleian Library, M.S. Talbot.

The Marriage Certificate of James Stuart III and Queen Maria Clementina Stuart, Trinity College Dublin, Manuscript 7574.

The Wogan Manuscript, housed at the Galway, Kilmacduagh and Kilfenora Diocesan Archive.

Wogan's military service record: Archivo General de Simancas, Secretaría de Guerra, Legajo 2598, 2, expediente 2.

Secondary Sources

18th Century Britain, 1714–1815 – 'Britain from 1715 to 1742: The Supremacy of the Whigs', in *Britannica*, accessed 28/6/2023, available at https://www.britannica.com/place/United-Kingdom/18th-century-Britain-1714-1815#ref483223.

Amhurst, N. (ed.), 'An Epistle from the Princess Sobieski [sic] to the Chevalier de St. George', in *Poems on Several Occasions*, (London,1721).

Anonymous, *The Secret History of the Rebels in Newgate*, (London, 1717).

Ayre, W., *Memoires of the Life and Writings of Alexander Pope*, (London, 1745).

Bartlam Smith, Lawrence, *Spain and Britain, 1715–1719: The Jacobite Issue*, (London, 1987).

Bartlett, T., *Ireland: A History*, (Cambridge, 2010).

Black, J., 'The Catholic Threat and the British Press in the 1720s and 1730s', *Journal of Religious History*, Vol. 12, Issue 4 (December 1983).

Blaikie, W. B., *Itinerary of Prince Charles Edward Stuart from his landing in Scotland July 1745 to his departure in September 1746*, (Edinburgh, 1897).

Bruce, N. 'The Duke of Mar in Exile, 1716–32', in *Transactions of the Royal Historical Society*, Fourth Series, Vol. 20 (December, 1937).

Carroll, C. L., 'The Romance and Disillusionment of Exile: Charles Wogan and his Memoir of Clementina Sobieska', in Carroll, C. L., *Exiles in a Global City: The Irish in Early Modern Rome, 1609–1783*, (Boston, 2018).

Corp, E., 'Murray, James, Jacobite first earl of Dunbar (1690–1770)', in *Oxford Dictionary of National Biography*, accessed 25/07/2014, available at http://www.oxforddnb.com/view/article/92615.

Corp, E., 'The Location of the Stuart Court in Rome: The Palazzo del Re', in Monod, Pittock and Szechi, *Loyalty and Identity: Jacobites at Home and Abroad*, (Basingstoke, 2010).

Corp, E., *The Jacobites at Urbino: An Exiled Court in Transition*, (Basingstoke, 2009).

Corp, E., *The Stuarts in Italy 1719–1766: A Royal Court in Permanent Exile*, (Cambridge, 2011).

Cruickshanks, E., and Erskine-Hill, H., *The Atterbury Plot*, (Edinburgh, 2004).

D'Arcy, F., 'Exiles and Strangers: The Case of the Wogans', in O'Brien, Gerard, (ed.), *Parliament, Politics and People: Essays in Eighteenth-Century Irish History*, (Dublin, 1989).

Defoe, D., *The History of the Press Yard*, (London, 1717).

Dilworth, W. H., *The Life of Alexander Pope*, (London, 1760).

Downey, D. M., 'Beneath the Harp and Burgundian Cross: Irish Regiments in the Spanish Bourbon Army, 1700–1818', in O'Donnell, H., (ed.), *The Irish Presence in the Spanish Military – 16th to 20th Centuries*, (Madrid, 2014).

Downey, D. M., 'The Habsburg-Hanoverian Alliance and its perspective on the Stuart-Sobieski match' in Maher, R. K. (ed.), *The Irish to the Rescue: the Tercentenary of the Polish Princess Clementina's Escape*, (Oxford, 2021).

Female Fortitued, exemplify'd, in an impartial narrative, of the seizure, escape and marriage of the Princess Clementina Sobieska, as it was particularly set down by Mr. Charles Wogan ... who was a chief manager in that whole affair, (London, 1722, reprinted in USA by Gale, Eighteenth Century Collection Online, Print editions).

Flood, J., *The Life of Chevalier Charles Wogan, an Irish Soldier of Fortune*, (Dublin, 1922).

Garnham, N., 'How Violent Was Eighteenth-Century Ireland?', *Irish Historical Studies*, Vol. 30, No. 119 (May, 1997).

Geange, K. E., 'Lieutenant-General Arthur Dillon: Jacobite at the Regency Court 1715–1725', (unpublished thesis, Trinity College, Dublin, Ireland, Department of History).

Giblin, C. OFM, 'Irish Exiles in Catholic Europe' in Corish, P. & Brady, J. (eds.), *The Church Under the Penal Code*, (Dublin, 1971).

Gilbert, J. T., *Narratives of the Detention, Liberation, and Marriage of Maria Clementina Stuart, styled Queen of Great Britain and Ireland, with contemporary letters and papers for the first time published*, (Dublin, 1894).

Glickman, G., *The English Catholic Community, 1688–1754*, (Woodbridge, 2009).

Harris, E. T., 'Farinelli', in Stanley, S. and Tyrrell (eds.), *The New Grove Dictionary of Music and Musicians*, 2nd Edition, Vol. VIII, (London, 2001).

Harrison Ainsworth, W., *Preston Fight or the Insurrection of 1715*, (London, 1875).

Hatton, R., *George I*, (Yale, 2001).

Heddle de La Caillemotte de Massue de Ruvigné, Melville Amadeus Henry Douglas, 9th Marquis of Ruvigny and 15th of Raineval, *The Jacobite Peerage, Baronetage, Knightage, and Grants of Honour*, (Edinburgh, 1904).

Hora, K., 'A Critical Discourse Analysis on Jonathan Swift's *Drapier's Letters*: Public advocacy and nationalism in Ireland, 1724–1725', in Somerville I., Edwards, L., and Øyvind I., (eds.), *Public Relations, Society and the Generative Power of History*, (London, 2019).

Keith Schuchard, M., 'Jonathan Swift, The Earl of Rosse, Duke of Wharton, and Sir Charles Wogan: the Irish-Spanish Masonic Connection' in *Revista de Estudios Históricos de la Masonería Latinoamericana y Caribeña*, Vol. 13, No. 1 (January–June, 2021).

Keith-Schuchard, M., *Masonic Rivalries and Literary Politics: from Jonathan Swift to Henry Fielding*, (2018).

Kenyon, J. and Ohlmeyer, J. (eds), *The Civil Wars: A Military History of England, Scotland, and Ireland, 1638–1660*, (Oxford, 1998).

Kernan, V., *The Duel in European History: Honour and the Reign of Aristocracy*, (London, 2016).

Lallement, L., 'Le Maréchal de Camp Baron de Warren, Correspondence et Notes (de 1740 à 1775)', in Warren et Le Prince Charles-Édouard, *Extrait de Bulletin de la Société Polymathique du Morbihan 2 September 1892*, Vol.1, (Vannes, 1893).

Law, H. A., 'Sir Charles Wogan', *The Journal of the Royal Society of Antiquaries of Ireland*, Seventh Series, Vol. 7, No. 2 (31, Dec, 1937).

Mackay, Ronan, 'Wogan, John' in *Dictionary of Irish Biography*, accessed 02/07/2024, available at https://www.dib.ie/index.php/biography/wogan-john-a9102.

Maher, R. K. (ed.), *The Irish to the Rescue: the Tercentenary of the Polish Princess Clementina's Escape*, (Oxford, 2021).

Maher, R. K., '"No Good Deed Goes Unpunished": Charles Wogan and his Removal from the Jacobite Court in Rome, June 1719', (M.A. Thesis, University College Dublin, 2013, unpublished).

Maher, R. K., 'Poems from the prison yard – a poetic correspondence between Charles Wogan and William Tunstall', *History Ireland*, Issue 2 (March/April 2017), Vol. 25.

Maher, R., 'A Duel Between Jacobites' at 8th Annual Tudor and Stuart Ireland Interdisciplinary Conference, Queen's University Belfast (August, 2018). Available at https://soundcloud.com/history-hub/richard-maher-a-duel-between-jacobites.

McCabe, J., *A Candic History of the Jesuits*, Vol. I, (London, 1913).

McGrath, Charles Ivar, 'Securing the Protestant Interest: The Origins and Purpose of the Penal Laws of 1695', *Irish Historical Studies*, Vol. 30, No. 117 (1996).

McLynn, F., *The Jacobites*, (London, 1985).

Miller, P., *A Wife for the Pretender*, (London, 1965).

Murdoch, S., 'Tilting at Windmills: The Order del Toboso as a Jacobite Social Network', in Monod, P., Pittock, M., and Szechi, D. (eds.) *Loyalty and Identity, Jacobites at Home and Abroad*, (Basingstoke, 2010).

Ó Briain (ed.), 'The Chevalier Gaydon's memoir of the regiment of Dillon, 1738' [In thirteen parts: III (11), pp.98–106 to VI (24)] in *The Irish Sword*.

Ó Ciardha, Éamonn, *Ireland and the Jacobite Cause, 1685–1766: A Fatal Attachment*, (Dublin, 2001).

O'Callaghan, J. T., *A History of the Irish Brigades in the Service of France*, reprinted & published by Forgotten Books (London, 2018).

O'Donovan, J., O'Conor, T., and O'Keefe, P., *Ordnance Survey of Ireland: Letters, Kildare*, Vol. 1 (Ordnance Survey Office, 1861).

O'Kelly de Galway, Alph. (Cte.), *Mémoire historique et généalogique sur la famille de Wogan, avec une relation inédite de l'évasion de la princesse Marie-Clémentine Sobieska, femme de Jacques III, roi de la Grande-Bretagne et d'Irlande (1719)*, (Paris, 1896).

Oates, J. *The Last Battle on English Soil, Preston 1715*, (Oxon, 2015).

Ottoman Turkish Tents, Wawel Castle, accessed on 10/11/2024, available at https://wawel.krakow.pl/en/exhibition-constant/ottoman-tukish-tents.

Patten, R., *The History of the Rebellion in the Year 1715*, (London, 1745).

Royle, T., *The British Civil War: The Wars of the Three Kingdoms, 1638–1660*, (London & New York, 2004).

Sanchez Doncel, G., *Presencia de España en Orán, 1509–1792*, (Toledo, 1991).

Scott, Sir Walter, *The Works of Jonathan Swift: containing additional letters, tracts, and poems not hitherto published; with notes, and a life of the author*, 2nd Edition, 19 Volumes, (A. Constable & Co., 1824).

Seccombe, T., 'Oxburgh, Henry', in *Dictionary of National Biography*, 1885–1900, Vol. 43.

Storrs, C., *The Spanish Resurgence, 1713–1748*, (Yale, 2016).

Szechi, D., 'The Political Consequences of the Cuckoldy German Turnip Farmer' in Sirota, B. and Macinnes, A. (eds.), *The Hanoverian Succession in Great Britain and its Empire*, (Woodbridge: Boydell Press, 2019).

Szechi, D., *1715: The Great Jacobite Rebellion*, (Yale, 2006).

Szechi, Daniel, '"Cam Ye O'er Frae France?" Exile and the Mind of Scottish Jacobitism', *Journal of British Studies*, Vol. 37, No. 4 (October, 1998).

Tayler, H., *Jacobite Epilogue*, (London, 1941).

Tayler, H., *Lady Nithsdale and her Family*, (London, 1939).

Tayler, H., *The Jacobite Court at Rome, 1719*, (Publications of the Scottish History Society, Third Series, Volume XXXI, Edinburgh, 1938).

Tornabene, Hugh, 'Jacobite Rebellion Ships', Immigrant Ships Transcribers Guild, accessed 28/10/2024, available at https://www.immigrantships.net/jacobite/indexjacobite.html.

Walsh, Micheline (ed.), *Spanish Knights of Irish Origin: documents From Continental Archives*, Vol. I, (Dublin, 1960).

Whelan, K., 'An underground gentry? Catholic middlemen in eighteenth-century Ireland', in *Eighteenth-Century Ireland*, Vol. 10 (1995).

Williams, B., *Stanhope: A Study in Eighteenth-century War and Diplomacy*, (Oxford, 1932).

Wills, R., *The Jacobites and Russia 1715–1750*, (East Lothian, 2002).

Winch, C., (trans.), *The Rescue of Princess Clementina (Stuart): A 1719 Adventure of the Irish Brigades*, by Sir Charles Wogan, (Belfast Historical & Educational Society, 2008).

Woolley, David, (ed.), *The Correspondence of Jonathan Swift, D.D.*, Vol. III, (Frankfurt, 2007).

References

1. Downey, D. M., 'Beneath the Harp and Burgundian Cross: Irish Regiments in the Spanish Bourbon Army, 1700–1818', in O'Donnell, H., (ed.), *The Irish Presence in the Spanish Military – 16th to 20th Centuries*, (Madrid, 2014), p. 89.
2. D'Arcy, F., 'Exiles and Strangers: The Case of the Wogans', in O'Brien, Gerard (ed.), *Parliament, Politics and People: Essays in Eighteenth-Century Irish History*, (Dublin, 1989), p.175.
3. The original maps are made available by Tailte Éireann, an Irish government body with responsibility for valuation, registration and surveying of land. Tailte Éireann, *Historical Maps & Data*, accessed 15/7/2024, available at https://www.tailte.ie/en/surveying/products/professional-mapping/historical-maps-and-data/.
4. O'Donovan, J., O'Conor, T., O'Keefe, P., *Ordnance Survey of Ireland: Letters, Kildare* (Vol. 1), (Ordnance Survey Office, 1861), p.75; accessed on 15/7/2024, available at https://askaboutireland.ie/reading-room/digital-book-collection/digital-books-by-subject/ordnance-survey-of-irelan/.
5. O'Kelly de Galway, Alph. (Cte.), *Mémoire historique et généalogique sur la famille de Wogan, avec une relation inédite de l'évasion de la princesse Marie-Clémentine Sobieska, femme de Jacques III, roi de la Grande-Bretagne et d'Irlande (1719)*, (Paris, 1896), pp.1–2.
6. Ibid., pp.2–3.
7. Mackay, Ronan, 'Wogan, John', in *Dictionary of Irish Biography*, accessed 02/07/2024, available at https://www.dib.ie/index.php/biography/wogan-john-a9102.

8. 'Wogan to James III', 23 September 1729, Jaca (RA/SP/MAIN/130 f.167–166).
9. There were two palatinates as well, those of the Earls of Desmond in Kerry and the Earls of Ormond in Tipperary.
10. Royle, T., *The British Civil War: The Wars of the Three Kingdoms, 1638–1660,* (London & New York, 2004) pp. 368–381; Kenyon, J. and Ohlmeyer, J. (eds.), *The Civil Wars: A Military History of England, Scotland, and Ireland, 1638–1660*, (Oxford, 1998), pp.93–94.
11. Edward Wogan died in Scotland after receiving a light wound to the shoulder during a skirmish. The wound festered and no medical treatment was available.
12. Richardstown is often listed as Mainham; both placenames are used for the same area. The author thanks Dr Harman Murtagh for providing these details about Charles's father and uncle ahead of the publication of his new book *Regimental Lineages and Officer Lists of the Irish Jacobite Army*, publishing in 2025.
13. 'Schedule of deeds relating to the Wogan property' dated 11 July 1802, Bodleian Library, M.S. Talbot b. 132/17.
14. Charles II's representative and head of government in Ireland.
15. 'Schedule of deeds relating to the Wogan property' dated 11 July 1802, Bodleian Library, M.S. Talbot b. 132/17.
16. 'Wogan to Swift', 27 February 1732, in Scott, W., *Swift's Works*, Vol. XVIII, pp. 472–473.
17. Lenihan, P., *The Last Cavalier: Richard Talbot (1631–91)*, (Dublin, 2014), p. 2.
18. This is evidenced by the extant documents of the Archive of the Talbot family, Barons Talbot de Malahide housed at the Bodleian Library wherein family connections between the Wogans, Talbots, Brownes and Aylmers are indicated in a schedule of deeds. See Bodleian Library, M.S. Talbot b. 132/17.
19. The Flight of the Wild Geese.
20. Archivo General de Simancas, Secretaría de Guerra, Legajo 2598, folio 4. This has already been shown by D'Arcy, F., 'Exiles and Strangers: The Case of the Wogans', in O'Brien, Gerard, (ed.),

Parliament, Politics and People: Essays in Eighteenth-Century Irish History, (Dublin, 1989), p.182, and by another means in Law, H. A., 'Sir Charles Wogan', *The Journal of the Royal Society of Antiquaries of Ireland*, Seventh Series, Vol. 7, No. 2 (31 December 1937), pp. 257–258.

21. 'Wogan to Edgar', 23 August 1746, Madrid, The Royal Archive, Stuart Papers/MAIN/276 f.109; accessed digitally at The National Archive in Kew, London.
22. McGrath, Charles Ivar, 'Securing the Protestant Interest: The Origins and Purpose of the Penal Laws of 1695', *Irish Historical Studies*, Vol. 30, No. 117, 1996, pp. 25–46. JSTOR, http://www.jstor.org/stable/30008727, accessed 15 July 2024, p. 26.
23. Glickman, G., *The English Catholic Community, 1688–1754*, (Woodbridge, 2009), pp.71–76, 253.
24. Scott, Sir W., *The Works of Jonathan Swift: containing additional letters, tracts, and poems not hitherto published; with notes, and a life of the author*, Vol. 19 (Edinburgh, 1824), pp. 458–459, 495. Wogan's correspondence with Swift is printed there in full (Vols. 16–19). Where Wogan mentions his acquaintance with Alexander Pope, Scott notes that knowledge of this connection had escaped Pope's early biographers. To date I have not been able to find mention of Wogan in any of Pope's early biographies.
25. Originally built in the sixteenth century, the large house and estate were owned by the Gawdy family of Redenhall, Norfolk. In 1666 the house and estate passed by marriage to the Wogan family, whose main holdings were in Pembrokeshire since their arrival from Normandy. The Wogans retained this large estate in Norfolk until 1778. See O'Kelly de Galway, Alph. (Cte.), *Mémoire historique et généalogique sur la famille de Wogan, avec une relation inédite de l'évasion de la princesse Marie-Clémentine Sobieska, femme de Jacques III, roi de la Grande-Bretagne et d'Irlande (1719)*, (Paris, 1896), p.35.
26. D'Arcy, F., 'Exiles and Strangers', p.182. For Wogan's proficiency in Latin, the author refers to *The Wogan Manuscript*, housed at the Galway, Kilmacduagh and Kilfenora Diocesan Archives.

27. Dilworth, W. H., *The Life of Alexander Pope*, (London, 1760), pp.3–11.
28. Ayre, W., *Memoires of the Life and Writings of Alexander Pope*, (London, 1745), pp.1–4.
29. *Contrôles des Officiers 1706–1710, Service Historique de la Défense, Chateuax de Vincennes, Maison du Roi, troupes à pied, Gardes françaises, gardes Suisses et infanterie, Gardes françaises gardes suisse, regiments d'infanterie (ancienes regiments).* Microfilm GRyB78, folio 373. The spelling of Wogan's name in the continental archive sources can vary between Ugan, Ogan, Ughi, Bogan, Woghan, de Wogan, Woughan and Vaughan. In this case it was spelled Woghan. Scholars in the past have claimed that he was an officer in Dillon's Regiment but his name does not appear on any list for Dillon's between 1702 and 1715. Ruvigny stated in his 1904 *Jacobite Peerage* that Wogan served in Dillon's after his escape from Newgate, possibly giving us the origin of this error; see Heddle de La Caillemotte de Massue de Ruvigné, Melville Amadeus Henry Douglas, 9th Marquis of Ruvigny and 15th of Raineval, *The Jacobite Peerage, Baronetage, Knightage, and Grants of Honour*, (Edinburgh, 1904), p.210.
30. Two soldiers named Nicholas Wogan appear in the French military archive in the early and mid-eighteenth century. It is probable that the earlier refers to Nicholas, son of John Wogan, heir of Rathcoffey as Charles's younger brother would have been too young. The other Nicholas was perhaps a distant relative from Galway which was the place of origin given on that particular record. The latter was wounded at Fontenoy resulting in the amputation of his arm and was made a Chevalier de Saint Louis in 1745. See Cullen, Séamus, 'The Wogans and Brownes: Two 18th-Century North Kildare Jacobite Families', published in two parts by *Liffey Champion*, Part I – 13 July 2024; Part II – 20 July 2024. See also Service Historique de la Défense, Château de Vincennes, GR1 YE 25792, 'Woghan (Nicholas)'
31. Corp, E., *The Stuarts in Italy 1719–1766: A Royal Court in Permanent Exile*, (Cambridge, 2011), pp.121–136.

32. Giblin, C. OFM, 'Irish Exiles in Catholic Europe' in Corish, P. and Brady, J. (eds), *The Church Under the Penal Code*, (Dublin, 1971), p.50.
33. National Library of Ireland, Microfilm Reel P519. Further to this, a letter from the Stuart Papers between a T. Southcott and John Paterson from April 1716 mentions Wogan by name, misspelled (Oughan). The fact that two high ranking members of James III's court in exile knew him further supports the idea that he was a regular at the court and well acquainted with those in high positions. See Southcott to Paterson, 29 April 1716, *RA SP*, Main, 7 f.96–7; or *Calendar of Stuart Papers*, Historical Manuscript Commission, March–September 1716, (London, 1904).
34. O'Callaghan, J. T., *A History of the Irish Brigades in the Service of France*, reprinted & published by Forgotten Books (London, 2018) p.299; see also Szechi, D., 'The Political Consequences of the Cuckoldy German Turnip Farmer' in Sirota, B. and Macinnes, A. (eds.), *The Hanoverian Succession in Great Britain and its Empire*, (Woodbridge: Boydell Press, 2019), pp.20–37; see also Hatton, R., *George I*, (Yale, 2001), pp.6, 211.
35. Szechi, D., *1715: The Great Jacobite Rebellion*, (Yale, 2006), p.92.
36. Patten, R., *The History of the Rebellion in the Year 1715*, (London, 1745), p.50.
37. Ibid., p.97.
38. Ibid., p.110.
39. In one of Charles Wogan's military service records from Spain, it mentions that he held the rank of a captain of a cavalry detachment during the 1715 insurrection: Archivo General de Simancas, Secretaría de Guerra, Legajo 2598, 2, Expediente 2.
40. Patten, R., *The History of the Rebellion*, p.80; see also Szechi, D., *1715, The Great Jacobite Rebellion*, (Yale, 2006), p.176.
41. Szechi, *1715, The Great Jacobite Rebellion*, (Yale, 2006), pp.177–183.
42. Harris Library, Preston, Community History Pamphlet Collection, Item Number LE75 LET, Anonymous, 'A Letter about the occurrences in the way to, and at Preston, by a gentleman who was

an eyewitness to the said transactions'. The manager of the Harris Library confirmed to the author (Latimer, S., email communication, 7/4/2016) that the document was printed for private circulation among Scottish Jacobites from a letter sent by an individual referred to as the Merse Officer, the apparent author of the letter, to a Jacobite friend in Scotland. From the content it can be deduced that he was part of the troop raised in Berwickshire known as the Merse troop, commanded by the Hon. James Hume, which had joined the Northern English Jacobite forces at Kelso. It is one of the only surviving contemporary accounts by an eyewitness on the Jacobite side. Another, but rather more literary, account of the 1715 rebellion by William Harrison Ainsworth titled *Preston Fight or The Insurrection of 1715* echoes that Nicholas was a captain and also that he defended a barricade with a troop of Northumbrian soldiers.

43. Whether it was Charles or Nicholas is not clear, but it seems that Nicholas was more often referred to as a captain in sources concerning the rebellion consulted during this study.
44. Patten, R., *The History of the Rebellion*, pp.97–99.
45. Ibid., p.97.
46. Ibid.
47. Patten, R., *The History of the Rebellion*, pp.134–135; Murray was known for overplaying his position as was revealed by this author in previous work. See Maher, R. K., '"No Good Deed Goes Unpunished": Charles Wogan and his Removal from the Jacobite Court in Rome, June 1719', (M.A. Thesis, University College Dublin, 2013, unpublished), pp.11–22.
48. Tayler, H., *Jacobite Epilogue*, (London, 1941), p.278.
49. Tornabene, Hugh, 'Jacobite Rebellion Ships', Immigrant Ships Transcribers Guild, accessed 28/10/2024, available at https://www.immigrantships.net/jacobite/indexjacobite.html.
50. Ibid.
51. O'Callaghan, John C., *A History of the Irish Brigades in the Service of France*, (London, 1875), p.207.
52. Estado 3494, 'Socorro al rey Jacobo sobre el socorro doda a dicho rey 1711–1715' in Archivo Nacional Historico (Madrid). See

also Bartlam Smith, Lawrence, *Spain and Britain, 1715–1719: The Jacobite Issue*, (London, 1987), p.30.

53. Geange, K. E., 'Lieutenant-General Arthur Dillon: Jacobite at the Regency Court 1715–1725', (unpublished thesis, Trinity College, Dublin, Ireland, Department of History), pp. 59–60.
54. Defoe, D., *The History of the Press Yard*, p.65.
55. Ibid., p.71.
56. Ibid., p.78.
57. Oates, J. *The Last Battle on English Soil, Preston 1715*, (Oxon, 2015), p.113; see also Patten, R., *The History of the Rebellion*, pp.67, 112.
58. Patten, R., *The History of the Rebellion*, pp.112–113.
59. *Poems of Love and Gallantry, Written in the Marshalsea and Newgate by Several of the Preston Prisoners*, (London, 1716), p.5. See also Maher, R. K., 'Poems from the prison yard – a poetic correspondence between Charles Wogan and William Tunstall', *History Ireland*, Issue 2 (March/April 2017), Volume 25.
60. The work was published in 1716 by the London printer John Grantham of Paternoster Row.
61. For more detailed treatment of this poetic exchange see Maher, R. K., 'Poems from the prison yard – a poetic correspondence between Charles Wogan and William Tunstall', *History Ireland*, Issue 2 (March/April 2017), Volume 25.
62. Anonymous, *The Secret History of the Rebels in Newgate*, 1717, p.7.
63. Ibid., p.8.
64. Ibid.
65. Ibid., p.9.
66. Ibid., p.10.
67. Tayler, H., *Jacobite Epilogue*, p.276.
68. *The Wogan Manuscript*, Galway, Kilmacduagh and Kilfenora Diocesan Archives, p.6.
69. Ibid.
70. Anonymous, *The Secret History*, p.38.
71. Seccombe, T., 'Oxburgh, Henry', in *Dictionary of National Biography*, 1885–1900, Volume 43.

72. Tayler, H., *Jacobite Epilogue*, p.277. Wogan was detained for a further year.
73. Ó Ciardha, Éamonn, *Ireland and the Jacobite Cause, 1685–1766: A Fatal Attachment*, pp.171–172.
74. *The Wogan Manuscript*, p.7.
75. Ibid., pp.6–7.
76. Winch, C., (trans.), *The Rescue of Princess Clementina (Stuart): A 1719 Adventure of the Irish Brigades*, by Sir Charles Wogan, (Belfast Historical & Educational Society, 2008), p.47.
77. Norfolk himself was held in 1722 under suspicion of involvement in the Layer Plot, in which both Nicholas and Charles Wogan were involved. See Ó Ciardha, Éamonn, *Ireland and the Jacobite Cause*, pp.200–201. See also Cruickshanks, E., & Erskine-Hill, H., *The Atterbury Plot*, pp.107 and 166–167.
78. *The Wogan Manuscript*, p 4.
79. Winch, C., *The Rescue*, p.47.
80. 'Gordon to Paterson', Paris, 8 July 1716, Historical Manuscript Commission, *Calendar of Stuart Papers* Vol. II, (London, 1904), p.261; hereafter HMC, *Stuart Papers*.
81. Gaydon provided a valuable avenue of intelligence to Wogan while the latter was based in Lyons. The subjects varied from international relations relating to George I and his Hanoverian territory, ongoing talks between major powers at the time, and the rumours of the break-up of the Irish regiments in the French service as a result of the Treaty of Utrecht. Wogan to Mar, Lyons, 18th December 1716, HMC, *Stuart Papers*, II, pp 322–323.
82. 'Wogan to Mar', Lyons, 21 November 1716, HMC, *Stuart Papers*, Vol. II, p.242.
83. 'Mar to Wogan', Avignon, 1 February 1717, HMC *Stuart Papers*, Vol. II, p.496. It appears that assassins had been intercepted *en route* to Avignon and that was the reason for the relocation of James's court to Bologna. Also see Corp, E., *The Jacobites at Urbino, An Exiled Court in Transition*, (Basingstoke, 2009), p.20 and McLynn, F., *The Jacobites*, (London, 1985), p.162.

84. 'Patterson to Mar', 5 June 1717, HMC, *Stuart Papers*, Vol. IV, (London, 1910), p.319.
85. Wills, R., *The Jacobites and Russia 1715–1750*, (East Lothian, 2002), p.57.
86. 'Mar to Ormonde', Friday, 22 July 1718, HMC, *Stuart Papers*, Vol. VII, (London, 1923), p.73. Therein, passing reference is made to Wogan having taken trips into the countryside around Rome in the recent past.
87. For thorough treatment of the political, diplomatic, strategic and military situation in Europe at that time, see Downey, D. M., 'The Habsburg-Hanoverian Alliance and its perspective on the Stuart-Sobieski match' in Maher, R. K. (ed.), *The Irish to the Rescue: the Tercentenary of the Polish Princess Clementina's Escape*, (Oxford, 2021), pp.95–119.
88. Wills, R., *The Jacobites and Russia*, (East Linton, 2002), pp.57–60.
89. Ibid.
90. Tayler, H., *The Jacobite Court at Rome, 1719*, (Publications of the Scottish History Society, Third Series, Volume XXXI, Edinburgh, 1938), Part I, pp.6, 7.
91. Ohlau (Oława) is in modern-day Poland, but at the time was a part of the Holy Roman Empire.
92. Tayler, H., *The Jacobite Court at Rome, 1719*, Part I, pp.7–8.
93. 'Mar to Ormond', 22 July 1718, HMC, *Stuart Papers*, Vol. VII, p.73.
94. Corp, E., *The Jacobites at Urbino*, (Basingstoke, 2009), p.57.
95. 'Mar to Ormond', 22 July 1718, HMC, *Stuart Papers*, Vol. VII, p.73.
96. Ibid.
97. Kernan, V., *The Duel in European History: Honour and the Reign of Aristocracy*, (London, 2016), pp.165–184.
98. 'Mar to Ormond', 22 July 1718, HMC, *Stuart Papers*, Vol. VII, p.73.
99. Maher, R., 'A Duel Between Jacobites' at 8th Annual Tudor and Stuart Ireland Interdisciplinary Conference, Queen's University Belfast (August, 2018). Available at https://soundcloud.com/history-hub/richard-maher-a-duel-between-jacobites.
100. Flood, J., *The Life of Chevalier Charles Wogan, an Irish Soldier of Fortune*, (Dublin, 1922), p.27.

101. Tayler, H., *The Jacobite Court at Rome, 1719*, Part I, p.22.
102. Ibid.
103. Bruce, N. 'The Duke of Mar in Exile, 1716–32', in *Transactions of the Royal Historical Society*, Fourth Series, Vol. 20, (December, 1937), pp.61–82.
104. Despite his indignance, he had written in cipher to the Duke of Mar while at Ohlau that 'this is a terrible weight for Wogan to carry. Wogan wishes most ardently that some person of more merit and conduct were charged with it'. See 'Wogan to Mar', 30 December 1718, Ohlau, HMC Stuart Papers VII, p.695.
105. Winch, C., *The Rescue*, p.43.
106. Tayler, H., *The Jacobite Court at Rome, 1719*, Part I, p.25.
107. Winch, C., *The Rescue*, p.45.
108. Williams, B., *Stanhope: A Study in Eighteenth-Century War and Diplomacy*, (Oxford, 1932), p.273.
109. Black, J., 'The Catholic Threat and the British Press in the 1720s and 1730s', in *Journal of Religious History*, Vol. 12, Issue 4, (December 1983), p.371.
110. Williams, B., *Stanhope*, p.33.
111. The details of Clementina's detention requires further investigation. I contacted the curator of the Schloss Ambras who confirmed that the princess had not been detained there. He suggested that the Palais Spaur was far more likely at that time. In her book, Cathy Winch refers to an article titled *An Unwilling Polish Guest* authored by Ms Josefine Justic in which this location is mentioned. It is corroborated by Wogan's own account placing this location just outside the old city walls; see Winch, C., (trans.), *The Rescue of Princess Clementina (Stuart): A 1719 Adventure of the Irish Brigades*, by Sir Charles Wogan, (Belfast Historical & Educational Society, 2008), p.25.
112. Flood, J., *The Life of Chevalier Charles Wogan*, pp.28–29.
113. Williams, B., *Stanhope*, p.338. See also Wogan, C., *Female Fortitude*, (London, 1722), p.10.
114. Corp, E., 'The Location of the Stuart Court in Rome: The Palazzo del Re', in Monod, Pittock, and Szechi, *Loyalty and Identity*, pp.180–181.

115. Amhurst, N. (ed.), 'An Epistle from the Princess Sobieski [*sic*] to the Chevalier de St. George', in *Poems on Several Occasions*, (London,1721), Bodleian Library, Oxford.
116. Gilbert, J. T., *Narratives of the Detention, Liberation, and Marriage of Maria Clementina Stuart, styled Queen of Great Britain and Ireland, with contemporary letters and papers for the first time published*, (Dublin, 1894).
117. Miller, P., *A Wife for the Pretender*, (London, 1965), p.7.
118. Winch, C., *The Rescue*, p.73.
119. Ibid., pp.150–151.
120. Carroll, C. L., 'The Romance and Disillusionment of Exile: Charles Wogan and his Memoir of Clementina Sobieska' in Carroll, C. L., *Exiles in a Global City: The Irish in Early Modern Rome, 1609–1783*, (Boston, 2018), pp.232–256. See also *Female Fortitude, exemplify'd, in an impartial narrative, of the seizure, escape and marriage of the Princess Clementina Sobieska, as it was particularly set down by Mr. Charles Wogan ... who was a chief manager in that whole affair*, (London, 1722), reprinted in USA by Gale, Eighteenth Century Collection Online, Print editions.
121. Winch, C., *The Rescue*, p.51.
122. The tent itself is on display to the public at Wawel Castle in Kracow, Poland. See *Ottoman Turkish Tents*, Wawel Castle, accessed on 10/11/2024, available at https://wawel.krakow.pl/en/exhibition-constant/ottoman-tukish-tents.
123. Wogan mentions this 'priceless' item in his 1744 version of the rescue. However, in his correspondence with the Stuart court in Rome, he wrote that the snuff box was only worth ten pistoles in value and later wrote that after he accepted it he'd promised to give it to King James, see 'Wogan to Mar', 30 December 1718, Ohlau, HMC, Stuart Papers VII, pp.694–696. The snuff box is not listed among King James's possessions at the time of his death in 1766 as published in Edward Corp's *The Stuarts in Italy, 1719–1766*.
124. The order is signed: Made in our castle of Ohlau in Silesia, this 2nd January, 1719 – Jacques Louis, royal Prince of the Kingdom

of Poland and the grand Duchy of Lithuania; see Winch, C., *The Rescue*, p.151.

125. Corp, E., *The Stuarts in Italy*, p.133. In the account of Clementina's rescue and escape titled *Female Fortitude* (1722), the very same Vizzozi is identified as having been instrumental in the escape of William Maxwell, fifth Earl of Nithsdale, from the Tower of London in 1716.
126. Wogan, C., *Female Fortitude*, (London, 1722), p.17.
127. Winch, C., *The Rescue*, p.77.
128. The author is grateful to Peter Lang Ltd for granting their permission to reuse a section of a chapter already published in Maher, R. K., 'The Rescue and Escape of Princess Clementina', in Maher, R. K., (ed.), *The Irish to the Rescue: The Tercentenary of the Polish Princess Clementina's Escape*, (Oxford, 2021), pp.61–72. ISBN 978-1-78997-932-9.
129. Eau de Carmes is still produced today.
130. I am grateful to Mr Alexander von Peez for his inquiry into this place name. There is no record of a town with this name on the escape route anymore. It is possible that the name of the town was changed in the intervening years. Possible other forms are Welschmuehle / Walhazmuehle. The term 'Walhaz' yields fascinating information reaching into antiquity relating to ancient people who inhabited the region. 'Muehle' can be translated as 'Mill'.
131. The public seminar which took place at Europe House in Dublin to celebrate the tercentenary of Clementina's rescue and escape was held on 30 April 2019, 300 years ago to the day that the rescue mission succeeded and Clementina escaped Imperial territory.
132. Ibid.
133. 'The Narrative of Lord Pitsligo', in Tayler, H., *The Jacobite Court at Rome, 1719*, Part I, p.61.
134. 'The Narrative of Lord Pitsligo', in Tayler, H., *The Jacobite Court at Rome, 1719*, Part I, p.61 (see footnotes indicated by * on page 61).
135. Ibid.
136. *NLI*, P 511, MS No. 19, p 846.

137. Flood, J., *The Life of Chevalier Charles Wogan*, p.101. See also *The Wogan Manuscript*, pp.22–23 passim.
138. 'Francesco Bianchini to James III', 16 June 1719, Archivio Segreto Vaticano, Segretaria di Stato, Inghilterra, 1700–1745, pp.21, 123–126. The author gives hearty thanks to Dr Declan Downey, who generously gave his time to accompany me to the Archivio Segreto Vaticano in search of further documents on Wogan.
139. Tayler, H., *The Jacobite Court at Rome, 1719*, Part II, p.169.
140. 'James Murray to the King', August 10, 1719, in Tayler, H., *The Jacobite Court at Rome, 1719*, Part II, p.173.
141. 'The Narrative of Lord Pitsligo', in Tayler, H., *The Jacobite Court at Rome, 1719*, Part I, pp 62–63 (see footnotes indicated by ‡ on pages 62–63).
142. Szechi, Daniel, '"Cam Ye O'er Frae France?" Exile and the Mind of Scottish Jacobitism', *Journal of British Studies*, Vol. 37, No. 4, (October, 1998), pp.373–374.
143. Tayler, H., *The Jacobite Court at Rome, 1719*, Part I, p.69.
144. Gilbert, J. T., '*Narratives of the Detention, Liberation and Marriage of Maria Clementina Stuart'*, p.207. TCD MS 7574, *The Marriage Certificate of James Stuart III and Queen Maria Clementina*, pp.207.
145. Flood, J., *The Life of Chevalier Charles Wogan*, p.110.
146. National Library of Ireland, MS 8340.
147. Tayler, H., *The Jacobite Court at Rome, 1719*, Part I, p.92.
148. The attendant who had been with the princesses during their captivity in Innsbruck.
149. Tayler, H., *The Jacobite Court at Rome, 1719*, Part I, p.95. Not only did Misset, a 37-year-old captain of Dillon's Regiment, recently knighted and made a Senator of Rome, entertain his new queen by effectively impersonating Murray and his haughty nonsense, he did it again for Lord Pitsligo at Leghorn. Nicholas Wogan had obviously paid his respects to the new queen in Rome before returning to France.
150. 'Mar to John Hay', April 19, 1722, Paris, in Tayler, H., *The Jacobite Court at Rome, 1719*, Part II, pp.210–214.

151. Corp, E., 'Murray, James, Jacobite first earl of Dunbar (1690–1770)', in *Oxford Dictionary of National Biography*, accessed 25 July 2014, available at http://www.oxforddnb.com/view/article/92615, accessed 25 July 2014.
152. Flood, J., *The Life of Chevalier Charles Wogan*, p.111.
153. 'The Narrative of Lord Pitsligo', in Tayler, H., *The Jacobite Court at Rome, 1719*, Part I, pp.74–75.
154. 'Wogan to Arthur Dillon', 27 December 1723, Royal Archive: Stuart Papers, Main Series.Vol.233, *Manuscript papers, May 20 – Jun 30 1720; hereafter RA SP/MAIN/47 f52–53.*
155. 'Wogan to James III', 28 May 1720, Villafranca (RA SP/MAIN/47 f32–33).
156. 'Wogan to James III', 3 June 1720, Villafranca (RA SP/MAIN/47 f52–53).
157. Ibid.
158. 'James III to Wogan', 21 July 1720, Rome (RA SP/MAIN/48 f.54–55).
159. 'Wogan to James III', 3 June 1720, Villafranca (RA SP/MAIN/47 f.52–53). See also Tayler, H., *Jacobite Epilogue*, p.281.
160. 'Wogan to Edgar', 31 May 1732, Valencia (RA/SP/MAIN/153 f.175–176).
161. Ibid.
162. For the full lineage of the Irlanda regiment, see Downey, D. M., 'Beneath the Harp and Burgundian Cross: Irish Regiments in the Spanish Bourbon Army, 1700–1818', in O'Donnell, H., (ed.) *The Irish Presence in the Spanish Military – 16th to 20th Centuries*, (Madrid, 2014), pp.92–93.
163. Downey, D. M., 'Beneath the Harp', p.91.
164. Tayler, H., *Jacobite Epilogue*, p.284.
165. This subject has been discussed in excellent detail by Professor Edward Corp in *The Stuarts in Italy, 1719–1766.*
166. Corp, E., *The Stuarts in Italy*, p.142; see also footnote 26, pp.142–143.
167. Ibid., p 140.

168. Ibid., p 141.
169. Ibid., p 142.
170. 'Wogan to James III', 20 February 1721, Cartagena, *RA SP/MAIN/52 f.37–38*.
171. Corp, *The Stuarts in Italy*, p.143.
172. Ibid.
173. Ibid.
174. Ibid.
175. Ibid., p.144
176. Carroll, C. L., *Exiles in a Global City*, p.248. The letter is quoted from the Lockhart papers, published 1887.
177. 'Wogan to Gualtiero', Livorno, 30 April 1722, *Papers of Cardinal Gualtiero*, British Library, Additional Manuscripts, 20310, f.308, 309. The final paragraph of this letter gives a bizarre account of an imposter from Vienna who posed as Wogan's brother, borrowing money from a 'German Prince' and getting his food and transportation paid for him to travel to Rome. James III, John Hay and Cardinal Gualtiero were asked to track him down and 'have him punished for trickery and arrogance'.
178. Tayler, H., *Lady Nithsdale and her Family*, (London, 1939), p.146.
179. Warrant to Sir Charles Wogan, (RA SP/MAIN/20 f.133.)
180. 'Wogan to James III', 19 December 1722 (RA SP/MAIN/64 f.21–22).
181. Ibid.
182. Odriscol, Ana, *Archivo General de Palacio*, ES.28079/AGP, Personal, Caja 16813 Exp. 03. Anne's first task in her position would be to meet the young Princess Mariana Victoria at the border with France to escort her back to Madrid. Princess Mariana had been betrothed to the young Louis XV from childhood. In 1725 Louis XV abruptly ended the betrothal , but she would go on to marry José Francisco António Inácio Norbérto Agostinho (Joseph I) to become queen of Portugal.
183. 'Wogan to James III', 19 December 1722 (RA SP/MAIN/64 f.21–22).

184. 'Wogan to Gualtiero', 12 April 1723, El Escorial (*Gualtiero*, BL, Add. Ms., 20310, f.337); and 'Wogan to Gualtiero', 12 April 1723, El Escorial (*Gualtiero*, BL, Add. Ms., 20310, f.337).
185. An interesting comment in Britannica states that the British secret service was more efficient during this period than during World War II; see 18th Century Britain, 1714–1815 'Britain from 1715 to 1742: The Supremacy of the Whigs', in *Britannica*, accessed 28/6/2023, available at https://www.britannica.com/place/United-Kingdom/18th-century-Britain-1714-1815#ref483223.
186. 'Mottram to Walpole', 11 October 1724, Fontainebleau, Newcastle Papers Vol. LVI. Brit. Mus. Add. Ms. 32741, 245, pp.108–116.
187. Extracts 24 April/5 May 1722, *Jacobite Correspondence 1722*, British Library, Brit. Mus., Stowe 250, f. 10.
188. Ibid.
189. Extract, June 1722, *Jacobite Correspondence 1722*, B.L., Brit. Mus., Stowe 250, f. 43.
190. Extract, Stanhope, 8 June 1722, Madrid, *Jacobite Correspondence 1722*, B.L., Brit. Mus., Stowe 250, f. 83.
191. Extract, 18 July 1722, Rome, *Jacobite Correspondence 1722*, B.L., Brit. Mus., Stowe 250, f. 85.
192. Extract, Crawford, 24 June 1722, Paris, *Jacobite Correspondence 1722*, B.L., Brit. Mus., Stowe 250, f. 85.
193. Extract, 10 August 1722, La Corunna, *Jacobite Correspondence 1722*, B.L., Brit. Mus., Stowe 250, f. 89.
194. Extract, 10 August 1722, Bilbao, *Jacobite Correspondence 1722*, B.L., Brit. Mus., Stowe 250, f. 89.
195. Extract, 12 August 1722, Bilbao, *Jacobite Correspondence 1722*, B.L., Brit. Mus., Stowe 250, f. 90.
196. Extract, 16 August 1722, Bilbao, *Jacobite Correspondence 1722*, B.L., Brit. Mus., Stowe 250, f. 95.
197. Tayler, H., *Jacobite Epilogue*, pp.289–290.
198. 'Wogan to Dillon', 24 January 1724 (RA SP/MAIN/47 f.45–46).
199. A note in one of Wogan's letters mentions that Anne had been born in St-Germain, so there should be an entry in the parish register there for her birth. Her maiden name and her age are unknown,

however. In order to find that information it will be necessary to find the entry of their marriage in the parish register of the church in which they were married. It may also be recorded on the papal dispensation, which should be archived in Toledo.

200. 'Hay to Wogan', 28 October 1724, Albano (RA SP/MAIN/47 f.71).
201. Charles's brother, Nicholas, visited the court a few days before Hay penned this letter; he said he was going to Naples in the company of a Mr Carrey and didn't expect to see him in Rome until after the winter.
202. 'Hay to Wogan', 9 December 1724, Rome (RA SP/MAIN/47 f.71–72). He also confirmed that the Stuart court would forward Lady Misset's pay for the new year as per Wogan's request. This might be further evidence of the delay of pay from the Spanish military for Sir John.
203. 'Wogan to Hay', 13 January 1725, Madrid (RA SP/MAIN/79 f.33–34).
204. This was quite a sum of money. To put it into perspective, Philip V sent 100,000 crowns to Prince Charles Edward in Scotland during the 'Forty-five'.
205. Tayler, H., *Jacobite Epilogue*, p.299.
206. There is no record of Anne having been married to her previous husband at the Royal Chapel of the Palace of Madrid. Other O'Driscoll men appear in the records at Simancas as military officers: Dionesio, Eneas and Alejandro but these appear in the records in the mid-seventeenth century. If Anne didn't marry Cornelius then it could be possible that she married the son of one of the other men.
207. Ibid. The author thanks Mr Rafael Torres of Madrid for explaining this cultural characteristic to me. He said that the term to describe it is *vuelva usted manaña* (come back tomorrow) and it was first described in writing in a short story by Mariano Jose de Larra.
208. 'Wogan to Hay', 13 January 1725, Madrid, RA SP/MAIN/79 f.33–34. As always, James III did everything he could to help, including sending a personal note to Philip V to expedite things. All the

correspondence referred to has cordial messages of good wished from the Missets in Spain, returned by James III and Hay in Rome.

209. Ibid.
210. Ibid.
211. Referred to by Kevin Whelan as an underground gentry, see Whelan, K., 'An underground gentry? Catholic middlemen in eighteenth-century Ireland', in *Eighteenth-Century Ireland*, Vol. X (1995). pp.7–68. See also Garnham, N., 'How Violent Was Eighteenth-Century Ireland?', *Irish Historical Studies*, Vol. 30, No. 119 (May, 1997), p.377, footnote 2.
212. 'Wogan to Hay', 13 January 1725, Madrid (RA SP/MAIN/79 f.33–34).
213. Ibid.
214. 'Hay to Wogan', 28 January 1725, Rome (RA SP/MAIN/79 f.104–105).
215. 'Wogan to Hay', 24 March 1725, Madrid (RA SP/MAIN/80 f.22–23).
216. Ibid.
217. 'Wogan to Hay', 13 April 1725, Madrid (RA SP/MAIN/81 f.79–80).
218. Ibid.
219. Ibid.
220. Ibid.
221. Though he had a lot more waiting to do in Spain, this early mention of Don Quixote might indicate his induction to the mock chivalric Order of Toboso.
222. 'Wogan to James III', 24 March 1725, Madrid (RA SP/MAIN/81 f.21–22).
223. 'Wogan to Gualtiero', 21 September 1725, Madrid, *Papers of Cardinal Gualtiero*, (B. L., Add. Ms. 20310 f.365).
224. Henry Benedict Stuart, Duke of York, was born in Rome on 6 March 1725.
225. 'Hay to Wogan', 2 June 1725, Rome (RA SP/MAIN/82 f.84–85).
226. Mar purportedly caused the failure of the Atterbury plot in order to obtain this and received a pension from the British government after that.

227. 'Wogan to Hay', 13 April 1725, Madrid (RA SP/MAIN/81 f.79–80).
228. 'Wogan to Hay', 15 July 1725, Madrid (RA SP/MAIN/84 f.43–44).
229. Ibid.
230. Ibid.
231. Ibid.
232. Ibid.
233. Ibid.
234. 'Wogan to Hay', 8 September 1725 (RA SP/MAIN/85 f.154–155).
235. Ibid.
236. Ibid.
237. 'Wogan to Hay', 21 September 1725 (RA SP/MAIN/86 f.46–47).
238. Ibid.
239. Ibid.
240. 'Wogan to Hay', 21 September 1725 (RA SP/MAIN/86 f.46–47). He also asks to be remembered to William Tunstall, the gentleman with whom he had a poetic correspondence while both were in imprisoned after the 'Fifteen'.
241. Ibid.
242. 'Wogan to Hay', 4 December 1725 (RA SP/MAIN/86 f.152–153).
243. 'Wogan to Hay', 27 March 1726 (RA SP/MAIN/91 f.105–106).
244. Ibid.
245. 'Wogan to James III', 3 April 1726, Mequinenza (RA SP/MAIN/92 f.100–101).
246. 'Hay to Wogan', 18 May 1726, Rome (RA SP/MAIN/94 f.7–8).
247. Melville, L., *The Life and Writings of Philip, Duke of Wharton*, (London, 1913), p.12. This source contains letters between the duke and high profile Jacobites and his unsteady relationship with James III. Wharton's relationship to Swift and Wogan, and their connections with the Freemasons is discussed in chapter 11.
248. 'Wogan to Hay', 23 April 1726, Mequinenza (RA SP/MAIN/93 f.20–21).
249. Melville, L., *Duke of Wharton*, p.191.
250. Raymond Macdonnell had a successful military career in Spain. He married a *camarista* of Queen Elizabeth Farnese and his

daughters, Clementina, Maria, and Maria Jacoba later became *camaristas* in the queen's household. Wogan corresponded with the Duke of Wharton as is seen in *The Wogan Manuscript*. John Hay wrote to Wogan in a letter that it was a pity he hadn't had the chance to meet him because he'd heard that he was 'one of the cleverest geniuses in Europe' – see 'Hay to Wogan', 18 May 1726, Rome (RA SP/MAIN/94 f.7–8).

251. 'Wogan to Hay', 24 April 1726, Mequinenza (RA SP/MAIN/93 f.22–23).
252. 'Wogan to Hay', 1 May 1726, Mequinenza (RA SP/MAIN/93 f.54–55).
253. Ibid.
254. 'Hay to Wogan', 18 May 1726, Rome (RA SP/MAIN/94 f.7–8). James Wogan would later inherit the knighthood/baronetcy after his father's death.
255. 'Wogan to Hay', 29 May 1726, Mequinenza (RA SP/MAIN/94 f.44–45).
256. 'Wogan to James III', 5 July 1727, Monzón (RA SP/MAIN/108 f.31–32).
257. 'Jaime Wogan', AGS, SGU, Leg. 2588, 003, f. 28.
258. 'Diego Wogan', AGS, SGU, Leg. 2668, 001, f. 53.
259. Ibid.
260. 'Wogan to James III', 23 August 1746, San Clemente (RA/SP/MAIN/276 f.110–111).
261. 'Wogan to James III', 8 December 1744, San Clemente (RA/SP/MAIN/260 f.118–119).
262. 'Wogan to James III', 5 November 1745, El Escorial (RA/SP/MAIN/271 f.5–6).
263. Odriscol Wogan Ana, AHN, Consejos, ES. 28079, OM-Casamiento_Santiago, Exp. 10319, accessed on [21/4/2025], available at https://pares.mcu.es/ParesBusquedas20/catalogo/description/1724364?nm.
264. 'Wogan to Hay', 6 August 1726 (RA/SP/MAIN/96 f.84–85).
265. 'Wogan to Edgar', 21 January 1730, Zaragoza (RA/SP/MAIN/132 f.129–130).

266. 'Wogan to Hay', 6 August 1726 (RA/SP/MAIN/96 f.18–19); see also 'Wogan to Edgar', 18 April 1732, Valencia (RA/SP/MAIN/143 f.126–127).
267. 'Wogan to Hay', 30 July 1726 (RA/SP/MAIN/92 f.139–140).
268. 'Wogan to Hay', 6 August 1726 (RA/SP/MAIN/96 f.18–19).
269. Ibid.
270. A unit of currency used in Hispanic America.
271. 'Wogan to Gualtiero', 17 January 1727, Monzón, *Papers of Cardinal Gualtiero*, (B. L., Add. Ms. 20310 f.392). Apparently the Duke of Wharton was present at the siege, walked right up to the British defences declaring King James III as the only true King of Britain and Ireland, showed the garter on his leg, and then had to withdraw from the field after getting wounded in the toe! Keith-Schuchard, M., 'Jonathan Swift, The Earl of Rosse, Duke of Wharton, and Sir Charles Wogan: the Irish-Spanish Masonic Connection' in *Revista de Estudios Históricos de la Masonería Latinoamericana y Caribeña*, Vol. 13, No. 1 (January-June), 2021, p.180.
272. 'Wogan to Edgar', 28 April 1730, Monzon (RA/SP/MAIN/136 f.30–31).
273. 'Wogan to Hay', 22 August 1726 (RA/SP/MAIN/96 f.84–85).
274. 'Wogan to Dillon', 6 December 1723 (RA/SP/MAIN/71 f.4–5).
275. Ibid.
276. 'Wogan to Dillon', 20 December, 1723 (RA/SP/MAIN/71 f.73–74).
277. Ibid.
278. Ibid.
279. 'Wogan to Hay', 22 August 1726 (RA/SP/MAIN/96 f.84–85).
280. The following year he would complain to James that some of his pay was twelve months in arrears; 'Wogan to James III', 10 December 1727, RA/SP/MAIN/122 f.102–103).
281. 'Wogan to Hay', 22 August 1726 (RA/SP/MAIN/96 f.84–85).
282. 'Wogan to Hay', 6 August 1726 (RA/SP/MAIN/96 f.18–19).
283. 'Wogan to Hay', 22 August 1726 (RA/SP/MAIN/96 f.84–85).
284. 'Edgar to Wogan', 6 December 1728, Bologna (RA/SP/MAIN/122 f.71–72). John Hay had recently been dismissed from his post as James III's secretary of state.

285. 'Wogan to Hay', 30 July 1726 (RA/SP/MAIN/92 f.139–140).
286. 'Wogan to Edgar', 20 December 1728, Jaca (RA/SP/MAIN/124 f.153–154).
287. Ibid.
288. 'Wogan to James III', 10 May 1729, Jaca (RA/SP/MAIN/127 f.152–153).
289. Ibid.
290. Ibid.
291. 'Wogan to Edgar', 18 May 1729 (RA/SP/MAIN/128 f.34–35).
292. 'Wogan to Hay', 22 August 1726 (RA/SP/MAIN/96 f.84–85).
293. 'Wogan to Edgar', 18 May 1729 (RA/SP/MAIN/128 f.34–35).
294. 'Wogan to Hay', 22 August 1726 (RA/SP/MAIN/96 f.84–85).
295. Ibid.
296. 'Wogan to James III', 10 May 1729, Jaca (RA/SP/MAIN/127 f.152–153).
297. Ibid.
298. 'Wogan to Hay', 22 August 1726 (RA/SP/MAIN/96 f.84–85); see also 'Wogan to Edgar', 21 January 1730, Zaragoza RA/SP/MAIN/132 f.129–130).
299. 'Wogan to Edgar', 21 January 1730, Zaragoza (RA/SP/MAIN/132 f.129–130).
300. 'Wogan to James III', 10 May 1729, Jaca (RA/SP/MAIN/127 f.152–153).
301. Gaelic for 'West Connaught'.
302. 'Wogan to James III', 10 May 1729, Jaca (RA/SP/MAIN/127 f.152–153).
303. Ibid.
304. Ibid.
305. 'Wogan to James III', 10 May 1729, Jaca (RA/SP/MAIN/127 f.152–153).
306. Ibid.
307. Ibid.
308. Part of that plot had been that his cousin, Nicholas, and brother, Nicholas, would ship battalions of Irish troops from the Mediterranean to Britain to join Ormonde's main landing there.

He mentions a Colonel O'Brian, then Governor of Malaga, had prepared this plot under the guise of preparing the Madagascar Expedition. 'Wogan to James III', 10 May 1729, Jaca (RA/SP/MAIN/127 f.152–153); see also 'Wogan to Edgar', 18 April 1732, Valencia (*RA/SP/MAIN/143* f.126–127).

309. 'Wogan to James III', 10 May 1729, Jaca (*RA/SP/MAIN/127* f.152–153); see also 18 April 1732, 'Wogan to Edgar', Valencia (RA/SP/MAIN/143 f.126–127).
310. 'Wogan to Edgar', 15 December 1730, Morella (RA/SP/MAIN/140 f.206–207).
311. 'Wogan to James III', 20 December 1728, Jaca (RA/SP/MAIN/140 f.113–114).
312. To lighten the mood, Hay told how he was currently working with a 'physick' because he had taken very little exercise over the previous months and had become enormously fat, of which 'the honest woman [his wife] complains heavily.' See Hay to Wogan, 20 November 1726, Rome (RA/SP/MAIN/99 f.59–60).
313. 'Wogan to James III', 23 September 1729, Jaca (RA/SP/MAIN/130 f.167–166). One wonders if it was used by O'Kelly-Galway to write his *Historique Genealogique de la Famille de Wogan* or if it was purchased by Baron Tanneguannay de Wogan during his research on his ancestors, in which case it could be in a private archive in Belgium.
314. 'Wogan to James III', 23 September 1729, Jaca (RA/SP/MAIN/130 f.167–166).
315. 'James III to Wogan', 12 November 1729, Rome (RA/SP/MAIN/132 f.14–15).
316. 'Wogan to Gualtiero', 17 January 1727, Madrid, Papers of Cardinal Gualtiero, (B. L., Add. Ms. 20310 f.392.)
317. Ibid.
318. Though Wogan's father would have been particularly challenged to provide for his 32 children.
319. D'Arcy, F., *Exiles and Strangers*, p.178. D'Arcy noted that his death appeared in the press in Dublin.

320. 'Wogan to Hay', 22 August 1726 (RA/SP/MAIN/96 f.84–85). Details on the identity and career of Brigadier Campbell are obscure.
321. 'Wogan to Hay', 30 July 1726 (RA/SP/MAIN/92 f.139–140).
322. Ibid.
323. Richard Gaydon, a member of Clementina's rescue mission, later wrote his eyewitness account of the Siege of Cremona. The battalion of Dillon's Regiment suffered a casualty rate of over fifty percent but refused to surrender the Po Gate to Prince Eugene of Savoy. O'Mahony had an hour-long private audience with Louis XIV at Versailles so that the king could get a full account of the engagement. He was elevated and promoted the same day by the king and joined the forces of his nephew, Philip, to win the Kingdom of Spain during the War of the Spanish Succession. At long last, a meticulous study of Count Daniel O'Mahony is underway at the hands of Mr Mario Luis Lopés Durán. Ó Briain (ed.), 'The Chevalier Gaydon's memoir of the Regiment of Dillon, 1738' [In thirteen parts: III (11), pp.98–106 to VI (24)] in *The Irish Sword.*
324. The O'Sullivans of Bearehaven, County Cork, held this hereditary title since the arrival of their ancestor to Spain. Domhnall Ó Súilleabháin Mór was created a knight of the order of Santiago there in 1607. Philip III also bestowed on him the hereditary title Count of Bearhaven in the Spanish nobiliary system. See Walsh, *Spanish Knights of Irish Origin*, p.1. See also O'Byrne E., 'O'Sullivan Beare, Domhnall' in *Dictionary of Irish Biography*, originally published 2009, accessed on 23/11/2024, available at https://doi.org/10.3318/dib.007078.v1 on 23-11-2024.
325. 'Wogan to Edgar', 18 April 1732, Valencia (RA/SP/MAIN/143 f.126–127).
326. Ibid.
327. 'James III to Wogan', 3 August 1731, Rome (RA/SP/MAIN/151 f.100–103).
328. 'Wogan to Edgar', 18 April 1732, Valencia (RA/SP/MAIN/143 f.126–127).

329. 'Wogan to Edgar', 2 April 1732, Valencia (RA/SP/MAIN/152 f.135–136).
330. Ibid
331. 'Wogan to Edgar', 2 April 1732, Valencia (RA/SP/MAIN/152 f.135–136).
332. 'Wogan to Edgar', 31 May 1732, Valencia (RA/SP/MAIN/153 f.175–176).
333. Ibid.
334. AGS, SGU, Legajo 2598, f.4.
335. 'Wogan to Edgar', 31 May 1732, Valencia (RA/SP/MAIN/153 f.175–176). Daniel was third Count of Berehaven, a noble title of Castille granted in 1607 to his ancestor, Dónal Ó Súilleabhán, in recognition of the part he played defending Ireland against Elizabeth I's onslaught during the Nine Years' War. See Walsh, Micheline (ed.), *Spanish Knights of Irish Origin: documents from continental archives*, Vol. I, (Dublin, 1960), p.1.
336. Sanchez Doncel, G., *Presencia de España en Orán, 1509–1792*, (Toledo, 1991), pp.259–260.
337. Ibid.
338. Storrs, C., *The Spanish Resurgence, 1713–1748*, (Yale, 2016), pp.137–138.
339. Sanchez Doncel, G., *Presencia de España*, p.259.
340. *Diario del Expedicion de Oran de Montemar*, Archivo General de Simancas, Secretaria de Guerra, Legajo 482 Supplemental, f.24. Hereafter AGS, SGU, LEG, SUP.
341. Exertico de Valencia, Relacion de las familias a quienes se ha de asistian por la Thesoriria de Valencia con las cantidades que se expresaran, las mismas que descuenttan a los oficiales de los regimientos qui pasan a l'exercito de la expedicion y de avignades a las familias (AGS, SGU, SUP LEG 483).
342. Montemar, *Oran* (AGS, SGU, LEG 482, SUP, f.27R).
343. August 1732, Noticias (AGS, SGU, LEG, 485 SUP).
344. Montemar, *Oran* (AGS, SGU, LEG 482, SUP, f.29).
345. Montemar, *Oran* (AGS, SGU, LEG 482, SUP, f.44).

346. 'Contaminna to Patino', 24 July 1732, Alicante (AGS, SGU, LEG, SUP, 484).
347. Don Zenón de Somodevilla y Bengoechea, Marqués de la Ensenada, later a letter of recommendation for Wogan in the 1740s.
348. 'Doctor Don Andres Dominguez Barrajo y Sozel to José Contaminna', 1 August 1732, Oran (AGS, SGU, SUP, LEG 484).
349. 'Don Alfonso Rojo to Patino', 3 September 1732, Seville (AGS, SGU, LEG 4728); see also *Noticias* 19 December 1732 (AGS, SGU, LEG 4728).
350. 'Montemar to José Contaminna', 1 August 1732, Oran (AGS, SGU, SUP, LEG 484).
351. Ibid.
352. Doncel Sanchez, *Oran*, 266.
353. 'Santa Cruz to Patiño', 25 August 1732, Oran (AGS, SGU, LEG 4728).
354. 'Santa Cruz to Patiño', 20 August 1732, Oran (AGS, SGU, SUP, 485).
355. 'Santa Cruz to Patiño', 11 August 1732, Oran (AGS, SGU, SUP, 485). A curious aside in this letter mentions how Santa Cruz had heard criticism directed at him by an unnamed officer under his command in Oran. He identified the officer to Patiño as the one 'who wrote 8 letters on the 11th' and that 'I hope your excellency will deign to insinuate the officer … for men of notoriety and honour, what do the troops know of me, such words are not accurate'. This is really serious, as the reputation of the officer in question would be damaged permanently.
356. Santa Cruz to Patiño, 6 September 1732, Oran (AGS, SGU, 4728).
357. Santa Cruz to Patiño, September, Oran (AGS, SGU, SUP, 485).
358. Ibid.
359. Santa Cruz to Patiño, 19 September, Oran (AGS, SGU, SUP, 485).
360. 'Don Alfonso Rajo to Santa Cruz', 30 October 1732, Seville (AGS, SGU, SUP, 485).
361. 'Santa Cruz to Patiño', 27 October 1732, Oran (AGS, SGU, LEG 4728).

362. A group called *Miquelets de Catalunya* was founded in 2005 as a Catalan living history and historical reenactment group.
363. 'Ladron to Patiño', 7 January 1733, Oran (AGS, SGU, LEG 4733).
364. 20 August 1732, Cartagena (AGS, SGU, LEG, SUP, 485).
365. 'Santa Cruz to Patiño', September 1732 (AGS, SGU, LEG, SUP, 485).
366. Ladron, 7 January 1733, Oran (AGS, SGU, LEG 4733).
367. 'Santa Cruz to Patiño', 18 August 1732, Seville, (AGS, SGU, LEG, SUP, 485). See also 'Ladron to Patiño', December 1732, Oran (AGS, SGU, LEG 4728).
368. Doncel Sanchez, *Oran*, p.267.
369. Doncel Sanchez, *Oran*, p.268.
370. 'Santa Cruz to Patiño', 1 October, Oran (AGS, SGU, LEG 4728).
371. 'Santa Cruz to Patiño', 6 October, Oran (AGS, SGU, LEG 4728).
372. Ibid.
373. Ibid.
374. 'Wogan to Campoflorido', 8 October 1732, Oran (AGS, SGU, LEG, SUP, 487).
375. 'Al Marqués de Santa Cruz', 12 October 1732, Sevilla (AGS, SGU, LEG, SUP, 485).
376. 'Wogan to Campoflorido', 8 October 1732, Oran (AGS, SGU, LEG, SUP, 487).
377. 'Wogan to Campoflorido', 8 October 1732, Oran (AGS, SGU, LEG, SUP, 487).
378. Ibid.
379. Ibid.
380. Campoflorido to Patiño, 8 November 1732, Oran (AGS, SGU, LEG, SUP, 487).
381. To Campoflorido, 30 November 1732, Alicante (AGS, SGU, LEG, SUP, 487).
382. 'Wogan to Campoflorido', 13 November 1732, Oran (AGS, SGU, LEG, SUP, 487).
383. Ibid.
384. 'Wogan to Campoflorido', 13 November 1732, Oran (AGS, SGU, LEG, SUP, 487).

385. 'Wogan to James III', 22 June 1741, Barcelona (RA SP/MAIN/233 f.170–171).
386. To the Marqués de Villadarias, 18 December 1732, Seville (AGS, SGU, LEG 4728).
387. 'Santa Cruz to Patiño', 20 October 1732, Oran (AGS, SGU, SUP 485).
388. 'Ladron Y Guevara to Patiño', 12 December 1732, Oran (AGS, SGU, LEG 4728.
389. 'Ladron y Guevara to Patiño', 23 December, 1732, Oran (AGS, SGU, LEG 4728.
390. Scott, Sir Walter, *The works of Jonathan Swift: containing additional letters, tracts, and poems not hitherto published; with notes, and a life of the author*, 2nd Edition, 19 Volumes, (A. Constable & Co., 1824). Scott provides some commentary and context for Wogan's letters to Swift, which were later edited out and dismissed as 'screed' by David Woolley (see footnote 4).
391. Ó Ciardha, Éamonn, *Ireland and the Jacobite Cause*, p.171.
392. Ibid., p.172.
393. Woolley, David, (ed.), *The Correspondence of Jonathan Swift, D.D.*, Vol. III, (Frankfurt, 2007), p.514.
394. *The Wogan Manuscript*, p.20.
395. Ibid.
396. In one of the letters to the Stuart court shortly after his arrival in Spain he mentions having made Crofton's acquaintance and send his regards to Rome. 'Wogan to James III', 28 May 1720, Villafranca (RA SP/MAIN/47 f32–33.
397. *The Wogan Manuscript*, pp.42–43.
398. *The Wogan Manuscript*, p.22.
399. *The Wogan Manuscript*, pp.23 and 25; see also Hora, K., 'A Critical Discourse Analysis on Jonathan Swift's *Drapier's Letters*: Public advocacy and nationalism in Ireland, 1724–1725', in Somerville I., Edwards, L., and Øyvind I., (eds.), *Public Relations, Society and the Generative Power of History*, (London, 2019), p.199.
400. *The Wogan Manuscript*, p.23, 'Wogan to James III', 23 September 1729, Jaca (RA/*SP/MAIN/130* f.167–166.

401. Wogan, C., *Female Fortitude*, (London, 1722), p.4; see also Winch, C., *The Rescue*, p.43.
402. *The Wogan Manuscript*, p.31.
403. *The Wogan Manuscript*, p.27.
404. On page 30 of *The Wogan Manuscript*, Wogan mentions that he is ready to embark for Italy. Since he already mentioned the battle of 4 October 1732, it means he was ready to leave Oran after his tour of duty was completed. He left in March 1733.
405. Ibid.
406. Woolley, David, *The Correspondence of Jonathan Swift*, p.515.
407. *The Wogan Manuscript*.
408. Woolley, David, *The Correspondence of Jonathan Swift*, p.515.
409. Ó Ciardha, Éamonn, *Ireland and the Jacobite Cause*, p.216.
410. Milller, Peggy, *A Wife for the Pretender*, (London, 1965), p.155.
411. Winch, C., *The Rescue*, p.162.
412. Ibid., p.163.
413. Ibid.
414. Ibid., p.165.
415. Ibid., pp.165–166.
416. This community more or less included Swift!
417. Tadhg is a Gaelic Irish first name, pronounced using English phonetics as 'Tie-g'. The word Wogan quotes is still used as a derogatory term for Irish nationalists in Northern Ireland today. For a more detailed account of the New English in Ireland and their relationship with the British authorities, see Bartlett, T., *Ireland: a History*, (Cambridge, 2010), pp.155–157.
418. Winch, C., *The Rescue*, p.166.
419. Walter Scott noted Wogan's acute prejudice against Clarendon and the New-Irish but his writings facilitated an understanding of the experience of the Irish exiles; see Winch, C., *The Rescue*, pp.193–194.
420. Winch, C., *The Rescue*, pp.185–188.
421. Ibid., p.188.
422. Ibid., p.185.
423. Ibid., p.163.

424. Ibid., p.189.
425. Ibid., p.190.
426. Reasons Humbly Offered to the Parliament of Ireland for Repealing the Sacramental Test, in Favour of the Catholicks, Otherwise Called Roman Catholicks, and By their Ill-Willers, Papists, Drawn Partly from their Arguments as they are Catholicks, and Partly from Argument common of their Brethren the Common Dissenters, (1733).
427. Keith-Schuchard, M., *Masonic Rivalries and Literary Politics: from Jonathan Swift to Henry Fielding*, (2018), Chapter 13, p.20.
428. Wogan may be referring to poetry he composed while at Newgate, *Poems of Love and Gallantry*, which was published in 1716 by the London printer, John Grantham of Paternoster Row. Both prisoners wrote poems to each other while detained.
429. Woolley, David, *The Correspondence of Jonathan Swift*, p.591.
430. Flood, J., *The Life of Chevalier Charles Wogan*, (Dublin, 1922), p.125.
431. Winch, C., *The Rescue*, p.191.
432. Ibid.
433. Winch, C., *The Rescue*, p.192.
434. Ibid.
435. Keith-Schuchard, M., 'Jonathan Swift, The Earl of Rosse', p.180.
436. *The Wogan Manuscript*, p.40.
437. Knights of the order wore special rings. See Murdoch, S. (2010), 'Tilting at Windmills: The Order del Toboso as a Jacobite Social Network', in Monod, P., Pittock, M., and Szechi, D. (eds.) *Loyalty and Identity. Studies in Modern History*, (Palgrave Macmillan, London), https://doi.org/10.1057/9780230248571_13.
438. Keith Schuchard, M., 'Jonathan Swift, The Earl of Rosse', p.179.
439. Ibid., p.190.
440. Ibid., p.191.
441. According to Schuchard, Prince Charles Edward had been initiated into the Order of Toboso in 1732 and in 1745 would write to Wogan using Tobosan and Masonic references. See Keith-Schuchard, M., 'Jonathan Swift, The Earl of Rosse': the 'Irish-Spanish Masonic Connection', p.197.

442. 'James III to Wogan', 13 February 1733, Rome (RA/SP/MAIN159 f.83–84).
443. 'Wogan to Edgar', 18 March 1733, Valencia (RA/SP/MAIN160 f.40–41).
444. Ibid.
445. Ibid.
446. Ibid. Again, this item might have been auctioned locally after the death of James III in Rome in 1766.
447. On his military service record, dated May 1735, the last two documents contain the following: 'This captain is ill in Valencia, for which reason he has not been able to present the papers of his merit and services; for which reason and because the colonel of this regiment sealed himself with the books of the most recent antecedents, this page has been left blank'. The last document of his record is undated but probably is from 1736 and only contains the comment, 'He is in court having taken his papers'. He needed them to present all of them to obtain promotion in Madrid.
448. 'James III to Wogan', 3 October 1733, Albano (RA/SP/MAIN165 f.70–71). Dr James Wogan was appointed to the canonicate of Lille in 1738; see 'James Edgar to Wogan', 12 July 1738 (RA/SP/MAIN208 f.4–5).
449. Ibid.
450. A cilice is a barbed band that one can strap around one's leg to inflict pain on oneself. This was practiced by nuns and monks in order to bring the wearers closer to God through pain, emulating the experience of Jesus on the last day of his life.
451. Edward Corp has shown her deterioration in an excellent review of her portraits. See Corp, E., 'Clementina Sobieska at the Jacobite Court', in Maher, R. K., *The Irish to the Rescue; the Tercentenary of the Polish Princess Clementina's Escape*, (Oxford, 2021), pp.121–145. See also Corp, E., *The Stuarts in Italy*.
452. 'Wogan to Edgar', 25 February 1735, Madrid (RA/SP/MAIN178 f.13–14).
453. Ibid.
454. Ibid.

455. 'Wogan to Edgar', 10 December 1735 (RA/SP/MAIN184 f.115–116).
456. Ibid.
457. Ibid.
458. 'Wogan to James III', 22 June 1741, Barcelona (RA/SP/MAIN233 f.170–171).
459. 'Wogan to Edgar', 10 December 1735 (RA/SP/MAIN184 f.115–116).
460. 'James III to Wogan', 13 January 1736 (RA/SP/MAIN185 f.57–58). James may also have feared that Wogan would seek an accommodation with the British government.
461. 'Wogan to Edgar', 15 December 1736 (RA/SP/MAIN192 f.83–84). Perhaps Wogan's refusal to serve under Bourke in the early 1720s was what had cost him dearly.
462. 'Wogan to Edgar', 15 December 1736 (RA/SP/MAIN192 f.83–84).
463. Ibid.
464. 'Wogan to James III', 15 December 1736, Barcelona (RA/SP/MAIN192 f.84–85).
465. 'Wogan to James III', 1 March 1737, Barcelona (RA/SP/MAIN194 f.117–118).
466. Ibid. See also McCabe, J., *A Candic History of the Jesuits*, Vol. I, (London, 1913), p.272.
467. 'Wogan to James III', 1 March 1737, Barcelona (RA/SP/MAIN194 f.117–118).
468. Ibid.
469. 'Edgar to Wogan', 20 July 1737 (RA/SP/MAIN199 f.100–101).
470. 'Wogan to James III', 18 August 1737, Barcelona (RA/SP/MAIN200 f32–33). This would not happen since the duke had become Ambassador Extraordinaire of Spain to the Kingdom of Naples and would die there shortly afterwards.
471. 'Wogan to Edgar', 18 August 1737, Barcelona (RA/SP/MAIN206 f.33–34).
472. 'Wogan to James III', 18 August 1737, Barcelona (RA/SP/MAIN200 f32–33).

473. 'Wogan to Edgar', 18 August 1737, Barcelona (RA/SP/MAIN206 f.33–34).
474. Ibid.
475. Ibid.
476. 'Wogan to James Butler', 20 May 1739, Barcelona (RA/SP/MAIN215 f.170–171).
477. Ibid.
478. Ibid.
479. 'Wogan to James III', 6 September 1739, Barcelona (RA/SP/MAIN217 f.52–53).
480. Ibid.
481. 'Edgar to Wogan', 17 January 1740, Rome (RA/SP/MAIN219 f. 165–166). This is the last letter in which any reference is made to Anne O'Driscoll where Edgar passes on his regards to 'Lady Wogan'.
482. 'Edgar to Wogan', 2 November 1740, Rome (RA/SP/MAIN228 f.54–55).
483. 'Wogan to James III', 22 June 1741, Barcelona (RA/SP/MAIN233 f.170–171).
484. Ibid.
485. Ibid.
486. Ibid.
487. 'James III to Wogan', 24 July 1741 (RA/SP/MAIN234 f.204–205).
488. 'Edgar to Wogan', 20 July 1737 (RA/SP/MAIN199 f.100–101).
489. 'Edgar to Wogan', 15 January 1742 (RA/SP/MAIN239 f.78–79).
490. 'James III to Wogan', 14 February 1742 (RA/SP/MAIN240 f.11–12).
491. Ibid.
492. *Archivo Histórico Nacional*, Consejos, 31801, Exp. 3 Autos generales de la residencia que en la villa de San Clemente (Cuenca) tomó Carlos Wogan a Salvador Antonio Barnuevo, corregidor de ella, y demás ministros que debieron darla. This document contains 534 digital images relating to Wogan's government of La Mancha, available online here: https://pares.mcu.es/ParesBusquedas20/catalogo/show/6473322?nm.

493. 'Wogan to Edgar', 9 December 1744, San Clemente de La Mancha (RA/SP/MAIN/260 f.119–120).
494. 'Wogan to James III', 8 December 1744, San Clemente de La Mancha (RA/SP/MAIN/260 f.118–119).
495. Ibid.
496. The War of Jenkins Ear.
497. 'Wogan to James III', 8 December 1744, San Clemente de La Mancha (RA/SP/MAIN/260 f.118–119).
498. Ibid.
499. 'Edgar to Wogan', 26 January 1745, Rome (RA/SP/MAIN/262 f.53–54).
500. Ibid.
501. 'James III to Wogan', 29 January 1744, Rome (RA/SP/MAIN/262 f.42–43).
502. The opposing commander was an Irishman, Maximilian Ulysses von Browne, commander of the Austrian forces.
503. Downey, D. M., 'Beneath the Harp', p.93.
504. Charles VI's will that should he die without a male heir, his Imperial title should pass to his daughter, Maria Theresa.
505. A Nicholas Wogan of Galway is listed as having lost an arm at the battle. He was made a Chevalier de Saint Louis for his bravery and would later join Prince Charles Edward in Scotland. Charles had a younger brother Nicholas and a cousin, the heir to Rathcoffey, also named Nicholas. This Nicholas Wogan whose place of origin is listed as Galway is probably another relative of the same name.
506. 'Wogan to James III', 5 October 1745, San Ildefonso (RA/SP/MAIN/269 f.49–50).
507. Ibid.
508. Ibid.
509. Ibid.
510. Ibid.
511. Ibid.
512. Ibid.
513. 'Wogan to James III', 16 November 1745, El Escorial (RA/SP/MAIN/271 f.5–6).

514. Ibid.
515. Ibid.
516. Ibid.
517. *Galien le Restoré*, an Old French late-medieval romance or *chanson de geste* (a song of heroic deeds) had Galien as its hero. After many trials and dangers, battles and voyages he eventually ends up Emperor of Constantinople.
518. 'Wogan to James III', 16 November 1745, El Escorial (RA/SP/MAIN/271 f.5–6).
519. Ibid.
520. Ibid. See also 'Wogan to Prince Charles Edward', 10 December 1745, Madrid (SP 36/75/2 f.55).
521. 'Wogan to Prince Charles Edward', 10 December 1745, Madrid (SP 36/75/2 f.55)
522. 'Wogan to James III', 16 November 1745, El Escorial (RA/SP/MAIN/271 f.5–6).
523. Ibid.
524. 'Wogan to Prince Charles Edward', 10 December 1745, Madrid (SP 36/75/2 f.55).
525. Ibid.
526. 'James III to Wogan', 24 January 1746, Rome (RA SP/MAIN/271 f.101–102).
527. 'Wogan to Edgar', 15 December 1745, Madrid (RA SP/MAIN/271 f.100–101).
528. D'Arcy, F., *Exiles and Strangers*, p 183.
529. 'James III to Wogan', 24 January 1746, Rome (RA SP/MAIN/271 f.101–102).
530. 'James III to Wogan', 7 February 1746, Rome (RA SP/MAIN/272 f.142–143).
531. 'James III to Wogan', 25 April 1746, Rome (RA SP/MAIN/273 f.130–131).
532. 'Sir John Graeme to James III', 27 May 1746, Paris (RA/SP/MAIN274 f.146-147).
533. 'Warren to Wogan', 7 February 1747, Paris, in Lallement, L., 'Le Maréchal de Camp Baron de Warren, Correspondence et

Notes (de 1740 à 1775)', in Warren et Le Prince Charles-Édouard, *Extrait de Bulletin de la Société Polymathique du Morbihan*, Vol.1, (2 September 1892, Vannes, 1893), pp.77–78 passim; accessed at the Bibliothèque Nationale de France in Paris.

534. 'Wogan to James III', 13 July 1746, Paris (RA SP/MAIN/275 f.139–140).
535. 'James III to Wogan', 9 August 1746, Rome (RA SP/MAIN/276 f.57–58).
536. 'Wogan to Edgar', 23 August 1746, Madrid (RA SP/MAIN/276 f.109).
537. 'Wogan to Henry Benedict Stuart', 15 December 1746, San Clemente (RA SP/MAIN/279 f.105–105a).
538. Blaikie, W. B., *Itinerary of Prince Charles Edward Stuart from his landing in Scotland July 1745 to his departure in September 1746*, (Edinburgh, 1897), pp.100–101 passim. This psychological condition had affected his mother during her life as well.
539. 'Captain Hay to Duke of Newcastle', 15 October 1746, Edinburgh, quoted from the State Papers Domestic in Blaikie, *Itinerary of Prince Charles*, p.109.
540. 'Wogan to James III' 23 August 1746, Madrid (RA SP/MAIN/276 f.110–111).
541. Ibid.
542. Ibid.
543. Sheridan was one of the seven men of Moidart.
544. 'Wogan to Thomas Sheridan', 15 September 1746, San Clemente (RA SP/MAIN/277 f.34–35).
545. 'Wogan to Henry Benedict Stuart', 15 December 1746, San Clemente (RA SP/MAIN/279 f.105–105a).
546. 'Wogan to James III', 15 December 1746, San Clemente (RA/SP/MAIN/279 f.106–107).
547. 'James III to Wogan', 10 February 1747, Rome (RA/SP/MAIN281 f.79–80).
548. Ibid.
549. Law, 'Sir Charles Wogan', p.236.

550. 'Wogan to Warren', January 1747, Madrid, in Lallement, L., 'Le Maréchal de Camp Baron de Warren', p.75.
551. Ibid., p.76.
552. 'Warren to Wogan', 7 February 1747, Paris, in Lallement, L., 'Le Maréchal de Camp Baron de Warren', p.76.
553. Peace negotiations were underway at Breda to bring an end to the War of Austrian Succession; so the 'Forty-five' really was a late-taken chance to secure a Stuart restoration during that war.
554. 'Wogan to Warren', 13 April 1747, San Clemente, in Lallement, L., 'Le Maréchal de Camp Baron de Warren', p.79.
555. Ibid. The wording of the last sentence in French is 'ni le vieux Racoffy que les farces de ma jeunesse m'ont fait perdre'. A direct translation could be, 'nor Old Racoffy whom the pranks of my youth have made me lose'. Richard Hayes translated the French word 'farces' as 'wildness' so that in English it read 'which I lost through the wildness of my youth'. The author can find many different meanings for the word but concludes that Hayes's preference for the word 'wildness' is generous and subtracts some of the negative connotation which could be contained in the French word 'farces'. Wildness suggests the bold and reckless acts of a young man who simply didn't know any better. 'Follies' or 'pranks' have a much more negative connotation. Accuracy is crucial because this could be the only direct surviving indication that Wogan regretted his actions in service to the Jacobite cause given that he lost his inheritance as a result of them.
556. Lallement, L., 'Le Maréchal de Camp Baron de Warren', p.80.
557. Harris, E. T., 'Farinelli', in Stanley, S. and Tyrrell (eds.), *The New Grove Dictionary of Music and Musicians*, 2nd Edition, Vol. VIII, (London, 2001), pp.565–569.
558. 'Wogan to Warren', 13 April 1747, San Clemente, in Lallement, L., 'Le Maréchal de Camp Baron de Warren', p.79.
559. 'Edgar to Wogan', July 18 1747, Rome (RA SP/MAIN/285 f.153–154).

560. 'Edgar to Wogan', 21 January 1749, Rome (RA SP/MAIN/286 f..120–121).
561. Ibid.
562. One wonders whether the prince had ever heard that some in Avignon had been very critical of his decision to launch an insurrection in Scotland in 1745, as reported by Wogan in his letter to James III. See 'Wogan to James III', 16 November 1745, El Escorial (RA/SP/MAIN/271 f.5–6).
563. 'James III to Wogan', 21 January 1749, Rome (RA SP/MAIN/296 f.108–190).
564. 'Edgar to Wogan', 2 December 1749, Rome (RA SP/MAIN/301 f.140–141).
565. Ibid. See also 'Wogan to Edgar', 15 September 1750 (RA SP/MAIN/310 f.138–139).
566. 'James III to Wogan', 23 February 1750, Rome (RA SP/MAIN/304 f.77–78).
567. Maher, R. K., '"No Good Deed Goes Unpunished": Charles Wogan and his Removal from the Jacobite Court in Rome, June 1719', (M.A. Thesis, University College Dublin, 2013, unpublished).
568. Papal Nuncio to Spain.
569. 'Wogan to Edgar', 15 September 1750 (RA SP/MAIN/310 f.138–139).
570. Ibid.
571. Ibid.
572. 'Wogan to Edgar', 25 September 1750, Barcelona (RA SP/MAIN/311 f.35–37).
573. Harris, E. T., 'Farinelli', in Stanley, S. and Tyrrell (eds.), *The New Grove Dictionary of Music and Musicians*, 2nd Edition, Vol. VIII, (London, 2001), p.568.
574. 'Wogan to Edgar', 25 September 1750, Barcelona (RA SP/MAIN/311 f.35–37). This remark about the occasion being ill-timed might be directed at the fact that Prince Charles Edward's insurrection in Scotland had not been, in Wogan's view, properly planned.

575. Warrant or Writ to Charles Wogan, 10 November 1750, Royal Archive, Stuart Papers, Additional and Miscellaneous Material, Miscellaneous Volumes. Vol. 21: Warrant Book, 1719–1744 f.23.
576. 1 March 2022, Professor Dedieu of the University of Lyons confirmed these details with the author by personal communication.
577. 1 March 2022, Jean-Pierre Dedieu to Richard Maher, email communication. By means of the Fichoz database, Professor Dedieu was able to find the information relating to Wogan and also the call numbers at Simancas in which the information is contained. It included an exact call number for the file at Simancas: AGS GM EXP, leg. 57, exp. 5. The author could not figure out how to use the database.
578. O'Kelly de Galway, *Mémoire historique*, pp.70–71.
579. 'Edgar to Wogan', 11 May 1751, Rome (RA SP/MAIN/321 f.78–79).
580. Ibid.
581. Tayler, H., *Jacobite Epilogue*, p.323.
582. Ibid.
583. Arxiu de la Catedral de Barcelona, *Libre de Obits*, *Tomo XXXIII, desde 1754–1759*, f.35.
584. The author extends his deep gratitude to Ms Lisset Jara, a resident of Barcelona, who kindly assisted in confirming the details of Wogan's burial on the grounds of the Cathedral of Barcelona. A cloistered area on the east side of the cathedral contains many large flagstones marking many burial places but there were none marked Charles Wogan. Access to the crypt is restricted. A plot used for graves adjacent the cathedral existed in Wogan's day, but has since been built upon.
585. The author is profoundly grateful for the help and patience of Sr Jordi Tor Azorín, Director de Gestió i Atenció a l'Usuari de l'Arxiu Colegio Notarial de Cataluña.
586. 'James Edgar to James Wogan', 10th September 1754, Barcelona (RA SP/MAIN/350 f.111–112).
587. 'James Wogan to James Edgar', 12 April 1755, Barcelona (RA SP/MAIN/356 f. 9–9a).

588. 'James Wogan to James Edgar', 14th December 1757, Barcelona (RA SP/MAIN/377 f.101–102). The fact that James refers to him as my 'uncle' Nicholas confirms that indeed his uncle had inherited Rathcoffey estate. His daughter, Frances, would marry John Talbot of Malahide in 1735 and would inherit Rathcoffey. She moved permanently to Malahide Castle in 1769 and brought the family heirlooms there, which included the surviving portraits of her grandfather John, her father Nicholas and her uncle Charles, all of which were passed on by the Talbot family to the National Gallery of Ireland where they exist today. The author leans here on the outstanding work of Séamus Cullen, a local expert of the Wogan family and of Clane, to state that it is most likely that Charles's brother inherited Rathcoffey after the death of his cousin. See generally www.seamuscullen.net; see also Cullen, Séamus, 'The Wogans and Brownes: Two 18th-Century North Kildare Jacobite Families', published in two parts by *Liffey Champion*, Part I – 13 July 2024; Part II – 20 July 2024. See also Cullen, Séamus, *A History of Christianity in Clane & Rathcoffey*, (Clane, 2011).
589. 'James Wogan to James Edgar', 11 February 1758, Barcelona (RA SP/MAIN/379 f.54–55).
590. No record exists to show that the patent was sent to James Wogan after James III's refusal to send the patent to his father. The actual patent itself was in the possession of the Bey family of Paris in the 1950s, a copy of which was shared with the National Library of Ireland and is available for consultation there. The Beys were the descendants of the exiled Wogans who had settled in France, but exactly how the patent came to travel from Rome to Paris, or from Spain to Paris is a mystery. It is possible that the Bey family of 1950s Paris might possess an archive of material relating to the Wogans. All documentation, including correspondence with the Bey family, are available for consultation at the National Archive of Ireland.

Index